Mandarin Chir
Dual Language
Immersion
Programs

BILINGUAL EDUCATION & BILINGUALISM

Series Editors: **Nancy H. Hornberger** *(University of Pennsylvania, USA)* and **Wayne E. Wright** *(Purdue University, USA)*

Bilingual Education and Bilingualism is an international, multidisciplinary series publishing research on the philosophy, politics, policy, provision and practice of language planning, Indigenous and minority language education, multilingualism, multiculturalism, biliteracy, bilingualism and bilingual education. The series aims to mirror current debates and discussions. New proposals for single-authored, multiple-authored, or edited books in the series are warmly welcomed, in any of the following categories or others authors may propose: overview or introductory texts; course readers or general reference texts; focus books on particular multilingual education program types; school-based case studies; national case studies; collected cases with a clear programmatic or conceptual theme; and professional education manuals.

All books in this series are externally peer-reviewed.

Full details of all the books in this series and of all our other publications can be found on http://www.multilingual-matters.com, or by writing to Multilingual Matters, St Nicholas House, 31–34 High Street, Bristol, BS1 2AW, UK.

BILINGUAL EDUCATION & BILINGUALISM: 119

Mandarin Chinese Dual Language Immersion Programs

Ko-Yin Sung and Hsiao-Mei Tsai

MULTILINGUAL MATTERS
Bristol • Jackson

DOI https://doi.org/10.21832/SUNG3958
Library of Congress Cataloging in Publication Data
A catalog record for this book is available from the Library of Congress.
Names: Sung, Ko-Yin, 1977- author. | Tsai, Hsiao-Mei, 1981- author.
Title: Mandarin Chinese Dual Language Immersion Programs/Ko-Yin Sung
    and Hsiao-Mei Tsai.
Description: Bristol; Blue Ridge Summit: Multilingual Matters, [2019] |
    Series: Bilingual Education & Bilingualism 119 | Includes bibliographical
    references and index.
Identifiers: LCCN 2018060940 (print) | LCCN 2019003985 (ebook) |
    ISBN 9781788923965 (pdf) | ISBN 9781788923972 (epub) | ISBN 9781788923989
    (Kindle) | ISBN 9781788923958 (hbk : alk. paper)
Subjects: LCSH: Mandarin dialects—Study and teaching—Immersion method. |
    Chinese language—Study and teaching—Immersion method.
Classification: LCC PL1893 (ebook) | LCC PL1893 .S86 2019 (print) |
    DDC 495.17—dc23
LC record available at https://lccn.loc.gov/2018060940

British Library Cataloguing in Publication Data
A catalogue entry for this book is available from the British Library.

ISBN-13: 978-1-78892-395-8 (hbk)
ISBN-13: 978-1-78892-864-9 (pbk)

Multilingual Matters
UK: St Nicholas House, 31–34 High Street, Bristol BS1 2AW, UK.
USA: NBN, Jackson, TN, USA.

Website: www.multilingual-matters.com
Twitter: Multi_Ling_Mat
Facebook: https://www.facebook.com/multilingualmatters
Blog: www.channelviewpublications.wordpress.com

The policy of Multilingual Matters/Channel View Publications is to use papers
that are natural, renewable and recyclable products, made from wood grown in
sustainable forests. In the manufacturing process of our books, and to further
support our policy, preference is given to printers that have FSC and PEFC Chain
of Custody certification. The FSC and/or PEFC logos will appear on those books
where full certification has been granted to the printer concerned.

Typeset by Deanta Global Publishing Services Limited.

Contents

1 Introduction

Introduction

In the increasingly multilingual and multicultural society of the United States, educational programs which promote biliteracy and cross-cultural learning are gaining in status. Among the different types of bilingual educational programs, dual language immersion (DLI) programs, which provide academic instruction in English and a second language, are increasing in popularity across the nation. In 2000, there were only about 260 DLI programs in K–12 US schools; however, the programs have flourished across the country since then and the number of programs reached 2000 in 2011 (Wilson, 2011). This is almost an eight-fold increase. In addition, the majority of states (39 of 50), and the District of Columbia, reported the implementation of DLI programs during the 2012–2013 school year. In other words, DLI programs in the US have grown rapidly, both in number and location.

Although US educators and administrators have recognized the importance and the urgency of investing in DLI programs in various languages, the pace of the current research on DLI programs does not seem to sync with the rapid program growth. The research in the DLI area is limited in terms of its scope, and the topics and languages covered. For instance, there tends to be a lack of focus on languages other than Spanish in DLI research, which is an issue as one cannot assume that all of the benefits identified and pedagogies suggested in Spanish programs can also be seamlessly applied to DLI programs of other languages. Taking Mandarin Chinese (hereafter referred to as 'Chinese'), a non-alphabetical language system, distinctive from Spanish, as an example, studies (Grenfell & Harris, 2015; Lee-Thompson, 2008) have shown that successfully learning how to read and write the language requires specific teaching and learning approaches. Therefore, the need for more research on DLI programs of languages other than Spanish is one reason that drove us to research Chinese DLI programs for this book. Moreover, the state of Utah, where the current studies described in this book were conducted, is the most ambitious state in growing DLI programs and is seen by other states as a model. At the same time, the state received many criticisms that its model targeted primarily white students for the purpose of world language enrichment, rather than for non-white students to maintain their heritage languages (Delavan *et al.*, 2017; Valdez *et al.*, 2016b). The large number of Chinese DLI programs, coupled with the controversial issues related to the Utah model, have made Utah a promising research site for Chinese DLI study.

This book consists of two major parts and delves into Chinese DLI programs in multiple aspects. Part 1 of the book, Chapters 2 to 5, involves parents, teachers and school administrators as they take important roles in aiding students' learning. This part of the book focuses on the participants' opinions regarding current DLI programs and how they collaborate with one another, and how Chinese DLI teachers position themselves in teaching through their teaching identities. Part 2 of the book, Chapters 6 to 9, emphasizes classroom research conducted in the second author's classes. As mentioned earlier, the Chinese language system is non-alphabetical, which is challenging and takes unique approaches to master; hence, Chinese DLI classroom research, which touches upon strategy use, corrective feedback, Chinese-character teaching and authentic teacher–student interaction, all offer unique findings and contributions to the current literature.

This book contains a few objectives. First, by researching the different stakeholders' opinions toward the rapidly expanding Utah DLI programs and how the stakeholders work independently and collaboratively under the newly developed structure of the Utah model, this book presents up-to-date information regarding the current operational state of the Utah model from the stakeholders' perspectives. The target audience for this information are DLI policymakers, administrators, teachers and researchers. The information about the current state of the model can be used as a checkpoint for our readers to be reflective and for them to continue developing or consider modifying their policymaking, teaching techniques and research agendas. Second, in the second half of the book, we lead our readers to pay attention to specific areas of classroom research that are identified as still lacking (e.g. effectiveness of separation of two languages, student performance beyond standardized tests, language teaching methods) in DLI research (Christian, 2016). At the micro level, the results of the classroom studies will offer useful teaching implications for DLI educators. At the macro level, the findings of the classroom research will prompt DLI policymakers and administrators to rethink whether the Utah DLI model is aiding the process of social reproduction and whether the structures and policies of the model promote minority educational equality and maximize teaching effectiveness for all student populations from distinct backgrounds. Finally, this two-year long book-length DLI research serves as an example of research in the rarely investigated, but rapidly growing, one-way foreign language immersion programs. This book can be seen as an invitation to call out DLI researchers to target their work toward gaps found in the newly developed one-way immersion research. As former and current Chinese DLI educators, we believe that this book will benefit not only Chinese DLI educators and administrators in the US, but will also offer some useful suggestions and thoughts to other educators and administrators of similar programs worldwide.

The rest of this chapter provides readers with the foundational knowledge necessary to understand the sociopolitical context of the Utah Chinese DLI programs. It starts with the definition of bilingual education, the introduction of the various types of bilingual education worldwide and a discussion of how US bilingual education has been formed and viewed through a political lens.

Bilingual Education

Bilingual education (BE) is a commonly and internationally used term in the education field; however, it is a 'simplistic label for a complex phenomenon' (Baker & Wright, 2017: 197). Freeman (2007) noted that 'there is considerable confusion and conflict about what bilingual education means, who is served by bilingual programs, (and) what the goals of a bilingual program are for its target populations...' (2007: 3). Indeed, because BE has been developed in distinct educational contexts globally, wide variations of BE exist, which serve different purposes to fulfill different populations' needs. Abello-Contesse (2013) sorted BE programs by their purposes and placed them into four major types.

The first type of BE is created to preserve a minority language through language revival programs. The languages in need of maintenance include indigenous, heritage and immigrant languages. In such programs, the minority languages are taught along with the majority languages. Abello-Contesse (2013) listed some program examples such as Spanish-Catalan in Spain, Spanish-Quechua in Peru, English-Welsh in Wales and English-Maori in New Zealand.

The second type of BE is intended to develop minority students' proficiency in majority languages, with the support of their first languages. Examples of such programs are the transitional BE programs for immigrant populations in the US. This type of program is not intended to develop the students' first language proficiency; rather, its main goal is to use the students' minority languages in assisting them to increase their fluency in the majority language so that they are able to return to mainstream classrooms in a few years.

The third type of BE, originally established in Sweden, is referred as the 'sign BE', which serves deaf students. The students receive instruction in sign language (their first language) and the written form of the majority language (their second language). This type of BE is implemented in different parts of the globe.

The fourth type of BE is intended to serve native speakers of the majority language in order to develop their proficiency in a second language, which is often an international or prestigious language (e.g. English, French and German). In the past, this type of BE was often offered in private bilingual schools, which were associated with the status of elite education; however, this type of BE has become more popular in public schools in the past few decades (Abello-Contesse, 1999).

Bilingual Education in the US Context

The historical context of BE in either the US or other parts of the globe is inseparable from immigration and politics (Baker & Wright, 2017). Different forms of BE cannot be understood without accounting for their social, cultural, economic and political settings. Simply put, BE is not only a pedagogical issue, but also a political matter often associated with the ideologies of policymakers and the general public, influenced by socio-economic and political factors of the time.

In the United States, language diversity was accepted in general in the 18th and 19th centuries. It was common to see monolingual or bilingual education offered in different languages (e.g. German, Norwegian, Polish, Spanish and Dutch) in both public and private schools (Malakoff & Hakuta, 1990). However, the political setting changed in the early 20th century when the number of immigrants, and anti-German sentiment, drastically increased. As a result, Americanization policies were put in place. Such policies called for harmonization and loyalty to the United States among immigrants and involved the process of assimilating diverse immigrant cultures by imposing monolingual English education. The restrictive attitude toward the use of languages other than English was eased when the Civil Rights movement, which intended to end racial segregation and discrimination against African-Americans, started in the 1950s. The movement, accompanied by the promotion of language and multiculturalism, resulted in the passing of the Bilingual Education Act. The Act legitimized bilingual programs and allocated funds for the programs, marking an important milestone in federal educational policy toward language minorities, and undermined the English-only policy in many states. Most importantly, 'it suggested that *equal education* was not the same as *identical education*, even when there was no difference in location or teacher' (Malakoff & Hakuta, 1990: 32).

Since BE began in its modern form in the 1960s in the US, it has been the subject of controversial debates, and policies and movements related to it have been frequently changing. For example, on the one hand, in many important cases (e.g. *Lau v. Nichols*, *Rios v. Read* and *Casteneda v. Pickard*) in the 1970s and 1980s regarding language and equal educational access of minority students, courts ruled in favor of BE and affirmed that school districts had to provide remedies to English language learners, including English as a second language instruction and some form of bilingual education (Wiley, 2007). In addition, the final version of the Bilingual Education Act in 1994 added an endorsement which stated the development of minority students' native language skills as a goal. This endorsement signified that, for the first time in law, BE was not seen only as a remedy for minority students to acquire the English language, but also an educational program to maintain and develop their heritage languages. However, in the late 1990s and early 2000s, anti-BE initiatives including Proposition 227 in California, Proposition 203 in Arizona and Question 2 in Massachusetts, which were approved by the state voters, all aimed to replace BE with English instruction for English language learners (Crawford, 2007).

Within the professional North American linguistic community, researchers have carried out studies on second language acquisition and understand the rationales of BE, almost all of the members are supporters of BE (Cummins, 1999). However, with the anti-BE initiatives in place, the BE debate has become tense. Advocates of BE believe that the most effective way to learn English is to use minority students' native language as support, while opponents of BE maintain that teaching no languages except English to minority students is the best way to acquire English (Medina, 2003). BE in the present time in the US has continued to be politicized. Baker (2003) explained,

> Many times, discussions have been conducted under the sponsorship of special-interest groups. Often, decisions have been made depending on who is in power in Washington, in the state capital, or the district. Bilingual education has been discussed alongside such volatile issues as nationalism, racism, immigration, and adoption of English as the official language of the United States as well as minority rights, cultural diversity, and the goals of education itself. (Baker, 2003: 8)

Indeed, anti-BE groups such as English Only, English First, and US English, along with anti-BE initiatives, were seen collectively as tools of the politics of enmity toward the influx of immigrants in recent years, especially the Hispanic and Asian populations (Ovando, 2003). Given that BE has long been a controversy in the nation, a form of BE, dual language education, has surfaced and served as a BE option since the 1960s. With the goals of bilingual and biliteracy development and the feature of additive orientation, dual language education is seen as having 'the potential to eradicate the negative status of bilingualism in the U.S.' (Lindholm-Leary, 2001: 1). The following sections introduce the concept of dual language education and studies conducted in the dual language education context.

Dual Language Education

Dual language education refers to programs which provide literacy and content area teaching (e.g. science, social studies and math) through the students' native language and the target language (also called the 'partner language'). Hence, second language acquisition is embedded in the daily academic curriculum, and the objectives of dual language education are to produce competent bilingual, biliterate and bicultural individuals who also achieve high levels of academic performance. Dual language instructional models take many forms, but current common programs are based on variations in student backgrounds, and can be categorized into four types (Christian, 2016): (1) developmental bilingual programs that target language minority students who are learning the majority language (e.g. English). The program goal is to develop not only the majority language, but also the students' native language. This type of program is also called 'maintenance bilingual education' or 'one-way immersion'. (2) Heritage language immersion programs enroll students who have ancestral ties with the target heritage culture. This type of program can be part of a language revitalization plan to provide students with opportunities to maintain or acquire the indigenous language related to their heritage. (3) Foreign language immersion programs, also called one-way immersion, include mostly language majority students. The program goal is to foster bilingualism and biliteracy. The target language chosen for the programs could be a global business language (e.g. Chinese) or a minority language commonly used locally (e.g. Spanish). (4) Two-way immersion programs consist of approximately equal numbers of language majority and minority students. Through such programs, language minority students are able to maintain and develop their heritage language while the language majority students have the opportunity to become fluent in a second language.

In terms of the ratio of time of instruction in the two languages, dual language programs in the United States are comprised of two major models. One model is the 90:10 model, in which students enter the program in kindergarten or first grade. Students receive 90% of daily instruction in the target language, with the remaining 10% in English in the first year of the program. The 90:10 model slowly increases the instruction in English each year, and by fourth grade and above, the instructional time between the English and the target language is balanced (Lindholm-Leary, 2016). This model has proven to be most successful for heritage learners (Thomas & Collier, 1997). The other model is the 50:50 model, which delivers daily instruction in English and the partner language with equal time throughout the program years. The decision on which model to implement often falls on the local education leaders.

Dual Language Studies in the United States

Recent dual language studies in the US have documented positive outcomes in terms of academic achievement and bilingual development for both language majority and minority students. A few major findings can be concluded. First, many studies reported that dual language students either performed equally well or outperformed their non-dual language peers in math and reading (Lindholm-Leary & Borsato, 2006; Lindholm-Leary & Howard, 2008; Snow, 1986). Second, most dual language students were rated as fluent bilinguals by the upper elementary grade levels and were more likely to be in higher level math courses (Genesee, 1987; Lindholm-Leary & Borsato, 2005) and less likely to drop out of school (Thomas & Collier, 2002). For language minority dual language students, the high performance both in language and content areas meant that they were more likely to close the gap with English native-speaking peers compared to their language minority peers in the mainstream curriculum. In sum, dual language studies conducted by different researchers in different locations with various socio-economic contexts in the US reported success for dual language students (Lindholm-Leary, 2012). BE expert Lindholm-Leary stressed that the fact that dual language education worked well in schools with different kinds of communities, especially ones with economically disadvantaged Hispanic students as the majority student population, illustrated that dual language education is a promising BE model for the nation.

While the results of dual language education appear positive in studies, researchers also point to a few issues that still need to be discussed and further researched in order to fulfill the promise of dual language education. A few areas of research needed to advance the knowledge in the dual language field include the need to research lesser-studied languages (as most dual language research emphasized the Spanish language), the need to investigate the effectiveness of separation of languages in instruction, especially when the bilingual phenomenon of translanguaging has been frequently noted in second language research, the need to investigate student academic outcomes beyond standardized tests, and the need to investigate whether dual language education aids the process of social reproduction in society (Christian, 2016). This book attempts to touch upon the current needs by including them as points for discussion in different chapters.

In the next sections of this chapter, the dual language education and the religious culture in the Utah context is discussed to offer readers essential background knowledge of the studies described in this book.

Utah Dual Language Immersion Programs and the Policy Context

In 2007, the Utah State Office of Education (USOE) established the Governor's World Language Council, which consisted of business and education leaders. The Council then created the Utah World Language Roadmap for K–12 students by addressing the need and importance of language skills in the world's marketplace (Roberts *et al.*, 2016). In the following year, Utah's DLI model was established when the Utah Legislature responded to the roadmap plan and passed Utah Senate Bill 41 International Education Initiatives - Critical Languages Program, which provided funding for Utah school districts to create DLI programs in numerous languages. In 2010, a goal stated by Governor Gary Herbert was that by 2015, Utah would implement 100 DLI programs with a target student number of 25,000. The stated goal was reached in 2015 and in the 2016–2017 academic year, there were a total of 160 DLI schools with an estimated 34,000 students learning one of the six different target languages: Chinese, French, German, Portuguese, Russian and Spanish.

Utah DLI programs adopt the 50:50 model, in which students receive equal instruction in English and the target language daily. The state requires that all programs sponsored by the state implement the 50:50 model with the hiring of two teachers, one of whom is assigned to teach exclusively in English for half of the day, while the other is assigned to offer instruction in the partner language for the other half of the day (Utah Dual Language Immersion, 2017a). The actual instructional medium allocation by subjects from grades one to six can be found in Table 1.1.

Table 1.1 shows that the Utah DLI model invests a significant amount of combined instructional time (a total of 50% of daily instructional time) in English Language Arts and target language literacy. The remainder of the instructional time is divided by content areas such as math, social studies and science. In addition, the instructional medium of a content subject changes every few years. For example, students receive math instruction in the target language from grades one to three. After that, the instructional medium changed from the target language to English. While the content subjects are taught in one language, reinforcement

Table 1.1 Utah's DLI model in grades 1–6

Grade Levels	Instructional Medium: Target Language	Instructional Medium: English
Grades 1–3	Math (20%) Social Studies (15%) Target Language Literacy (15%)	English (35%) Math and Social Studies Reinforcement (15%)
Grades 4–5	Math Reinforcement (8.5%) Target Language Literacy (25%) Science (16.5%)	Math (16.5%) English Language Arts (25%) Social Studies and Science Reinforcement (8.5%)
Grade 6	Science (12.5%) Target Language Literacy (25%) Social Studies (12.5%)	Math (20%) English Language Arts (25%) Science and Social Studies Reinforcement (5%)

Source: Utah Dual Language Immersion, 2017b.

in the other language is in place to ensure knowledge transfer between languages. From grades seven to nine, Utah DLI instruction is offered through courses such as World Language DLI honors, Social Studies, Science, and DLI Culture, History & Media, which emphasize critical thinking skills and use authentic teaching materials written for native speakers. For DLI tenth to twelfth graders, USOE has developed the DLI Language Bridge Project, which partners with seven universities in Utah to offer upper division college language courses to DLI high school students who pass the Advanced Placement Language and Culture exam. This project, which connects the K–12 DLI programs to advanced university courses, signifies the Utah DLI model's intent to prepare DLI students for higher education.

The rapid establishment and expansion of Utah's DLI program in the past few years has not only attracted much attention from the local news media, but it has also been noted in recent DLI literature (Christian, 2016; Curtain et al., 2016). More importantly, the Utah DLI model has received national attention and has since been a major influence on the decisions of DLI programs in other states. According to the Dual Language Immersion report prepared by Roberts et al. (2016), representatives from more than 30 other states visited Utah for its DLI programs, among which many of their local educational authorities adopted the design and curriculum materials of the Utah model. In their own words, Roberts et al. stated,

> It is inarguable that the Utah DLI model of instruction in which public-school children of all abilities and socio-economic conditions, from urban to rural areas of the country and from homes in which many languages are spoken, offers a new kind of 21st Century education, which is both rigorous and cost effective. (2016: 3)

Despite the positive remarks stated in the USOE's DLI report, Utah's DLI model is not without controversy. Based on the results of several studies which examined a wide variety of data, including the Utah DLI policy documents, school demographics, local newspapers, promotional materials produced by USOE DLI officials, and USOE-run websites, a group of scholars (Valdez et al., 2016a) claim that it is evident that the DLI programs in Utah target mostly student groups possessing the following three types of characteristics: Caucasian, wealthy and English-speaking. For example, a comparison of the student demographics between the period 1978–2005 when there was no Utah state model and the state-model period (2009–2014), illustrates that the DLI programs in the state-model period were more frequently located in schools with a higher number of white students, lower number of students in poverty and lower number of students who are English language learners. Moreover, the same group of researchers observed that the key discourse in the policy documents and promotional materials was predominantly globalized human capital (GHC)-based, which is defined as 'a preoccupation with economically conceptualized language skills' for 'competitively conceptualized individuals and nations and their workforces' (Valdez *et al.*, 2016a: 854). Keywords such as 'globalization', 'industry sectors', 'compete in a complex global economy', and 'international business languages' were frequently found in Utah's DLI GHC-based discourse (Delavan *et al.*, 2017). Such discourse with an emphasis on global economics draws attention away from local language and culture maintenance issues, and from the topic of inequality in language education. As a result, the benefits for the language minority students are marginalized and silenced, while the major interests are centered on the white English-speaking mainstream majority, with no heritage connection to the target language (Freire *et al.*, 2016).

Currently, the Utah model offers two types of bilingual programs: one-way and two-way. As stated on the Utah Dual Language Immersion (2017a) website, one-way programs intend to develop the target language fluency of English-speaking students. Two-way programs are offered only in Spanish and are comprised of both English- and Spanish-speaking students. To be more specific, according to the Utah Administration Code Rule R277-488 (2017), one-way programs should consist of mostly English language speakers and less than 30% of the students should have a native language other than English. The limit set on the number of heritage language minority students for the one-way programs sends a clear message that these programs deprioritize the need for minority language and culture maintenance. A brief on DLI program participation reported by the Utah Education Policy Center (2015) showed that in both one-way and two-way DLI programs in 2013, the majority population in the programs were Caucasian (89% in one-way and 64% in two-way). In addition, the one-way program model, which was 73% of all Utah DLI programs, was the dominant type. There is absolutely no one-way maintenance or heritage language immersion program in the Utah model.

Data gathered by the US Census Bureau (2018) reveal that the population of Utah was approximately 3.1 million people in 2017. The majority of the population identified as White (91%), followed by Hispanic or Latino (14%), Asian (2.5%), mixed-race (2.5%), American-Indian and Alaska Native (1.6%), African-American (1.4%), and Native Hawaiian and other Pacific Islander (1%). Besides English, which is spoken by the majority (85.6%) of the Utah population over five years old, the Utah Language Data Report (2016) identifies Spanish (9.6%, approximately 245,000 speakers) and Chinese (0.45%, approximately 10,000 speakers) as the first and second most commonly spoken minority languages, followed by 17 other languages. In sum, the current linguistic demographics in Utah show that one in seven Utah residents older than five years old speaks a minority language at home and that more than one-third of this population speak English 'less than very well'. In Utah public schools in 2014, there was a total of 36,175 (6.3%) students participating in programs for English Language Learners (ELLs) (National Center for Education Statistics, 2017). The results of the Student Assessment of Growth and Excellence (SAGE) test, a statewide comprehensive assessment in math, English language arts and science, show that ELLs in Utah performed poorly in all three subjects. For example, in the academic year of 2015–2016, current ELLs were 5.6% proficient in English, 8.8% in math and 4% in science, which were way below the average percentages of fluent English speakers (46%, 49% and 51% in English, math and science) (Utah State Board of Education, 2018). Even former ELLs, who had exited the ELL programs, perform poorly with 24.5% in English, 29.3% in math and 19.9% in science. There is an obvious gap in academic achievement between ELLs and other students even after the ELLs have received schooling in the United States for several years. Ruark (2012) pointed out that as Utah is the eighth fastest growing ELL population in the nation, the ELLs' poor academic performances should be seen as a noteworthy factor in the state's failure to satisfy federal guidelines for student performance.

According to the Utah administrative code Rule R277-716 (Utah Office of Administrative Rules, 2018), Alternative Language Services for Utah students, local education agencies (LEAs) must use Title III, a national Department of Education (ED) program that offers funding to assist ELLs and immigrant learners through dual immersion, ESL content-based, or sheltered instructions. Although DLI has been identified in research as the most effective type of instruction for minority students, the DLI student participation data reported by the Utah Education Policy Center (2015) showed that only 3% of third grade students in schools with one-way DLI programs were ELLs, and only 2% of third grade one-way DLI students were ELLs. In other words, DLI programs were not offered in areas with dense ELL populations and not every ELL in schools that offer DLI programs attends the programs. This, coupled with the fact that there is a restriction on the enrollment number of language minority students in the one-way immersion programs, and that there is no one-way immersion program for heritage students, illustrate that the Utah model appears to be in favor of a globalized language education and is unconcerned with the needs of, and education equality for, minority students. This is especially true for the largest minority group in Utah, the Spanish-speaking group, which comprises 10% of the total population. The figures presented here show that the statement in the state's DLI report, which argued that its DLI model offered innovative education to children of different socio-economic statuses and from homes in which different languages are spoken, is misleading. As education equality for minority students is an important issue, this book will include it as a point for discussion whenever relevant.

The Influence of Religion in the State of Utah

Utah is a unique state, whose majority population belongs to a single church, the Church of Jesus Christ of Latter-day Saints (also referred to as the Mormon Church or the LDS Church). The population of Mormon members in Utah reported by the Mormon Newsroom (2018) is 2,090,401, which is approximately 60% of the Utah population. The Mormon Church actively promotes the practice of missionary work. Most of the Mormon missionaries are young men and women between their late teens and early twenties, who are assigned to serve away from their homes in other states or overseas using a second language. The Mormon church prepares the missionaries in a missionary training center (MTC). Currently, there are a total of 15 centers worldwide, with the Provo Missionary Training Center in Provo, Utah, being the largest and the longest serving center since 1978. The center sits on 39 acres of land and has the capacity to house and train 3,700 missionaries. According to the center, 'over 600,000 missionaries from nearly every country in the world have come to the MTC for training' (Provo Missionary Training Center, 2018). The center teaches 55 different languages to Mormon missionaries before they depart for their missions. The Mormon church reports that in 2017, there were 67,049 full-time missionaries and 36,172 part-time church-service missionaries worldwide. Many Mormon missionaries return home speaking a language other than English fluently. In this very Mormon state of Utah, second language learning is commonplace. Language learning for the benefit of missionaries could have played a factor of the state's ambition to build the fastest growing DLI programs.

In the next three sections, we switch our focus from the DLI programs in Utah to discuss the history of Chinese language teaching, the Chinese language system and the reasons Chinese is challenging for English speakers. This should help readers understand why Chinese was chosen as one of the languages in the Utah DLI programs, and why research is needed in the programs.

Chinese Language Instruction in the United States

Since the 'Chinese fever' phenomenon (the increasing interest in learning Chinese as a foreign language (CFL) due to China's rising economic status) is recent, literature regarding the historical context of CFL in the US is limited. Wang and Ruan (2016) closely examined the evolution of CFL in the past 150 years and divided the history of CFL in the US into four periods. This section summarizes Wang and Ruan's key findings in each of the four periods.

The first period of CFL began in 1871 and ended when World War II erupted. The main purposes of CFL at the time were for individuals to become sinologists to study Chinese language, literacy and history, and to fulfill the needs of missionaries, businessmen and politicians to travel to China for various reasons. Prestigious schools such as Yale University, Harvard University, California State University, the University of Chicago and Stanford University were pioneers, offering Chinese instruction between the late 1800s and the early 1900s. The number of CFL students was very small and the grammar translation method was applied in language instruction, which had a focus on reading and writing. Subjects such as Chinese history, literature, customs and politics were also the topics of study.

The second period of CFL was during World War II and the post-World War II period between 1940 and 1960. During the war time, the need for the military to learn Chinese increased, as China and the US were allies against Japan. Due to the need for the military to be able to use Chinese in the war within a short time, the Audio-Lingual method, which emphasizes training in listening and speaking was utilized. By the end of the second period, approximately 25 universities in the US offered Chinese.

The third period of CFL was between 1960 and 2000. This period began with US governmental initiatives in support of the teaching of critical foreign languages, which included Chinese. Not only the government sector, but also professional organizations such as the Chinese Language Teachers Association (CLTA), and private foundations, such as the Carnegie Foundation and the Dodge Foundation, all contributed to the promotion of CFL learning. For example, the CLTA established the *Journal of the Chinese Language Teachers Association* for CFL researchers and organized annual national research conferences. On the other hand, private foundations funded Chinese programs for K–16 schools. During this period, a couple of political events also positively influenced CFL education in the US. One was the re-admittance of China to the United Nations, and the other was Ping-Pong Diplomacy, which entailed a group of American ping-pong players visiting China after 22 years of no contact or diplomatic relations between the two countries. This led to President Nixon's visit to China less than a year after the players' visit. In 1990, approximately 20,000 college students were studying Chinese. By the end of the third period, a small, but steady growth of CFL in K–16 education was observed (Wang, 2010).

The fourth period is considered the rapidly expanding period of CFL education from 2000 to the present. Many factors contributed to the fast growth. First, following the 9/11 terrorist attacks in 2001, an amendment was enacted for the National Security Education Act of 1991 to expand the NSA's funds in 2004 for critical language learning, and the National Security Language Initiative (NSLI) funded several K–16 critical language programs for the purpose of strengthening national security. An example of a critical language program is the Language Flagship Program, which partners higher education with the federal government to produce college students highly proficient in languages critical to the security and competitiveness of the United States (The Language Flagship, 2018). CFL education is also motivated by economic reasons. State and local education and business leaders foresee the impact of China being a global economic power in the 21st century and have urged schools to include CFL in K–12 curricula. Moreover, Confucius Institutes, commonly referred as 'Hanban' in Chinese, which are affiliated with the Chinese Ministry of Education with an aim to 'make policies and development plans for promoting Chinese language internationally' (Confucius Institute Headquarters, 2017), provide K–16 US schools funding and personnel resources for CFL education. According to the Hanban headquarters, in 2018, China had established 110 Confucius Institutes and 501 Confucius Classrooms in the US, which was the largest number compared to other countries, offering CFL classes and CFL professional development for teachers (Xu, 2014). In Utah, there are currently three Confucius Institutes in higher educational institutions. Due to the several factors discussed above, the number of CFL learners increased rapidly in the new millennium. An estimate of K–12 students studying CFL in the US during the 2014–2015 academic year was 227,086 (The State of Language in the United States, 2017) and the number is likely to continue to increase because of the political and economic climates in the current times.

The Chinese Language System

The Chinese language has a conceptually distinctive orthographic system compared to alphabetical languages such as English. The Chinese system is logographic and its structure consists of three layers of components: stroke, radical and character (Shen & Ke, 2007). Strokes, the smallest unit in a character, are a set of line patterns that follow certain positional constraints to combine in different ways to form radicals and characters. The second component, the radical, is considered the basic component of a character (Wang et al., 2003). A radical can be a semantic indicator (called 'semantic radical'), which hints at the meaning of a character, or a phonetic indicator (called 'phonetic radical'), which cues the pronunciation of a character. The third component, character, is a morpheme, which can be simple or compound. A simple character is comprised of a single radical, while a compound character contains at least two radicals, frequently with one being phonetic and the other being semantic. Although the majority (90%) of Chinese characters are compound characters, which gives readers hints to the characters' meanings and pronunciations, due to the evolution of the Chinese language, only 26% of the phonetic hints in modern characters are identical to the sounds of the characters they represent (Feldman & Siok, 1999). Due to the lack of correspondence between characters and their pronunciations, currently two Chinese phonetic systems are used as an aid to learning the pronunciation of Chinese characters. One is Zhuyin (mainly used in Taiwan) and the other is Hanyu Pinyin (mainly used in China).

In addition to the significant differences in the orthographic systems between Chinese and English, the tonal feature of the pronunciation system of the Chinese language is also unlike English. Every Chinese character is spoken as one syllable which carries a tone. Identical syllables carrying different tones are linked with different characters which differ in meaning. Mandarin Chinese consists of four regular tones (first, second, third and fourth tones) and a neutral tone. The first tone is a high-pitch tone; the second tone is a rising tone; the third tone is a falling, then rising tone; and the fourth tone is a falling tone. The neutral tone is a light tone and shorter than the other tones, whose pitch depends on the tone that came before it (Hao, 2012). Due to the conceptually distinctive nature of the Chinese phonetic and orthographic systems compared to alphabetic language systems, learners of Chinese who speak an alphabetic native language, such as the majority of the Chinese DLI learners investigated in this book, have to make a considerable effort to master the language. The next section details the particular challenges English-speaking students might face when learning Chinese.

English Speakers' Challenges in Learning the Chinese Language

English speakers' challenges in learning the Chinese language are related to the writing system, and the tonal feature (Sung, 2014). With respect to the writing system, one challenge is to acquire the knowledge of the strokes (including stroke sequences) and radicals that make up characters (Lee & Kalyuga, 2011). In order to function as a literate individual in a Chinese-speaking community, knowledge of three thousand common characters are needed (Wong et al., 2010), which is a large number of characters to be acquired for learners. Second, as the phonetic radicals in most of the characters no longer cue the pronunciations of the characters, the lack of correspondence between a character and its pronunciation makes the learning of reading and writing more difficult (Sung & Wu, 2011).

With regard to the Chinese tonal feature, researchers (Wang et al., 2003) found that English-speaking students encountered difficulty pronouncing Chinese with the correct tones because of the lack of the tonal feature in their native language. This difficulty was not only found with novice students, but also with advanced students who had studied Chinese for many years. The tonal feature of Chinese also created the challenge of having to learn a large number of homophones. It is common to find multiple characters, which have different meanings, carrying identical pronunciation and tone. For example, at least 14 different characters can be found that share the pronunciation /li/ with the fourth tone and at least six distinct characters can be found that share the pronunciation, /qi/ with the first tone (Sung & Wu, 2011).

Finally, the learning of the widely used phonetic system, Hanyu Pinyin, could confuse English-speakers (Lee & Kalyuga, 2011). Hanyu Pinyin contains 25 of the 26 English alphabet letters, but they are pronounced differently than in English. As a result, it demands extra effort for English-speakers to distinguish pronunciations between Hanyu Pinyin and English while learning Chinese. This is especially true for young English-speaking learners when they try to learn the English alphabet at the same time.

The identified challenges show how the learning of Chinese could be time-consuming and could cause learners' frustration. However, most of the current studies on Chinese as a foreign or second language learning emphasized older students (e.g. high school, college or adult learners) learning Chinese as a subject. Chinese language learning in the DLI context where Chinese is used as the instructional medium is seldom investigated, which illustrated the need for this book.

Next, this chapter presents the demographic information of the research sites of the studies in this volume, the detailed background information regarding the focal program and participants in the classroom studies in Chapters 6 to 9, and how we position ourselves in the research.

The Study Context

The context of the research studies in this book is the Mandarin Chinese DLI programs in Utah. According to the Chinese state director who was interviewed by us in 2017, there were nearly 30 Chinese programs in Utah, and Chinese programs, along with other languages in the DLI programs, are expanding each year. In fact, program growth was one of the requirements for receiving continued funding for the DLI programs.

The Chinese programs were located in eight different counties, with four (Box Elder: 78%, Cache: 71%, Davis: 68% and Utah: 78%) having more than the state average (60%) of Mormon population. The other four counties are close to the state average (Salt Lake: 51%, Tooele: 59%, Washington: 57% and Weber: 54%) (Canham, 2007) (see Figure 1.1).

According to the 2012 American Community Survey (ACS), an ongoing statistical survey by the US Census Bureau (2016), during the academic years of 2011–2012, the 12 school districts where the 30 Chinese programs were located (see Table 1.2) served a little more than 2 million students, among whom 90% (approximately 1.9 million) were Caucasian. On the other hand, Chinese heritage students comprised 0.4% (8,450) of the total student population (Proximity One, 2017).

In terms of the economic characteristics of the 12 districts, Table 1.3 shows that in 2010, eight out of the 12 school districts had median and mean household incomes higher than the average in Utah (median:

Utah Chinese DLI programs

Figure 1.1 Chinese DLI programs in Box Elder, Cache, Davis, Salt Lake, Tooele, Washington, Weber, and Utah counties.

Table 1.2 Student population information in the 12 districts which hosted the Chinese programs

School District	Total Student Population	Caucasian Student Population	Chinese
Alpine	284,131	262,392 (92.3%)	698 (0.2%)
Box Elder	49,660	46,316 (93.3%)	4 (0.0%)
Cache	64,125	60,642 (94.6%)	117 (0.2%)
Canyons	204,154	184,695 (90.5%)	1,930 (0.9%)
Davis	306,664	279,043 (91.0%)	1,085 (0.4%)
Granite	384,170	320,351 (83.4%)	2,258 (0.6%)
Jordan	222,083	203,265 (91.5%)	924 (0.4%)
Nebo	119,594	110,701 (92.6%)	48 (0.0%)
Provo	112,846	98,574 (87.4%)	832 (0.7%)
Tooele	58,158	549,14 (94.4%)	118 (0.2%)
Washington	139,484	129,149 (92.6%)	129 (0.1%)
Weber	148,191	135,896 (91.7%)	307 (0.2%)
Total	2,093,260	1,885,938 (90.0%)	8,450 (0.4%)

Table 1.3 Median and mean household incomes, and all families with income below poverty in the 12 school districts which hosted the Chinese programs

School District	Median Household Income ($)	Mean Household Income ($)	All families with income below poverty (%)
Alpine	66,489	81,353	7.9 %
Box Elder	55,918	64,860	6.7 %
Cache	61,443	74,327	5.7 %
Canyons	70,634	92,462	5.6 %
Davis	69,355	82,820	4.6 %
Granite	54,241	68,979	11.2 %
Jordan	75,579	85,745	5.0 %
Nebo	62,996	74,041	5.7 %
Provo	40,325	56,887	19.8 %
Tooele	61,933	71,875	7.0 %
Washington	49,145	61,298	10.1 %
Weber	63,998	74,461	5.0 %

$56,330; mean: $70,375) in the same year (American Community Survey, 2011). Relatively, the eight districts which were wealthier than average also had lower poverty rates than the average Utah families (7.7%) (American Community Survey, 2011).

A look at the occupation types in these 12 school districts revealed that the majority of occupations were management and professional, followed by sales and office. In sum, the racial and economic characteristics of the 12 school districts where the Chinese programs are located seem to echo Valdez *et al.*'s (2016b) findings that the majority of the Utah DLI programs serve wealthy Caucasian English-speaking students.

With regard to the study length, this research was a two-year long project, with the first year focusing on conducting the studies described in Chapters 2 to 5. For the classroom studies conducted in the second author's classrooms and discussed in Chapters 6 to 9, we made sure to spread them out in the two-year span so that no more than one study was conducted during the same time in the same classroom to avoid interactive effects of concurrent studies. The specific length of time and the particular methodology of each study is described in each chapter.

The Focal School

The Chinese DLI program involved in the classroom research in Chapters 6 to 9 was in Cache County, which is located in the northernmost area of Utah and extends to the Idaho border. Based on the data collected by the US Census Bureau (2016), in 2016, the majority (85.5%) of people in Cache County were Caucasian, while Hispanic (10.5%) and Asian (2.7%) were the second and third highest populations in Cache

County. In the same year, approximately 36% of the Cache County population had a bachelor's degree or above. The average median household income in Cache County during the years of 2011–2015 was $50,497 and the poverty rate was 16%. Compared to the household income data of the Cache County School District presented in Table 1.2 (median household income: $61,443; poverty rate: 5.7%) where the Chinese program was located, the people residing within the Cache County School District boundary were much wealthier than the total population residing in Cache County. The communities of Cache County include 13 cities and six towns. Logan is the county seat and is the largest city, and it is where the land grant university, Utah State University, is located. The elementary school where the Chinese program was located is in North Logan, which is adjacent to Logan City.

The Focal Teacher and Student Participants

The focal teacher participant is the second author, who had four years of experience teaching first-grade Utah Chinese DLI students prior to conducting the studies for the book. She is a native speaker of Chinese, who holds a US master's degree in second language teaching. The formal teaching and research training she received in the graduate program, coupled with her several years of DLI teaching experience in the context where the studies were conducted, made her an ideal teacher participant and researcher for the book.

The classroom studies involved two cohorts of first-grade students. Each cohort consisted of two classes. Cohort one had 53 first-graders in two classes. Class A consisted of 14 females and 12 males, and Class B had 12 females and 15 males. Cohort two consisted of 53 first-graders in two classes, with Class A having 15 females and 12 males, and Class B having 17 females and 9 males. All but one student in cohort one came from native English-speaking households. 'Alice' (a pseudonym), the student who did not come from an English-speaking home, was a Chinese heritage speaker. Both of her parents were blue-collar workers in the service industry. Alice's parents immigrated to Utah from China more than ten years ago. Alice has an older sister and a younger brother, who speak mainly Mandarin Chinese at home with their parents and grandparents. Due to the busy work schedule of the parents, they sent Alice to the Chinese DLI program hoping that she would learn how to write Chinese, as they did not have time to teach her at home. As with cohort one, cohort two also had only one student who came from a Chinese home. 'Laura' (a pseudonym), whose parents came to the United States more than 10 years ago for their higher education degrees, were working as a full-time professor (father) and a part-time research assistant (mother) at the nearby university. Laura has a younger sister and the family speaks a mix of English and Chinese at home. Laura's parents hoped that by enrolling

Laura in the Chinese program, she would know how to switch between Chinese and English well.

The English-speaking participants did not have any knowledge of the Chinese language before they entered the program. However, 24 of the students in cohort one and 29 of the students in cohort two had older siblings enrolled in the same DLI program; those parents were familiar with the program before the participants entered first-grade. Moreover, four parents in cohort one and five parents in cohort two spoke Chinese as a second language at various fluency levels.

This section discussed the Utah Chinese DLI programs in the local context. The next section places the programs within the larger international context.

The Utah Chinese DLI Programs Within the Global Context

To put the Utah Chinese DLI programs within the global context, the term 'globalization' plays a key role. Globalization refers to 'the forces that exercise pressure on standards and create demands in all societies' (Kheng & Baldauf, 2011: 952). These forces occur in many spheres, such as political, social and economic, and influence the ways and the places languages are utilized across the globe. Similar to other countries which responded to the changing global environment and its new demands, different entities (e.g. business leaders, policymakers and parents) in the United States have recognized the global change and requested that schools better prepare students' global competencies to meet the new demands. Since then, US DLI programs have become a choice to promote global education, which also conveniently serves as a reason to counter the anti-bilingual education attack (Stritikus & Varghese, 2012). In addition, viewed within the context of the global movement in the new millennium, the Chinese language is identified as a new emerging global language due to its large economic and diplomatic power. In order to assert itself as a superpower, China has been establishing Confucius Institutes worldwide since 2004. Chinese officials view these institutes as a way to help spread and glorify Chinese culture and use it as a propaganda strategy to increase their soft power around the world (Seib, 2016). According to Seib, as of 2015, Hanban had Confucius Institutes in 120 countries and has the goal of placing 1,000 Confucius Institutes around the world by 2020. Under the influence of globalization in the international political and economic spheres, Chinese, along with other global languages, boomed in the Utah DLI programs.

Now that the necessary background knowledge and the current status of the Utah Chinese DLI programs both from within the local and international contexts have been touched upon, the following sections wrap up this chapter by explaining the necessity of conducting research in the Utah Chinese context and introducing the content of this volume.

The Necessity of This Volume Regarding Utah's Chinese DLI Programs

Several reasons justify the importance and urgency of conducting research on Chinese DLI programs in the Utah context. First, the Utah model, which offers mostly one-way immersion programs serving mostly English-native speakers, develops its own target language materials and sets its own language teaching rules (e.g. Chinese teachers cannot be seen by students speaking English in the school environment, and no teaching of the Chinese phonetic system until the third grade), is fairly new and is less studied than other models. Second, with the rapid growth of the Utah programs and the popularity of the Utah model, which attracts other states to replicate it, more research is needed to support and help make suggestions for improvements to the model to benefit not only DLI students in Utah, but also those in the states that follow Utah. Third, despite the criticisms that the Utah model favors white mainstream students and is unconcerned with language minority students, the programs do serve a small number of heritage learners (e.g. there was one heritage student in each of the two cohorts in the current studies), and the quality of their learning deserves attention. Finally, although DLI instruction is seen as an effective form of bilingual education producing highly bilingual and biliterate students, DLI research has been focused on the Spanish language. Chinese, a structurally different language, is entitled to more investigation.

Introduction to This Volume

The chapters in this book give insights into the recently established Utah Chinese DLI phenomenon from multiple angles. All DLI stakeholders – such as students, teachers, parents, school administrators and the state director – who played important roles in the Chinese programs, were involved in the studies included in this book. The following paragraphs give short introductions to the chapters.

Chapters 2 and 3 report the findings on the Chinese DLI program benefits, challenges and suggestions identified by teachers, administrators and parents. Chapter 2 focuses on interviews with the state director of the Chinese DLI programs, principals whose schools offer Chinese DLI programs and Chinese and English partner teachers in Chinese DLI programs. Chapter 3 has an emphasis on interviews with Chinese DLI parents in different school districts in Utah. The objective of these two chapters is to present the perspectives of the parents, teachers, school administrators and the state director toward, and their first-hand experience with, Chinese DLI programs.

Chapter 4 explores four Chinese DLI teachers' identities through the method of in-depth interviews on their beliefs, perceptions and interpretations of events both in their personal and professional life experiences.

The four cases discussed in this chapter represent four typical types of Chinese DLI teachers. They are individuals who are (1) Chinese native speakers who received a degree in the US prior to teaching in DLI; (2) Chinese native speakers who married a US citizen or green card holder; (3) Chinese native speakers who were sent to the US from China by the Confucius Institute; and (4) English native speakers who speak Chinese fluently as a second language through an academic degree or immersion in Chinese language and culture overseas. Narrative inquiry, which focuses on the stories told by the teachers (Barkhuizen, 2016), was employed to investigate teachers' identities.

Chapter 5 has two foci. As the Utah model requires two teachers, one teaching through the target language and the other instructing in English, the effectiveness of the two partner teachers' communication is essential to aid to the success of the programs. In addition, in DLI programs which run the foreign language immersion model such as the Chinese DLI programs in Utah, almost none of the parents speak the target language; hence, ways to support parents to assist their children's study are necessary. In order to create an effective learning environment, not only the quality of instruction, but also communication among teachers, and communication between parents and teachers, are important elements. Through the theoretical lens of the Cultural-Historical Activity Theory (CHAT), this chapter reports the level of effectiveness of communication and assistance from a classroom teacher to the parents and examines how regular formal and informal communications between the Chinese and English partner teachers can build not only a professional, but a friendly team relationship, which positively influences the program quality.

Chapter 6 reports the language teaching and learning strategies employed in a first-grade Chinese DLI classroom. The roles of language teaching and learning strategies are of paramount significance in second language acquisition; however, research on strategies tends to focus only on the foreign language learning context and dismiss the DLI context. This chapter employs the method of classroom observation and Oxford's (1990) Taxonomy of Strategies as the framework. The reasons certain strategies are found to be used more frequently than others will be discussed. Based on the study results, teaching implications are suggested.

Chapter 7 tests the recently proposed concept of chunking for learning and teaching Chinese characters. One of the unique features of the Chinese language system is its ideographic written language, which is deemed difficult to master by native speakers of alphabetical languages such as English. The effectiveness of the chunking method based on the chunking theory was measured using students' character lesson tests, and a delayed comprehensive character test.

Chapter 8 explores Chinese DLI student errors, teachers' oral corrective feedback (CF) and students' subsequent responses (e.g. uptake and repair). CF is a teacher's response to a student's erroneous language production, which helps the student to pay attention to form while they try to communicate in the target language. By applying the view of the social interactionist theory, the daily oral interactions in a Chinese DLI classroom were recorded and analyzed. The one and only heritage student's utterances were analyzed and presented separately. Statistical tests were run to examine whether there were significant differences in the frequency of the teacher's feedback types, and whether the feedback types and learners' uptake and repair, which are often seen as indicators of learning effectiveness, were related.

Chapter 9 describes how translanguaging was used by a group of first-year Chinese DLI learners who entered the program speaking only English. Learning a new language involves learning 'a new way of being in the world' (Becker, 1995: 227). In the DLI classroom context, emergent bilinguals are found to use translanguaging (using two languages dynamically and simultaneously in communication), a bilingual phenomenon and a new developing theory, to facilitate learning and to make sense of their world (García, 2011). The findings documented how the emergent bilingual seven-year-olds used translanguaging to appropriate the new language and integrate the new language practices into their single linguistic repertoire.

The final chapter, Chapter 10, summarizes the major findings from the previous chapters. How these findings might be perceived within the national and the international contexts are discussed as well. This chapter closes by giving directions for future implementation and research in DLI programs.

The Overarching Theoretical Frameworks

In addition to the different frameworks applied in each chapter, this book draws on a couple of theoretical concepts as the underlying approaches that span across different chapters to examine how the different stakeholders define, position and act in the Chinese DLI programs in Utah. For the results found in Chapters 2, 3 and 5, the concept of policy ecology (Weaver-Hightower, 2008), which focuses on how a policy is situated within the sociocultural environment of the time (e.g. history, people, places, economic and political conditions, and institutions), is used to analyze the different participants' positions. For the results reported in Chapters 4, 6, 7, 8 and 9, which contain classroom and teaching identity research, the sociocultural theory is applied to understand the teaching and learning phenomena. As both the policy ecology approach and the sociocultural theory are based on the view that learning and policymaking are complex social practices and continuous processes of cultural production, the conclusions and implications made in the final chapter (Chapter 10) interweave the various results from the previous chapters, and should be seen as all-encompassing.

Our Positionalities

Approximately two decades ago, Freeman (1998) examined how a group of educators in a Spanish-English bilingual school in low-income Latino areas in Washington, DC went against the norm in mainstream educational practices to help minority students succeed academically. Through interviews and classroom interactions, Freeman positioned herself as a participant observer and a learner, who was eager to gain more understanding of the school's educational perspectives and practices and how they achieved their goals. We concur with Freeman's belief that 'it is important for bilingual education researchers to go beyond general discussions of *what* bilingual education means to investigate *how* and *why* actual bilingual programs function the way that they do in specific social and historical locations' (1998: 2). In contrast to researching how a bilingual program successfully functioned to aid the education of a minority population as Freeman did, this book takes readers in a different direction to examine the newly implemented, but fast-growing and nationally influential Utah DLI model serving a mostly English-speaking Caucasian population. In this book, we situate ourselves in several positions. First, we positioned ourselves as trained language teachers and second language acquisition researchers. The many years of teaching and researching experience we have ensure that the data is collected and interpreted based on sound theories and research methods. Second, we positioned ourselves as Chinese-speaking minority and current and future parents of Chinese heritage learners. Maintaining one's ethnic identity through its language and culture is essential to help heritage learners succeed in education and life in general. As we are minority stakeholders in the Chinese DLI context, we take the minority's educational equality to heart and critically examine issues related to it in the DLI context. Finally, we take both the insider and outsider roles in the Chinese DLI context. In Chapters 2 to 5, being both a current Chinese DLI educator in Utah and a researcher of this book, the second author considered herself to have the insider position when she interviewed and analyzed DLI educators. Also, Chapters 6 to 9 involved classroom research in which the second author acted as both the focal teacher participant in the classroom and as a researcher. Her insider position allowed her to investigate the particular issues in depth, and easy access to other participants and information further increased her insider knowledge regarding the studied situations. In addition, as an insider, the second author was able to be 'uniquely positioned to understand the experiences of groups of which they are members' (Kerstetter, 2012: 100), even in highly complex situations. In contrast, the first author took the outsider perspective, which is often valued for its neutral and detached views. As the outsider, the first author was able to observe and analyze the situations more objectively. Having both the insider and the outsider views in the classroom studies helped cancel out the disadvantages of only viewing the studies from a single perspective.

References

Abello-Contesse, C. (1999) El futuro de la enseñanza de lenguas extranjeras internacionales y la inmersión en L2 en la educación pública. In J.M. Becerra Hiraldo, P. Barros Garciá, A. Martinez Gonzalez and J.A. de Molina Redondo (eds) *La enseñanza de segundas lenguas* (pp. 83–90). Granada: Grupo de Investigación de Lingüística Aplicada (GILA).

Abello-Contesse, C. (2013) Bilingual and multilingual education: An overview of the field. In C. Abello-Contesse, P.M. Chandler, M.D. López-Jiménez and R. Chacón-Beltrán (eds) *Bilingual and Multilingual Education in the 21st Century: Building on Experience* (pp. 3–23). Bristol: Multilingual Matters.

American Community Survey (2011) Poverty status in the past 12 months of families 2006–2010 American Community Survey 5-Year Estimates. See www.census.gov/programs-surveys/acs/ (accessed 17 July 2017).

Baker, C. (2003) Bilingual education: A historical overview. In L. Medina (ed.) *Bilingual Education* (pp. 10–18). Farmington Hills, MI: Greenhaven Press.

Baker, C. and Wright, W. (2017) *Foundations of Bilingual Education and Bilingualism* (6th edn). Bristol: Multilingual Matters.

Barkhuizen, G. (2016) Narrative approaches to exploring language, identity and power in language teacher education. *RELC Journal* 47 (1), 25–42.

Becker, A.L. (1995) *Beyond Translation: Essays toward a Modern Philosophy*. Ann Arbor, MI: University of Michigan Press.

Canham, M. (2007) Utah less Mormon than ever. *The Salt Lake Tribune*, 18 November. See http://archive.sltrib.com/story.php?ref=/ci_7496034 (accessed May 17, 2018).

Christian, D. (2016) Dual language education: Current research perspectives. *International Multilingual Research Journal* 10 (1), 1–5.

Confucius Institute Headquarters (2017) Functions of Hanban. See http://english.hanban.org/node_7719.htm (accessed 22 July 2017).

Crawford, J. (2007) Hard Sell: Why is bilingual education so unpopular with the American public? In O. García and C. Baker (eds) *Bilingual Education: An Introductory Reader* (pp. 145–164). Clevedon: Multilingual Matters.

Cummins, J. (1999) Research, ethics, and public discourse: The debate on bilingual education. Presentation at the national Conference of the American Association of Higher Education. University of Toronto. See www.languagepolicy.net/archives/cummins2.htm (accessed 22 July 2017).

Curtain, H., Donato, R. and Gilbert, V. (2016) Elementary school foreign language programs in the United States. In B. Steven (ed.) *Foreign Language Education in America* (pp. 19–41). Hampshire: Palgrave Macmillan.

Delavan, M.G., Valdez, V.E. and Freire, J.A. (2017) Language as whose resource?: When global economics usurp the local equity potentials of dual language education. *International Multilingual Research Journal* 11 (2), 86–100.

Feldman, L.B. and Siok, W.W. (1999) Semantic radicals in phonetic compounds: Implications for visual character recognition in Chinese. In J. Wang, C. Chen, R. Radach and A. Inhoff (eds) *Reading Chinese Script: A Cognitive Analysis* (pp. 19–35). Mahwah, NJ: Lawrence Erlbaum Associates.

Freeman, R. (2007) Reviewing the research on language education programs. In O. García and C. Baker (eds) *Bilingual Education: An Introductory Reader* (pp. 3–18). Clevedon: Multilingual Matters.

Freire, J.A., Valdez, V.E. and Delavan, M.G. (2016) The (dis) inclusion of Latina/o interests from Utah's dual language education boom. *Journal of Latinos and Education* 16, 1–14.

García, O. (2011) Translanguaging of Latino kindergarteners. In K. Potowski and J. Rothman (eds) *Bilingual Youth: Spanish in English Speaking Societies* (pp. 33–55). Amsterdam: John Benjamins.

Genesee, F. (1987) *Learning Through Two Languages*. Cambridge, MA: Newbury House Publishers.

Grenfell, M. and Harris, V. (2015) Memorisation strategies and the adolescent learner of Mandarin Chinese as a foreign language. *Linguistics and Education* 31, 1–13.

Hao, Y.C. (2012) Second language acquisition of Mandarin Chinese tones by tonal and non-tonal language speakers. *Journal of Phonetics* 40 (2), 269–279.

Kerstetter, K. (2012) Insider, outsider, or somewhere in between: The impact of researchers' identities on the community-based research process. *Journal of Rural Social Sciences* 27 (2), 99–117.

Kheng, C.C.S. and Baldauf, R.B. (2011) Global Language: (De)colonisation in the new era. In E. Hinkel (ed.) *Handbook of Research in Second Language Teaching and Learning* (pp. 952–969). New York, NY: Routledge.

The Language Flagship (2018) *About Us*. See www.thelanguageflagship.org/content/about-us (accessed 16 May 2018).

Lee, C.H. and Kalyuga, S. (2011) Effectiveness of different pinyin presentation formats in learning Chinese characters: A cognitive load perspective. *Language Learning* 61 (4), 1099–1117.

Lee-Thompson, L. C. (2008) An investigation of reading strategies applied by American learners of Chinese as a foreign language. *Foreign Language Annals* 41 (4), 702–721.

Lindholm-Leary, K.J. (2001) *Dual Language Education*. Clevedon: Multilingual Matters.

Lindholm-Leary, K.J. (2012) Success and challenges in dual language education. *Theory Into Practice* 51, 256–262.

Lindholm-Leary, K.J. (2016) Students' perceptions of bilingualism in Spanish and Mandarin dual language programs. *International Multilingual Research Journal* 10 (1), 59–70.

Lindholm-Leary, K.J. and Borsato, G. (2005) Hispanic high schoolers and mathematics: Follow-up of students who had participated in two-way bilingual elementary programs. *Bilingual Research Journal* 29, 641–652.

Lindholm-Leary, K.J. and Borsato, G. (2006) Academic achievement. In F.G. Genesee, K. Lindholm-Leary, W.M. Saunders and D. Christian (eds) *Educating English Language Learners: A Synthesis of Research Evidence* (pp. 176–222). New York, NY: Cambridge University Press.

Lindholm-Leary, K.J. and Howard, E.R. (2008) Language development and academic achievement in two-way immersion programs. In T.W. Fortune and D.J. Tedick (eds) *Pathways to Multilingualism: Evolving Perspectives on Immersion Education* (pp. 177–200). Clevedon: Multilingual Matters.

Malakoff, M. and Hakuta, K. (1990) History of language minority education in the United States. In A.M. Padilla, H.H. Fairchild and C.M. Valadez (eds) *Bilingual Education: Issues and Strategies* (pp. 27–43). Newbury Park, CA: Sage Publications.

Medina, L. (2003) *Bilingual Education*. Farmington Hills, MI: Greenhaven Press.

Mormon Newsroom (2018) 2017 statistical report for 2018 April conference. See www.mormonnewsroom.org/article/2017-statistical-report-april-2018-general-conference (accessed 15 May 2018).

National Center for Education Statistics (2017) Number and percentage of public school students participating in English language learner (ELL) programs, by state: Selected years, fall 2004 through fall 2014. See https://nces.ed.gov/programs/digest/d16/tables/dt16_204.20.asp (accessed 11 May 2017).

Ovando, C.J. (2003) Bilingual education in the United States: Historical development and current issues. *Bilingual Research Journal* 27 (1), 1–24.

Oxford, R.L. (1990) *Language Learning Strategies*. New York, NY: Newbury House.

Provo Missionary Training Center (2018) See www.mtc.byu.edu/about/ (accessed 15 May 2018).

Proximity One (2017) School district demographic. See http://proximityone.com/sd11dp1.htm (accessed July 16, 2017).

Roberts, G., Suddreth, D. and Dickson, S. (2016) Dual language immersion: Prepared by the Utah State Office of Education. See http://le.utah.gov/interim/2016/pdf/00000674.pdf (accessed 15 July 2017).

Ruark, E.A. (2012) English language learners and public education in Utah. See https://fairus.org/issue/societal-impact/english-language-learners-and-public-education-utah-2012 (accessed 15 May 2018).

Seib, P. (2016) *The Future of Diplomacy*. New York, NY: John Wiley & Sons.

Shen, H. and Ke, C. (2007) An investigation of radical awareness and word acquisition among non-native learners of Chinese. *The Modern Language Journal* 91, 97–111.

Snow, M.A. (1986) Innovative second language education: Bilingual immersion programs, Education Report No. 1. Los Angeles, CA: UCLA Center for Language Education and Research.

The State of Language in the United States (2017) The National K–12 Foreign Language Enrollment Survey Report. See www.americancouncils.org/sites/default/files/FLE-report-June17.pdf (accessed 16 May 2018).

Stritikus, T. and Varghese, M. (2012) Global movements in education and their impact on diverse students. In D.A. Urias (ed.) *The Immigration & Education Nexus* (pp. 37–55). Rotterdam: Sense Publishers.

Sung, K.Y. (2014) Novice learners' Chinese-character learning strategies and performance. *Electronic Journal of Foreign Language Teaching* 11 (1), 38–51.

Sung, K.Y. and Wu, H. (2011) Factors influencing the learning of Chinese characters. *International Journal of Bilingual Education and Bilingualism* 14 (6), 683–700.

Thomas, W.P. and Collier, V. (1997) *School Effectiveness for Language Minority Students* (NCBE Resource Collection Series No. 9). Washington, D.C.: National Clearinghouse for Bilingual Education.

Thomas, W.P. and Collier, V. (2002) A national study of school effectiveness for language minority students' long-term academic achievement. See http://cmmr.usc.edu/CollierThomasExReport.pdf (accessed 20 July 2017).

U.S. Census Bureau (2016) Quick facts. See www.census.gov/quickfacts/fact/table/cachecountyutah/EDU685215#viewtop (accessed 19 July 2017).

U.S. Census Bureau (2018) Quick facts Utah. See www.census.gov/quickfacts/UT (accessed 15 May 2018).

U.S. Department of Education (2015) Dual language education programs: Current state policies and practices. See www.air.org/sites/default/files/downloads/report/Dual-Language-Education-Programs-Current-State-Policies-April-2015.pdf (accessed July 18, 2017).

Utah Administration Code Rule R277-488 (2017) Critical languages program. See https://rules.utah.gov/publicat/code/r277/r277-488.htm (accessed July 21, 2017).

Utah Dual Language Immersion (2017a) Why immersion? See www.utahdli.org/whyimmersion.html (accessed July 10, 2017).

Utah Dual Language Immersion (2017b) Dual language immersion instructional time. See www.utahdli.org/instructionalmodel.html (accessed 10 July 2017).

Utah Education Policy Center (2015) Dual language immersion program participation. See http://l2trec.utah.edu/research/DLI%20partipation_2015_final.pdf (accessed 1 July 2017).

Utah Language Data Report (2016) See www.health.utah.gov/disparities/data/ohd/UtahLangaugeDataReport2016.pdf (accessed 7 May 2017).

Utah Office of Administrative Rules (2018) Utah Administrative Code. See https://rules.utah.gov/publicat/code/r277/r277-716.htm#T4 (accessed 14 May 2018).

Utah State Board of Education (2018) Utah State Board of Education Release of the 2015–16 School Year SAGE English Language Arts, Mathematics, and Science

Assessment Results. See www.schools.utah.gov/file/c2d00ec1-61cc-4999-8a2e-4ab91 700edc1 (accessed 15 May 2018).

Valdez, V.E., Delavan, G. and Freire, J.A. (2016a) The marketing of dual language education policy in Utah print media. *Educational Policy* 30 (6), 849–883.

Valdez, V.E., Freire, J.A. and Delavan, G. (2016b) The gentrification of dual language education. *Urban Rev* 48, 601–627.

Wang, S. (2010) Chinese language education in the United States. In J. Chen, C. Wang and J. Cai (eds) *Teaching and Learning Chinese: Issues and Perspectives* (pp. 3–32). Charlotte, NC: Information Age Publishing.

Wang, M., Perfetti, C.A. and Liu, Y. (2003) Alphabetic readers quickly acquire orthographic structure in learning to read Chinese. *Scientific Studies in Reading* 72, 183–207.

Wang, J. and Ruan, J. (2016) Historical overview of Chinese language education for speakers of other languages in China and the United States. In J. Ruan, J. Zhang and C.B. Leung (eds) *Chinese Language Education in the United States* (pp. 1–28). Cham, Switzerland: Springer International Publishing.

Weaver-Hightower, M.B. (2008). An ecology metaphor for educational policy analysis: A call to complexity. *Educational Researcher* 37 (3), 153–167.

Wiley, T.G. (2007) Accessing language rights in education: A brief history of the US context. In O. García and C. Baker (eds) *Bilingual Education: An Introductory Reader* (pp. 89–107). Clevedon: Multilingual Matters.

Wilson, D.M. (2011) Dual language programs on the rise: 'Enrichment' model puts content learning front and center for ELL students. *Harvard Education Letter* (27) 2. See http://hepg.org/hel-home/issues/27_2/helarticle/dual-language-programs-on-the-rise (accessed 27 April 2018).

Wong, K., Li, W., Xu, R. and Zhang, Z. (2010) *Introduction to Chinese Natural Language Processing*. San Rafael, CA: Morgan & Claypool Publishers.

Xu, L. (2014) 2014 Hanban annual report. See www.handban.edu.cn/report/pdf/2014.pdf (accessed 14 July 2017).

2 Benefits, Challenges and Suggestions: Voices From Teachers and Administrators

Introduction

Since the popularity of DLI programs rose in the United States, DLI research has documented students' success in reaching high language proficiency and academic achievement mostly through the analysis of DLI students' testing scores in the subjects of English Language Arts, Math and the target language (Lindholm-Leary, 2012). On the other hand, current literature rarely investigated positive student outcomes other than testing scores, or the challenges faced by DLI programs. Without knowing the full benefits of DLI programs and challenges encountered in the programs, better DLI implementations and promotions in the future are difficult. Thus, Chapters 2 and 3 present a study which interviewed Utah DLI parents, teachers and administrators regarding their perceptions of the benefits of enrolling in Chinese DLI programs, the challenges they faced in the programs and suggestions they offered for improvements. This chapter first summarizes the findings from current literature about the benefits and challenges of, and suggestions for, DLI programs. Next, this chapter reports the findings of the few studies which focused on the DLI teachers' views. Finally, the findings based on the Utah Chinese DLI teachers' and administrators' interviews are discussed. The results of the Utah Chinese DLI parents' interviews are discussed in Chapter 3.

Benefits of DLI Programs

One major benefit promoted by DLI programs is that the students in the programs will become fluent bilinguals. Results from research (Howard et al., 2004; Howard & Christian, 1997; Lindholm-Leary, 2001) examining DLI students' language proficiencies have confirmed that programs with adequate design and implementation produce proficient bilingual speakers. One study which illustrated this outcome is Lindholm-Leary's (2001), in which she used the Student Oral Language Observation Matrix (SOLOM) to test the English and Spanish oral proficiency levels of Spanish DLI students. The study results showed that the majority of the students were rated as proficient in both languages when they reached the upper elementary grade levels. High levels of proficiency in two languages were not only found in the students' oral skills, but also in their literacy skills. For example, Howard *et al.* (2004) analyzed the scores of English and Spanish reading comprehension tests taken at different grade levels by more than 300 Spanish DLI students in 11 programs across the US, and reported a native language effect. In other words, English-speaking students performed better on English tests while Spanish-speaking students performed better on Spanish tests; however, further analysis showed that the gap between the two groups diminished over time. By the fifth grade, the English and Spanish test scores of the two groups of students were only slightly different, implying that both groups of students were fluent in their second languages. In a different study, Howard and Christian (1997) focused on the analysis of eight upper elementary grade Spanish DLI students' English and Spanish writing. The researchers found that even though the writing was not without errors, both the English and Spanish writing samples examined were equally sophisticated in terms of their topic development, organization, language use and mechanics.

Becoming a fluent bilingual is not the only benefit of enrolling in a DLI program. Research has shown that proficiency in two languages correlates with academic achievement in both languages. Many studies (García, 2003; Lindholm-Leary & Genesee, 2010; Lindholm-Leary, 2012) illustrated that by fifth grade, the standardized English reading and math test scores of both English-speaking and heritage-speaking DLI students were at or above grade level. In addition, both groups of students also performed at or above grade level in the partner language. The high academic achievements were also shown in the test scores of the English language learners (ELLs) enrolled in DLI programs. For example, Alanís and Rodriguez (2008) analyzed the test results of the English Texas Assessment of Knowledge and Skills (TAKS) in reading, mathematics and science taken by fifth grade ELLs, who were enrolled in a two-way Spanish DLI program in a school with a high percentage of economically disadvantaged and non-English speaking student population. The study results illustrated that the ELLs' scores were significantly higher than other students in the district and across the state. Alanís and Rodriguez, along with other scholars (Thomas *et al.*, 1993), concluded that the amount of the students' first language used in their formal schooling could be a strong predictor for ELLs' academic achievement. Hence, DLI programs, which utilize an extensive amount of time in teaching through ELLs' first language is a particularly effective education model, which benefits ELLs' academic learning tremendously.

Challenges of DLI Programs

Lindholm-Leary (2012) identified a couple of issues documented in current research that DLI programs need to overcome. The first issue is the debate about instructional time allocated for each language. In a Korean DLI study, even though the program stated the required time for each language, Lee and Jeong (2013) described how the Korean parents preferred that their children received more English instruction, while the non-Korean parents opposed the idea and believed that their children needed more instruction in Korean. The same debate occurred among the educators and school administrators when they needed to help their students comply with the requirements of the No Child Left Behind Act, which stated that all students from third- to eighth- grades, including non-native English speakers who have been in the US for one or more years, need to reach the standard competency in English language arts and other content subjects. Some school personnel believe that increasing the instructional time in English will help students pass the standardized tests more easily, discounting that current research has pointed out that it takes more than a year for DLI students, especially heritage students, to catch up on English tests.

The other challenge that Lindholm-Leary identified is the lack of instructions or guidelines for educators to follow to help students develop high academic language and literacy proficiency in two languages. Although an objective of DLI programs is to produce highly fluent bilinguals, current state standards and curricula are designed for English-only classrooms. Moreover, even though there are studies (Genesee & Riches, 2006; Saunders & Goldenberg, 2009) which offer insights into instructional methods for promoting literacy skills in a second language, they were conducted in the context of learning English as a second language and did not focus on DLI settings. Hence, due to a lack of DLI research and state guidelines for DLI classrooms, it is challenging for educators and administrators to implement well-designed DLI programs.

Suggestions for DLI Programs

A successful DLI program requires many key components. Through her prior work experience, the former bilingual teacher and teacher trainer, Montague (1997), identified several crucial elements that need to be thought through before starting a DLI program. First, school administrators need to carefully select the type of DLI model to be implemented in the community, with consideration for local minority languages and the sociocultural and sociopolitical atmosphere in the community. Second, slowly implementing a DLI program grade by grade each year rather than initiating multiple levels in the same year will ease the pressure on the English-speaking students needing to speedily adapt to the learning of the second language. Third, the proportion of the population of English and target language speakers needs to be balanced. In some DLI programs, the ratio of English to target language speakers can be as high as 9:1. Such imbalanced ratios would negatively affect the quality of the program, as there are not enough peers to be models of the target language. Fourth, it is often the case that due to a lack of resources, the teaching materials for a target language are made by classroom teachers themselves. It becomes time-consuming when the teachers need to spend time not only on lesson planning, but also making classroom materials. This might create pressure on the teachers and may affect the quality of their instruction. In addition, the self-made materials might send the message that the target language is not an important language to the students. Therefore, it is imperative that school administrators allocate necessary resources for teaching materials before a DLI program begins operating. Fifth, as mentioned in the Challenges of DLI Programs section above, teachers need more guidance on how to help develop students' bilingual competencies. Montague (1997) stated that offering professional training to bilingual teachers is essential to ensure the success of DLI programs. Sixth, as the leaders of the schools, school principals' support toward DLI programs in various areas, such as explaining the DLI model to parents whose children are new to the program and assisting in finding solutions for teaching or classroom management issues, are all critical for the programs. Finally, Montague suggested that researchers should look into how to encourage English-speaking DLI students to more actively participate in class in the target language, as she observed that many of these students did not see the importance of learning the target language and would not speak up unless the teacher elicited answers from them.

Studies on Teachers' and Administrators' Perspectives Toward DLI Programs

DLI studies on the views of current DLI professionals are rare. Lee and Jeong (2013) conducted a small-scale qualitative study on the perceptions of two teachers in a newly instituted Korean dual language immersion program. The teachers identified several benefits of the program, such as the students' development of bilingualism, reinforcement of ethnic identity and culture for the heritage students and respect for other languages and cultures. In terms of the concerns for the program, one issue the teachers worried about was the high program dropout rate. Due to some of the Korean parents' strong preference for their children to receive more instruction in English, 10 out of 36 students were transferred to English-only classrooms from the DLI classroom when the students completed the kindergarten level. The other challenge the teachers faced was insufficient support and resources for the program. The teachers stated that there was no state-developed curriculum specifically for the DLI program, the Korean books in the library were outdated (e.g. books containing old Korean orthographic conventions) and there were no age-appropriate books for teaching culture. In addition, the teachers sensed tension between them and the parents due to the distinct expectations among the parents (e.g. some hoped for more instruction in English, while the rest demanded more instruction in Korean).

Another study reporting DLI teachers' views of DLI through their professional experiences is Howard and Loeb's (1998) questionnaire and interview study. The results of the analysis of the 181 questionnaires and eight interviews by Spanish-speaking DLI teachers showed that the teachers believed that DLI promoted equality and fairness. In DLI classes, English-speaking and minority language-speaking students are each other's language model, which offers them equal opportunities to learn from each other. Moreover, the teachers stated that by learning and modeling their heritage language, the Spanish-speaking students had raised their self-esteem and confidence. Moreover, the teachers observed that the Spanish-speaking students seemed to learn English faster than students in English-only classes and that their parents tended to be involved in school more.

On the other hand, the teachers also listed a few challenges. Just like in the previously mentioned studies by Lee and Jeong (2013), the teachers in Howard and Loeb's (1998) study also identified a lack of teaching resources as a challenge. Many teachers indicated that they needed to make their own teaching materials, which made preparation too time-consuming for them. Moreover, teachers' working time got even tighter in programs which required English and Spanish teachers to alternate between two classes, resulting in these teachers having twice as many students to manage compared to teachers in other programs. Besides challenges encountered within the area of teaching, the teachers also identified multiple challenges in other areas. One was communication with parents. It was difficult to make clear to parents that acquiring a second language is a long process. Another challenge was the tension between DLI programs and general programs within schools, as non-DLI teachers complained about the DLI programs receiving more funding.

Elaborated discussions about DLI programs by DLI teachers and administrators, such as in Lee and Jeong's (2013) and Howard and Loeb's (1998) studies, are few and far between in the literature. Hence, this chapter is intended to assist in understanding more about the benefits, challenges and suggestions for DLI programs through the eyes of DLI professionals, including DLI teachers and administrators.

Data Collection and Analysis

This study used the method of one-on-one interviews in examining the perspectives of parents, teachers and administrators toward the

Chinese DLI programs in Utah. The parents, the Chinese DLI director from the Utah State Office of Education and all school administrators and Chinese DLI teachers in the districts in Utah which approved our study proposal were contacted to inquire about their interest in participating in the study. All participants who agreed to participate in the study signed the consent form. A 20–30 minute face-to-face or phone interview was conducted with each participant. Codes were used as pseudonyms to protect the participants' identities. Each parent was assigned the letter 'P' followed by a number. Each teacher was assigned either the letter 'C' (Chinese) or 'E' (English), depending on the language they taught, followed by a number. Each school administrator was assigned the letters 'SA' followed by a number. The interviews were semi-structured, with the main objective of eliciting detailed discussions on the benefits and challenges of, and suggestions for, Chinese DLI programs. A total of 20 parents, 25 teachers, two school administrators and the state director were involved in this study.

The interviews were audio-recorded and transcribed. The transcripts were read carefully and separately by us for themes which addressed the benefits and challenges of, and suggestions for, the programs. After that, we compared the coded themes. The inter-rater reliability for the coding was 95%. Interview excerpts were drawn from the data for use as examples to illustrate the participants' perspectives.

Who are the DLI Teachers and Administrators?

The teacher participants involved in this study were 22 female and 3 male teachers, among whom 10 were English teachers and 15 were Chinese teachers (see Table 2.1). Among the 15 Chinese teachers, 12 were Chinese native speakers, while three spoke Chinese as a second language. In terms of teaching experience, 11 teachers were fairly new teachers

Table 2.1 DLI teacher participants' background information

Gender	Male: 3
	Female: 22
Instructional Language	Teaching in English (English Teachers): 10
	Teaching in Chinese (Chinese Teachers): 15
Native Language	Chinese: 12
	English: 13
Years of Teaching Experience	1–5 Years: 11
	6–10 Years: 7
	11–20 Years: 4
	More Than 20 Years: 3
Highest Academic Degree	B.A.: 12
	M.A.: 13
Major	Education: 23
	Others: 2

who had only taught for 1–5 years, while the rest of the 14 teachers' experiences ranged from six to 20 years. One teacher majored in Exercise Science and a second majored in Business; the rest majored in Education with either bachelor's or master's degrees.

In addition to the teacher participants, this study also involved two school administrators and the Chinese DLI director for the state. The two school administrators were both male. One had five years of K–12 teaching experience and three years of administration experience, while the other had four years of K–12 teaching experience and five years of administration experience. Both of them had three years of experience managing the Chinese DLI programs in their schools. The director for the state was female and had over 25 years of teaching experience both locally and internationally. Prior to becoming the Chinese DLI director, she managed the world language program in a school for three years. At the time of the interview, she had been the Chinese director for three years and managed the Chinese DLI programs in 31 elementary and 12 junior high schools in Utah.

Benefits Identified by the Teachers

The top three benefits of enrolling in the Chinese DLI programs were identified and agreed by most of the English and Chinese teacher participants (thereafter referred as C1–C15 and E1–E10).

More work opportunities

The number one benefit identified is that the students will have more work opportunities in the future (see Table 2.2). This benefit is based on the teachers' belief that 'Knowing more languages will help the students gain more work opportunities in the future' (C1). Moreover, many of the participants also pinpointed the rising economy in China and how knowing Chinese as a second language is especially advantageous for future employment. Comments such as 'China is more and more powerful' (C9), 'Chinese is the language of the business world right now' (E5) and 'Chinese being such a super power can open a lot of doors' (E3) all suggest that the teachers recognize the importance of learning a second language, and particularly Chinese, for the students' future competitiveness.

Knowing more than one culture

The second most frequently mentioned benefit by the teachers has to do with knowing more than one culture. For example, a teacher mentioned, 'Anyone who knows more than one language knows more than one culture and knows where they are living is not the only way they live. And I think it is valuable for kids to learn' (C15). The teachers believed that the students would become 'more open-minded' (E2) as they know

Table 2.2 Teachers' perspectives on the benefits of the Chinese DLI programs

Ranking	Chinese Teachers' Perspectives	# of Chinese Teachers Who Believed in the Benefits	English Teachers' Perspectives	# of English Teachers Who Believed in the Benefits
1	More Work Opportunities in the Future	9	More Work Opportunities in the Future	4
2	Knowing More Than One Culture	7	Knowing More Than One Culture	4
3	Brain Development	3	Brain Development	4
			Confidence	3
			Learning a Second Language at a Young Age	3

there is more than one way to live. They will also be 'more tolerant toward different cultures' (C12), have 'more sophisticated thinking' (C11), know to 'be more flexible' (C11), have 'a wider world view' (C13) and be 'more compassionate toward other people'. (E4)

Brain development

The third benefit mentioned by some of the English and Chinese teachers is the students' brain development. The teachers described the advantages for children's brain development when learning a second language at a young age. The following excerpt is a good example.

Receiving dual language instruction at a young age helps form their brains in a more sophisticated way and enrich their language development. The brain functions differently when it's exposed to the language learning method such as the ones they experienced in the DLI setting. According to various research done previously, DLI students showed the same or even better development after a certain amount of time. The beginning progress might not be obvious; however, given time, parents, teachers, and students will all witness the great success of their performance. (C9)

Confidence booster

Besides the aforementioned three benefits, a few English teachers also reported that the DLI programs helped boost their students' confidence level. One observed, 'It makes them very confident, and I think confidence is a huge thing' (E7). Another English teacher also observed higher confidence in the students. She explained that it could be the success they felt about knowing two languages. She stated, 'It helps them from the beginning to feel successful about something that is maybe a little unusual, or something that their parents don't have' (E10). A different teacher attested that learning in the DLI programs boosted the students' confidence because they realized that they could overcome the challenge of learning a second language. She said,

> A lot of times, when a child can't read and I'm trying to teach a child to read, in the general education program, they would just say 'I can't do it' and sometimes they wouldn't try. But because these kids [DLI students] know that they can do hard things. They're learning Chinese and that's hard...They fight through and they tend to succeed because they know that, even though it's a challenge, it's something that they can work through. (E5)

It was evident to teacher E5 that, based on her past teaching experiences in both DLI and non-DLI settings, a big difference she saw in the two settings was that the challenging tasks the DLI students completed in the programs helped build the students' self-confidence and self-assurance.

Learning a second language at a young age

The next benefit that some of the English teachers mentioned is related to the advantages of learning a second language at a young age. One teacher stated, 'I think it is an amazing opportunity for them to be able to learn a second language, especially being so young where their minds are easily able to absorb new information and absorb a second language' (E1). Another teacher believed that it would be easier for young learners to learn additional languages. She said, 'It makes it easier for them to learn another language when they've learned a second one' (E4). The other belief related to starting in the DLI programs at a young age is that 'If it follows them all through high school...they'll be way higher than the other kids' (E9).

Challenges Identified by the Teachers

Most of the challenges perceived by the English and Chinese DLI teachers were distinct. Moreover, the Chinese teachers seemed to have more diverse challenges while the challenges identified by the English teachers were fewer (see Table 2.3). This section first discusses the challenges encountered by the Chinese teachers, followed by the ones found by the English teachers.

Limited resources

Eight out of the 15 Chinese teachers identified the lack of resources as a challenge for their teaching. One resource which was lacking was standardized teaching materials for the upper grade levels. One teacher explained, 'The biggest challenge for me is the lack of teaching resources. I left the 6th grade teaching position because it was difficult to teach

Table 2.3 Teachers' perspectives on the challenges of the Chinese DLI programs

Ranking	Chinese Teachers' Perspectives	# of Chinese Teachers Who Encountered the Challenge	English Teachers' Perspectives	# of English Teachers Who Encountered the Challenge
1	Limited Resources	8	Limited Time to Accomplish All Tasks	8
2	Curriculum Changes Frequently	6	Communication with the Chinese Teachers	4
3	Gap between Students	6		
4	Limited Time and Large Class Size	5		
5	Lack of Support from Parents and Administrators	4		
6	Chinese-Only Rule	3		

humanities without teaching materials' (C3). Another area lacking teaching resources was the subject of science. One Chinese teacher pointed out that the science class 'still doesn't have a textbook or materials. It all depends on the teachers to do PPT, find pictures, and make short clips' (C5), while another Chinese teacher stated that 'the resources for teaching science are scarce' and that she had to 'spend a lot of time making lesson plans and materials' (C4). One teacher thought that it would be helpful if someone other than the teachers could be responsible for 'mak[ing] all the pictures, all the supplies, and even some ready-to-go PPT' (C7). The lack of resources was also identified in the supplemental materials and technology tools. One teacher described how she tried to find supplemental materials for teaching science on the DLI website, but 'the descriptions for the science experiments are still in English only' (C4). The same teacher further elaborated,

> There are teaching suggestions on how to interact with students in Chinese, but the simulated conversations shown are unrealistic. My students wouldn't respond the way as described in the simulated conversations. (C4)

Curriculum changes frequently

The second challenge mentioned by the Chinese teachers is that the curriculum changed every year, making it hard for them to understand the objectives and make new teaching materials. A repetitive excerpt found in the Chinese teachers' interview data was that 'the curriculum changes every year' (C4, C5, C6, C14, C15), and it was often followed by complaints such as 'This makes me feel frustrated' (C5), 'That makes it hard for us to understand the objectives' (C6), 'If it is not systematic, students and teachers can get lost'. (C9) and 'I am kind of exhausted and really discouraged that every year I need to redo all curriculum materials' (C15). However, one Chinese teacher who was in an administrative position in the Chinese DLI programs before expressed the views from both the teachers and the administrators. He said,

> I think being involved in a new program, just brings lots of changes every year, and there's going to be lots of figuring out, and not quite sure exactly how things are working and the best way to do things, and I think that presents challenges. But I've been on the administrative side of that. You see why changes need to happen, and you see that you can't just keep doing the same thing that is not the best way going forward, even though it's hard for teachers to change. (C14)

Gap between students

The third challenge identified by the Chinese teachers is the gap between students. Several teachers mentioned that a small group of students lagged behind in their classes and had low motivation to learn Chinese. They often observed that the students 'just sit in the classroom everyday not knowing what's going on because they don't understand the instruction' (C2), and 'just kind of shut down and draw all the time' (C5). The teachers indicated that the gap became bigger between students when they moved to the upper grade levels; as one teacher said, 'When they reach 6th grade, the students who aren't doing well, their level is similar to first graders in the program' (C4). A few teachers expressed their desire to help the students, but some felt that the program was fast-paced and they did not have time to offer extra help, while some of them did not know how to help. For example, one teacher noted,

> Figuring out how to not just let them slide through or slip through the cracks, and how can you help them…And those kids really give me, just like lots of anxiety. I really want to help them. I do a lot to help them, but they are really challenging to help. (C14)

The low-performing students were seen as a problem for the whole class especially when 'they get bored and some of them start to misbehave and affect other students' learning'. (C4)

Limited time and large class size

The fourth challenge identified is having to pay attention to all students' needs when the teachers needed to teach fifty-plus students a day. Feelings such as the following are frequently found in the interviews. 'I feel it is difficult to care for each of the students' (C6), 'I can't make sure all of them absorbed the knowledge equally well' (C8) and 'I think

I never found the best way to give good feedback to 56 kids' (C15). The Chinese teachers also believed that the limited time to pay attention to students and the large class size affected the students' learning. Some of the teachers complained that 'we don't have much time for students to practice writing in school', 'It is very hard to cover all subjects every day' (C5) and 'I feel their writing is very weak because we don't have enough time to practice it' (C2).

Lack of support from parents and administrators

The fifth challenge the Chinese teachers mentioned is a lack of administrative and parental support. One teacher hoped that her school principal could be more actively involved in the DLI program. She expressed,

> I feel my principal is nice, but it is the way he does things. He doesn't observe our classes often. Most of the time he assigned the Assistant Principal to do it. I feel he understands the classroom situations, but he couldn't do anything. (C3)

Sometimes the need for administrative support comes from a call for respect for cultural difference. One teacher explained,

> The principal needs to understand where we are from in order for us to feel respected. We are from a different culture and family background. Instead of picking our mistakes, he needs to understand why we do things a certain way. (C9)

The other area that lacked support was parental support. A teacher expressed her concern that 'some parents do not provide any support at home at all, and some of them sometimes blame the teachers' (C11). Another teacher believed that parental support was essential. She stated, 'If parents want their children to be in the DLI program, they should also support them, correct?'. (C12)

Chinese-only rule

The sixth challenge perceived by the Chinese teachers is that the state-required Chinese-only rule for Chinese teachers could sometimes be ineffective in certain situations. The state requires that when Chinese DLI teachers are in the school environment, regardless of whether they are in class teaching or not, they can speak only Chinese. A few Chinese teachers pointed out that in most situations, this rule was good for the students; however, in certain situations, speaking in English was more efficient. For example, one 6th grade teacher said,

> I feel the Chinese-only rule works well in the elementary levels, but when they get to the 6th grade, the content and vocabulary are more abstract.

If you need to spend an hour to use purely Chinese to explain a word, do you think this is meaningful? And there are students who still don't understand. (C3)

A couple of teachers felt that when applying the Chinese-only rule outside the Chinese classroom, accommodations and support were needed in order for it to work. For example, a Chinese teacher described, how 'When the school office makes a classroom broadcasting call to a Chinese teacher in English, the teacher has no choice but to reply to the call in English. But the Chinese teacher can be accused of breaking the Chinese-only rule' (C5). The other Chinese teacher said, 'Same with bus duty and recess duty. Sometimes when an issue occurs during duty time, it is more efficient to respond in English to solve the problem, but the Chinese teacher might be reprimanded again' (C6). The issues the two teachers faced created stress for them as one of them said, 'Sometimes having ideals are good, but they need to give teachers time and space to breathe' (C5).

Limited time to accomplish all tasks

As for the challenges identified by the English teachers, limited teaching time seemed to be the major challenge for most of them. Eight out of the ten English teachers touched upon this issue. For example, one teacher explained, 'I really have to focus on getting to the heart of whatever the lesson is. I have to streamline things because I don't have much time' (E2). Another teacher mentioned how the limited teaching time affected her instructional style. She said,

I have very little time to do any small group instruction in both language arts and in math. So, most of my instruction is whole group and then I check on individuals. So, that would be the biggest obstacle that I faced, is finding the time to do small group instruction. (E6)

The limited time also created other issues. For example, a few teachers mentioned not having time to help with struggling students, to get to know their students, to assess students and to make individualized learning available. The teachers expressed frustration, with comments such as 'I don't have as much time during the day to help those low kids' (E2), 'Just time-wise with 50 students to begin with, and then to try and come up with more individualized things, it's overwhelming' (E4) and 'I just have that three hour block of time, so sometimes classroom management is difficult to do because you have so many bodies' (E10).

Communication with the Chinese teachers

The second major challenge faced by the English teachers was communication with their Chinese partner teachers. The challenge derived from the language barrier. One English teacher stated,

It's definitely a little different with the language barrier and being able to communicate in, or to make sure we are on the same page in terms of going to recess at the same time, and/or leaving the school when the bell rings. So, that has been a little bit of a challenge. (E1)

Cultural difference is another reason for the communication challenge with the Chinese teachers. An English teacher described her experience with the Chinese partner teacher and how the partnership was difficult for her. She indicated,

She's struggling just with the cultural difference. And being a first-year teacher, a lot of that ends up becoming my burden and stress because I'm working twice as hard to teach her the district policies, and the school policies. It's so hard for them, but a lot of that ends up falling on me as the English partner because we are a team, and watching her struggle is very hard. (E3)

Due to the cultural difference, it was difficult for some of the Chinese teachers to know how to use proper class management in American classrooms. As a result, their English partner teachers were often called for help by the Chinese teachers. A different English teacher described her experience working with a Chinese teacher who did not know how to manage her class,

Because she did not have any behavior management, so every day, she would call me and needed my help to control the kids. So I'd always have to put my class on hold and run down there. Like literally daily to try and get kids to behave for her, because they behaved for me but they did not behave for her. Sorry this sounds negative. I don't blame her at all. She never taught elementary school. She said she was a college lecturer, never worked with elementary kids, and then they just throw her into a first grade classroom. She had no idea how to do it. No idea. (E9)

Teachers' Suggestions

With the exception of the Chinese teachers suggesting the hope of receiving more teaching resources, the other suggestions were identical from both the Chinese and the English teachers. Both groups recommended more proper training for various types of DLI teacher groups and more flexibility and support from various entities in the DLI programs (see Table 2.4).

Teacher training

Both the English and the Chinese teachers made suggestions on improving teacher training. First, 'the content of the teacher training

Table 2.4 Teachers' suggestions for the Chinese DLI programs

Ranking	Chinese Teachers' Perspectives	# of Chinese Teachers Who Made the Suggestion	English Teachers' Perspectives	# of English Teachers Who Made the Suggestion
1	Teacher Training	6	Teacher Training	7
2	More Flexibility and Support	4	More Flexibility and Support	2
3	Teaching Resources	4		

needs to fit different teachers' needs' (C4). Some of the teachers mentioned that the current training did not distinguish between the diverse needs of Chinese and English teachers, and between new and more experienced teachers. As a result, they did not feel that the training was useful to them. A teacher described how the training she attended was useful because it separated groups of teachers who had different needs. She said, 'half the day we were working both English and Chinese [teachers], and then the second half just English [teachers] together and just Chinese teachers together' (E6). More of this type of training is needed. Second, both the Chinese and the English teachers believed that the Chinese teachers fresh from overseas, sent by Hanban, the Confucius Institute affiliated with the Chinese Ministry of Education, needed to be well-trained and supported before coming to the programs. One Chinese teacher described what she observed.

> I've seen some, just the difficulties they go through…they didn't have a home, they didn't have a car. Those things should be taken care of before school. They should be incorporated into American society before school. And receive some training where they can interact with real American students. And find a lot of training before they start school or even have an aide with them to teach them in the beginning of school how to interact with the children. (C15)

Due to the lack of living experience in the US, the teacher interviewees thought that the training for the Chinese teachers should not be restricted only to teaching methods, but should extend to other areas such as American cultural knowledge, teaching and learning styles in the US, school and district policies, classroom management and interactions with students and parents. One teacher suggested,

> Definitely if you're having a Hanban teacher coming to the country for the first time, a little bit more time before school starts to be able to meet with them and talk to them about the program, and discuss just the structure of the day, and what it should look like, and expectations, so they are aware of it before the school year starts. Otherwise, it starts off rushed and uncomfortable. (E1)

The other teacher suggested that the state should 'get them [Hanban teachers] over here earlier in summer', so they have more time to adjust. The same teacher observed how overwhelming it was for the Hanban teachers to teach in a new program while trying to settle down at the same time. She said, 'They are living with a host family, they are trying to find an apartment, they don't have a bed, they don't have dishes. You know, they don't have a car' (E2). Her suggestion to the state was that the state could also assist the Hanban teachers by 'giving them a furnished apartment, so that they can focus on learning the programs and getting ready to teach' (E2).

More flexibility and support

A couple of teachers asked for more support from the state and the school administrators by giving them more flexibility in making teaching decisions. One Chinese teacher gave a few examples.

> For example, you don't let English teachers speak English in the Chinese classrooms. It has been hard for both of us. We already do not have time. If we need to communicate, we have to go to the hall and if my partner has an emergency, I would say speaking English in the Chinese class would not be a big problem. I don't think students' Chinese will degrade by that. Educators sometimes need to apply whichever method better fits the needs of the situation. Without empowerment from above, teachers might often experience difficulties. (C11)

The other type of support the teachers needed was classroom support. More teaching assistants and substitute teachers were requested. One teacher said, 'We need teaching assistants, especially us teachers who teach lower grade levels. We need to do center activities. Without TAs, it is hard to do' (C2). The last type of support mentioned by the teachers was monetary support. The DLI teachers felt that they spent more time and effort compared to teachers in regular classrooms; hence, there was a sense of entitlement that they should be paid more. One teacher said, 'I think as teachers, we put in so much time I think that it would be nice to have a stipend like coaches have, even just a stipend' (E5). One other teacher explained the reason increasing teachers' pay is important. She stated,

> If the teachers at the lower grade levels don't teach well, it will affect my teaching when the students move up to my grade level. If I don't teach well, it will be challenging for the teacher who teaches them next year and then it becomes a vicious cycle. So, in order to increase the quality of the DLI teaching faculty, increasing teachers' salaries is a good way to recruit quality teachers. (C8)

Teaching resources

The Chinese teachers suggested that more teaching resources are needed and that they need to be more systematic. One teacher hoped that 'the school can send in more Chinese multi-media materials to address the lack of materials in Chinese' (C9), while the other teacher stated that using unified materials which share the same teaching objectives, is important.

Administrators' Perspectives

Learning new language/culture and child development

Both school administrators (referred as SA1 and SA2) mentioned the DLI programs being significantly beneficial for the students, exposing them to a second language and culture. SA1, who grew up in a bilingual home, said, 'Speaking two languages is not abnormal. It's a great skill to have, so our kids are benefiting a ton from that. They're learning new culture. They're learning new language. They're getting a lot of opportunities'. In addition to the gain of a second language and culture, the school administrators also believed that DLI helped children's overall development. SA2 added, 'There are some great things that we do psychologically and developmentally for kids in the program that are almost unmeasured. I think there are things that are pretty hard to keep your thumb on or pinpoint or measure by standard tests'.

Finding and retaining qualified teachers

In terms of challenges, both SA1 and SA2 identified finding and retaining qualified teachers as a challenging task. SA2 explained that finding Chinese teachers locally who were qualified to work with kids was not easy. He said, 'I'll get a lot of candidates who have a master's degree or a bachelor's degree and want to teach but they don't have an education background'. As a result, it was common for the schools to hire Chinese teachers from overseas. For example, SA1 mentioned, 'Every year we are having guest teachers come from China. We are having to pull left and right'. However, the teachers from overseas usually do not have a legal status to permanently stay and work in the US. Thus, it is difficult to retain teachers in the Chinese DLI programs.

DLI is the most work-intensive program

Both SA1 and SA2 commented on the huge amount of work for DLI teachers and administrators as being a challenge. SA1 gave an example of how the large amount of work demanded by the DLI program resulted in a lack of interest from the current general education teachers in the school for working as the English teachers in the DLI program. He explained,

> They [DLI teachers] have 60 kids. They do all of the assessments. They have to do 60 parent-teacher conferences. They have to review 60 of the same assessments versus 28 or 30, so there is a component where those teachers feel like, man, I'm going to get all of this extra work for no real added bonus to them personally.

SA1 observed that every year the teachers who were required to be the English teachers for the DLI program reacted as 'who got the short straw to be the partner, and not who wants it'. SA1 stated that the amount of work was so overbearing that even a current English DLI teacher in his school, who believed in the program, did not feel that she could continue the work much longer after teaching in the Chinese DLI program for three years. Not only teachers, but also the school administrators felt the intensity of the amount of work. For example, SA2 stated, 'It is the most work intensive program that I have ever been engaged with in my career'. SA1 also mentioned how managing the DLI program such as dealing with staffing issues and responding to the DLI parents' demands on top of the other administrative work could be work intensive. He said,

> As far as dual language goes, being able to manage fairly demanding parents at times, just being able to manage two different programs [general education and DLI] within your school, plus I have two emotional needs units so I have Special-Ed in my school too, that is a little bit more intense than other schools.

Communication with and collaboration between teachers

Communication between the school administrators and the Chinese teachers was a challenge identified by SA2. Before he hired a full-time Chinese mentor to assist the Chinese teachers (most of them from overseas) with language and cultural barriers, and pedagogy in the classroom, he found himself having difficulty with effectively communicating with the Chinese teachers. He described,

> I think that one of the biggest problems was my teachers didn't want to look like they weren't competent, so they would tell me they understood something when they really didn't. So, I think there were really cultural and language…were the two biggest problems.

The other communication-related challenge was to have the Chinese and the English teachers fully engaged in their collaboration. SA1 mentioned that since each teacher was only responsible for teaching part of the curriculum (e.g. the Chinese teachers only focused on Chinese and math and the English teachers only focused on English), when they met as a team, they sometimes were not attentive. He described,

Every time, one of those partners is basically tuning out because they are not part of that conversation at that point. The information that is being discussed at that moment isn't pertinent. So, I have had some teams [where] that is frustrating to them, that that teacher isn't fully engaged in the whole conversation.

The use of the lottery system

SA1 felt that using the lottery system to help decide which students could enter the DLI programs was not the best method. He stressed,

It's a public school…with a lottery that's weird. You know we are excluding kids. It's not that we want to, but we are excluding kids, which then gives parents some bitter feelings toward the school. If they are still in our boundaries and they still come here and they've been excluded. They feel a little burnt by it.

According to SA1, approximately 20% of schools in the school district offered DLI programs; hence, some of the students who were interested in the programs may not be able to enroll if the number of interested students was larger than the number of students the programs could include.

Communication with the state

The last challenge identified was communication with the state. SA1 was concerned with the way the state communicated with the schools. He expressed the view that there was a 'punitive way' in which the state handled some of the concerns the school administrators had. He described,

'You will do this or we will pull your funding'. I've heard that a few times, like 'you'll teach it this way or there won't be money available for you' or 'you use this program or there won't be things available for you'.

It seems that to SA1, the state needed to be more patient and tolerant toward the DLI staff's and school administrators' ideas and be more convincing of the state's requirements and ideas. This is evident when SA1 elaborated, 'They're not saying this is the best method. They're not saying this is why this is a great strategy. They're just saying "this is what we've agreed to do and you will do it", and that kind of communication'.

Suggestions

For suggestions, SA2 mentioned how difficult learning the Chinese language could be and recommended that the Chinese teachers utilize positive reinforcement more frequently. He said, 'I think the teachers need to work extra hard at saying "Wow, look what you've done and show me where you started and show me where you are now" and recognizing that progress'. On the other hand, SA1 thought that in order for DLI programs to grow, the state should not simplify, but revisit the components of the DLI programs and have better communication with teachers and administrators. He stated,

> When the state presents it [DLI], they present it as if there is nothing different any other place. You just have two teachers and they just trade the kids in the middle of the day, and you don't have to hire differently...but I think it's kind of a simplistic approach and I think it's not really looking at the details of running that program.

The State Director's Perspectives

Developing cultural sensitivity

The director believed that the DLI programs prepared students for the modern world where everyone was connected through the internet and where cultural sensitivity was needed. She stated,

> In America, language study has never been a priority really. We are sort of insulated from the rest of the world, so I think it gives our students an advantage to already be able to interact with other places and other people and have a cultural sensitivity that so many others don't.

Positive influence on other states

The director also mentioned that the DLI programs in Utah were the fastest-growing and the largest in the nation, which 'has given the chance for the community in Utah to really be a beacon to other states'. The huge amount of attention received from other states gave Utah 'the opportunity to help influence other places to follow a similar course'. It was evident to the director that in national language conferences, when she stated that she was from Utah, positive comments such as 'Oh I wish I was there' illustrated to the director that other states recognized the efforts made for DLI programs in Utah.

Chinese-American cultural difference

A major challenge the director identified was the distance between Chinese and American cultures, creating the opportunity for misunderstandings to occur. The director saw it happen between teachers and students, teachers and parents, teachers and administrators, and teachers and partner teachers. She stated,

When you bring a culture that has got the distance that this one does from western culture, there's no way you can anticipate all the little things that are going to pop up. There is no way you can prepare an administrator, a teacher, a student, for things that might happen as a result of that gap.

The director realized that conflicts derived from cultural differences would naturally continue to occur when two cultures clashed, and her team's job was to minimize that to a certain degree by offering support to school administrators and help them realize that they were going through a cultural experience. She said,

You're going to be offended at some point. You are going to be frustrated at some point. You're not going to know the answer at some point, and so that's where, as a state team, we try to help guide that process, because our goal is for principals to feel confident and comfortable in making the decisions they need to build their program and we're there to support them all the way.

Finding quality teachers

The director understood that the quality of the teachers had a large impact on the programs. Hence, finding quality teachers was the state's priority. It had been challenging for the state to find consistency in the quality of the Chinese teachers and the director was attempting to try new channels to bring in better qualified teachers. She stated, 'I'm excited about some of the new channels that we are working on with universities as well as private agencies and we've tried out a couple of new ones this year and have been really pleased'. The new recruiting method was to use multiple channels to bring in teachers from overseas, rather than looking for qualified local teachers. The director explained, 'the starting salary for a brand new elementary teacher is like $35,000, and that's not really appealing to most [local] people'. The director quoted a local student they tried to recruit as an example to show the salary expectation of the local people. She said, 'he was like, "you know, I understand you guys need teachers, but in my field the starting salary is like $80,000 or $90,000"'. The director further elaborated that the low salaries were actually attractive to people overseas, therefore, she believed that 'the future is not in front of us here. It's across the ocean'.

Being highly supportive

According to the director, the Chinese DLI programs grew very quickly in the past eight years, currently having almost 30 programs. With extremely limited resources and limited teacher supply, the director believed that being highly supportive towards the school administrators and teachers was one of the keys to program success. She explained,

> You might notice there's a lot of things the teacher needs to change, but if they sense your support, a lot of times they'll start recognizing, they're open to seeing things they need to change and it can sort of happen in a little more natural way, when there is an environment of support for them to be open to that. So, for me, as an administrator, that's the key message that I try to put out there is to communicate and be supportive.

The director also mentioned that the support from the state is multi-layered. In addition to the support from the state team, some of the districts also received support from the local schools, such as on-site coaches, who trained the new teachers in their districts.

Being flexible

As the brand new Chinese DLI programs quickly expanded in Utah in a short time, many of their components were at the experimental stage. For example, the director mentioned,

> We pilot something for two or three years and you know it gives us some information and we decide, 'is this something we want to continue or no?', and a lot of the time it's like, no. It's helped us to this point, but it's not where we want to keep going.

Due to the programs being at the developmental stage, the director advised the teachers to be more flexible and always be ready to change. She noted,

> It's hard for the people on the ground sometimes to be part of something that's still in motion and sorry if I just tell the teacher, 'if you don't like change then you're in the wrong place because this program is going to constantly be changing because we're trying to make it better all the time, so don't get too comfortable'.

The high level of flexibility was also suggested by the director in terms of encountering cultural conflicts in the programs. As mentioned earlier, due to the Chinese-American cultural differences, cultural misunderstandings are inevitable. Therefore, the director encouraged the school administrators and teachers to operate with a high level of flexibility.

Principals' investment in the Chinese programs

The director believed that the key to growing successful DLI programs are the school principals. The director elaborated,

Utah is a local-control state, and so that means that we are here to set standards, to guide things, to provide resources and support, but in terms of the local outcomes, it comes down to the principal and their level of investment in the program.

Indeed, the state had approximately 200 Chinese teachers, and it would not be realistic to have the state team, which included the director herself and three other trainers, to be with the teachers every day to help them succeed. The success will rely primarily on the local leadership, with the support of the state on occasion. The director recognized the amount of effort needed from the principals for the programs to work. She said,

> It's not a turnkey operation where it's like 'Ok, great. Here you go. Here's your teacher. Here's the curriculum', and you know, 'Good luck!' It's a program that requires constant close oversight and support and a principal who is connected to their teachers and is there to support them.

Finally, the director stated that she was aware of the concerns and challenges the parent and teacher interviewees mentioned, but she stressed again that 'it all comes down to the communication from the principal to his or her local community about what's going on'.

This study continues in the next chapter, Chapter 3, with the report of the parents' perspectives toward the Chinese DLI programs, followed by conclusion and discussion sections based on the study results.

References

Alanís, I. and Rodriguez, M.A. (2008) Sustaining a dual language immersion program: Features of success. *Journal of Latinos and Education* 7 (4), 305–319.

García, Y. (2003) Korean/English two-way immersion at Cahuenga Elementary School. *NABE News* 26, 8–11, 25.

Genesee, F. and Riches, C. (2006) Instructional issues in literacy development. In F. Genessee, K. Lindholm-Leary, W. Saunders and D. Christian (eds) *Educating English Language Learners: A Synthesis of Research Evidence* (pp. 109–175). New York, NY: Cambridge University Press.

Howard, E.R. and Christian, D. (1997) The development of bilingualism and biliteracy in two-way immersion students. Paper presented at the 1997 Annual Meeting of the American Educational Research Association (pp. 1–28). Washington, D.C.: Educational Resources Information Center.

Howard, E.R. and Loeb, M. (1998) In their own words: Two-way immersion teachers talk about their professional experiences. Berkeley, CA: University of California Berkeley, Center for Research on Education, Diversity & Excellence. See http://escholarship. org/uc/item/9td4m00c (accessed 12 June 2017).

Howard, E.R., Christian, D. and Genesee, F. (2004) *The Development of Bilingualism and Biliteracy from Grade 3 to 5: A Summary of Findings from the CAL/CREDE Study of Two-Way Immersion Education*. Santa Cruz, CA: Center for Research on Education, Diversity & Excellence.

Lee, J.S. and Jeong, E. (2013) Korean–English dual language immersion: Perspectives of students, parents and teachers. *Language, Culture and Curriculum* 26 (1), 89–107.

Lindholm-Leary, K.J. (2001) *Dual Language Education*. Clevedon: Multilingual Matters.

Lindholm-Leary, K. (2012) Success and challenges in dual language education. *Theory into Practice* 51 (4), 256–262.

Lindholm-Leary, K. and Genesee, F. (2010) Alternative educational programs for English language learners. In California Department of Education (ed.) *Research on English Language Learners* (pp. 323–367). Sacramento, CA: California Department of Education Press.

Montague, N.S. (1997) Critical components for dual language programs. *Bilingual Research Journal* 21 (4), 409–417.

Saunders, W. and Goldenberg, C. (2009) Research to guide English language development instruction. In D. Dolson and L. Burnham-Massey (eds) *Improving Education for English Learners: Research-Based Approaches* (pp. 21–81). Sacramento, CA: California Department of Education.

Thomas, W.P., Collier, V.P. and Abbott, M. (1993) Academic achievement through Japanese, Spanish, or French: The first two years of partial immersion. *The Modern Language Journal* 77 (2), 170–179.

3 Benefits, Challenges and Suggestions: Voices From Parents

> It's like magic, you go to that first grade parent teacher conference and you don't understand what they're [the Chinese teacher and her child] saying, and they do. I just think it's really neat.
>
> (A Chinese DLI parent in Utah)

This chapter is a continuation of Chapter 2 regarding the benefits and challenges encountered in Chinese DLI programs, with a switch of focus from the teachers' and administrators' perspectives to those of the parents. This chapter begins with a review of studies on DLI parents' perspectives toward DLI programs in the US, which is followed by the report of this study's findings on the Chinese DLI parents' views about the programs in which their children were enrolled in Utah.

Studies on DLI Parents' Perspectives

A few studies addressed DLI parents' perspectives toward DLI programs. One example is Craig's (1996) parent attitude survey study in an elementary school in an east coast metropolitan area with a dense Spanish-speaking immigrant population. The findings in Craig's study illustrated that all 120 parents (50% English-speaking and 50% Spanish-speaking) had similar positive attitudes toward the DLI programs and agreed that such programs would enhance their children's multicultural awareness and future work opportunities. However, there was a difference in opinion between English- and Spanish- speaking parents on their rating of the importance of minority language maintenance. The Spanish-speaking parents rated 'maintaining the minority language' with much higher importance compared to the rating by the English parents. The attitude difference between the two language groups could be explained by the reasons they enrolled their children in the DLI program. For the English-speaking parents, the main reasons for DLI were the exposure to other cultures, the opportunity of intellectual stimulation through learning a second language at a young age and the expectation of a better future career. In contrast, the main reason for the Spanish-speaking parents to enroll their children in the DLI programs was Spanish language and cultural maintenance. The heritage maintenance would assist them with communicating with their family, keep their mother tongue, appreciate their own cultural origin and be proud of their ethnic and cultural heritage. Other research in the US (Lao, 2004; Parkes, 2008; Young & Tran, 1999) on DLI parental perceptions reported similar findings, which illustrated that minority parents identified the maintenance of their home languages and cultures as the major benefit of DLI programs, whereas English-speaking parents tended to acknowledge becoming multilingual and multicultural, and increasing future job opportunities as the key benefits of DLI programs. Moreover, two studies (Leung, 2018; Yang et al., 2018) conducted in Cantonese DLI programs found that some of the parents' perspectives (e.g. job benefits) were so strong that the ideas were passed onto their young students.

While most studies on DLI parents' perspectives had a focus on their attitudes and reasons for enrolling their children in DLI programs, Parkes and Ruth's (2011) study identified a few concerns toward DLI programs expressed by 724 parents in Spanish DLI programs in the southwest United States. First, the parents were unsure whether their children were making good progress in one or the other language. Second, some of the parents were concerned about communication from the schools, such as giving parents updates when there was an issue with their children. Some parents also questioned the level of rigorousness of the programs, with specific concerns regarding large class sizes which made the classrooms overcrowded, and with teaching materials not being critically engaging. Finally, some of the English-speaking parents expressed that they were having a difficult time helping their children with Spanish homework and concluded that maybe knowing how to speak Spanish was the only way to overcome the frustration.

The current literature which presented the DLI parents' views on their children's learning in DLI is restricted mostly to the context of Spanish programs. There was only one study (Lao, 2004), which investigated Chinese DLI programs; however, the programs were only for pre-school age students. Moreover, while the studies learned about parents' thoughts regarding DLI programs, there was a lack of investigation such as Parkes and Ruth's (2011) study on the challenges parents encountered. Hence, the current study reported in this chapter, which involved parents whose children were in elementary and middle school Chinese DLI programs, regarding their perspectives on the benefits and challenges encountered in the DLI programs will add new insights to the current literature.

The Parent Participants

The 20 Chinese DLI parent interviewees (referred to as P1–P20) were from the seven districts in Utah which had approved our study.

Table 3.1 Grade level information of parent interviewees' children

Grade Level	# of Children
First grade	6
Second grade	10
Third grade	5
Fourth grade	11
Fifth grade	1
Sixth grade	2
Seventh grade	2

All parents were asked for their consent to conduct the interview. There were two male and 18 female parent interviewees, most of whom had more than one child in the Chinese DLI programs. Among the 20 parents, four of them or their spouses were Chinese heritage speakers, while the rest of the parents were English-speaking. Table 3.1 summarizes the grade levels of the interviewees' children.

Benefits Identified by the Parents

The parent interviewees identified a wide variety of benefits they believed their children received or would receive in the long run. The list of benefits identified is ranked and shown in Table 3.2.

Future opportunities

The top ranked benefit, which was mentioned by 11 interviewees, relates to the children's future, in particular, their future work opportunities. The parents recognized that China is 'the next major first world economy' (P18) and that Chinese is an important business language to learn. Hence, choosing to enroll in Chinese DLI programs rather than other languages made the most sense to the parents. One parent explained,

Table 3.2 Parents' perspectives on the benefits of the Chinese DLI programs

Ranking	Benefits	# of Parents
1	Future Opportunities	11
2	Features of the Chinese DLI programs	8
3	Globally Minded	5
4	Interest in Chinese Culture and People	5
5	Curiosity, Confidence, and Adaptability	5
6	Brain Development	4
7	Preserve Heritage Language and Culture	4
8	Fast Learning at a Young Age	4

I am strongly drawn to Mandarin because of the increased trade deals happening with China and there just seems to be more and more. It just seems that in the world right now that there is just going to be more interactions between the US and China. (P17)

The keywords and key phrases such as 'amazing work opportunities' (P1), 'an advantage in the workforce' (P17), 'a better career' (P14) and 'good for future job prospects' (P12) were frequently found in the interviews when the parents mentioned that knowing Chinese would help their children in the future.

Features of the Chinese DLI programs

One feature that the parents liked about the programs was that a lot of the Chinese teachers were native speakers from overseas. One parent thought that it was an interesting experience. She said,

I love the students to have their Chinese speaking teachers come from another country. That's fun for them and it's fun for us at the school to be able to interact with people from different cultures. I just learned about that culture, so I'd say that is a big benefit. (P16)

Another reason the parents liked the idea of having native Chinese-speaking teachers is associated with having diversity. One parent expressed the view,

I love that our kids are being exposed to native speakers. Some of them are from Mainland China. Some of them are from Taiwan. So just like we have accents in the United States based on where you grew up, I love that I feel our kids are being exposed to that based on where their teachers are from and I think that has been great. (P15)

The Chinese native-speaking teachers not only brought their culture and diversity into the Chinese programs, according to the parents, they also set a higher standard for their children. One parent said,

Here you have these teachers from China or Taiwan who come over and they take this seriously and they have high expectations for themselves and they set the bar really high for our kids and they push our kids, but they also have a great understanding that our kids are kids. (P8)

Another feature which the parents advocated was the Chinese-only rule in the programs. One parent stated,

I love that they are only allowed to speak Chinese in the classrooms, I think we all tend to take the path of least resistance and if there is a way to communicate more easily in another language we do. (P17)

The Chinese-only rule was strictly applied in the programs. The Chinese teachers could only speak Chinese when the students were present. One parent described such an occasion:

> I think that it is great that they only speak Chinese. I think it's pretty impressive. I was going to speak to the teacher one time, but if you go to talk to them and your kid is standing next to you, they won't talk to you in English because they are not allowed to talk in English around the kids, only Chinese. (P12)

The parents thought that the strict restriction of speaking Chinese only in the classrooms had a positive effect on their children's learning. One parent said,

> I'm surprised at how quickly they learn it...My son, he doesn't know that any of his teachers have ever been able to speak English because they strictly speak Mandarin and I think that has really benefited him. (P14)

The parents also liked the structure of the 50/50 DLI model, where the students spend half of the day in Chinese and the other half in English.

> I like that structure. It doesn't lopside different amounts of Chinese and English instruction. And they have a breakdown as to which classes are taught in which language throughout the six-year program. When I studied that [the breakdown], it looked like it was a good idea. (P9)

Another parent thought that the program structure gave students the opportunity to be immersed in the target language. He said,

> I think it is necessary at that age to get them as much exposure as possible. Complete immersion is by far the best way to learn another language...and we are not in a region where Chinese is spoken in the community, so just to be around Chinese speakers just for the amount of time that it takes that's important. (P18)

Another feature the parents liked about the programs was that they had seen program improvements over the years. One parent mentioned about the improvements she witnessed,

> It has changed hugely. At the beginning it almost was like the expectation on how much Chinese they were expected to know and what they were supposed to have passed off was kind of on the lower end... But since there is a three-year gap between my oldest and my second, through that they got more materials...I feel like they set the bar pretty high, like

we are going to get our kids above target level on whatever that sheet thing [informational sheet] that we are given, but they just had a higher expectation. (P13)

Another parent believed that the state fixed some of the program issues and since then the program has been more established. She said,

I feel it is getting more organized. I felt like at first, they were working out the kinks in the program for our school district, but it felt like there were several times that curriculum would change as they were trying to figure out what worked best and so I feel like now they have a system that works well...and then we see more and more resources becoming available for dual immersion students, whereas the first couple of years those resources just weren't known or hadn't been developed yet. (P15)

Finally, a parent moved her child from one Chinese DLI program to another in a different city in Utah. She was happy about the consistency of the state-wide Chinese DLI programs. She said,

One thing that I am super happy about is there seems to be a lot of state-wide consistency. I was worried that things would be done differently at different schools and she would be behind or she would be ahead. I'm really happy that they use a consistent model state wide, that has enabled us to move. (P6)

Globally minded

A few parents believed that the DLI programs had expanded their children's minds and opened the door to other cultures. One parent explained how this opportunity was especially unique in Utah. She said, 'The impact on their education is opening their eyes to an entire new part of the world and part of the diversity that we just don't have in Utah' (P3). Indeed, in a state whose population is mostly Caucasian and LDS, learning a second language and its culture on a daily basis was almost impossible before the DLI programs were established less than 10 years ago. The parents observed that this opportunity had made their children more accepting of diversity and more globally minded. One parent testified,

My children are a lot more open to differences no matter what they are. Because they see so much difference on a day to day basis, like cultural differences, language differences, so they are accepting of new and different things in general. So, I feel like they are more globally minded because they are learning a second language. (P19)

Interest in Chinese culture and its people

The Chinese DLI programs have increased the students' interest in knowing more about Chinese culture and people. Several parents mentioned how their children noticed and desired to interact with Chinese when they spotted them locally or overseas while they were traveling.

One parent described, 'I have noticed that when we are at places where someone is speaking Chinese, like in a grocery store or in public, they will pick up on it, they will notice, and they will want to interact' (P15). A different parent expressed that she thought that her children 'already feel a connection to those [Chinese] people' and 'take an interest in their culture'. (P2)

Curiosity, confidence and adaptability

The trait of being curious toward Chinese had extended to the children's general learning. Several parents observed that learning Chinese made their children more curious and open to exploring the unknown. One parent said, 'They are just more open to challenges and when they are exposed to something new, they kind of just embrace it because that's kind of a normal part of their learning style right now' (P15). In addition, knowing a second language helped develop the children's confidence. A few parents reported that the level of their children's self-confidence increased because they 'feel proud that they can communicate well in another language' (P17). Moreover, the fact that the children often were exposed to things unfamiliar to them, they learned to adapt to this learning situation and became more adaptable. One parent described,

> They just kind of go 'OK, this is normal so we are just going to try to learn as much as we can.' and so I do feel like I have seen situations both academically and in social settings, I think because of the dual immersion program they are more adaptable. (P15)

Brain development

A few parents learned about the positive effects from research about learning two languages at a young age. This benefit was one reason that drew their interest in the Chinese DLI programs. One parent described, 'I just did a lot of research on what happens to the brain as it learns languages at an early age and so even just for her developing brain we really loved that idea' (P6). Another parent pinpointed how learning a tonal language like Chinese could exercise both sides of a brain. She said,

> Learning a second language overall, especially Chinese where it uses both sides of your brain because of the tones, it uses sort of one side for

language and one side for sort of the musical side of it, all of the tones. I know that it works their brain and they do great in school. (P8)

A different parent was supportive of the above claim and described how a teacher observed that the DLI students did better in the music class. She said,

She recognized the kids in the dual immersion, that they caught onto the music patterns a lot faster. She hadn't expected that; she's like 'I just felt they caught onto those rhythms and patterns faster.' And that's kind of the things that they say when they're trying to sell the program so that was exciting to hear a teacher say that. (P2)

Preserving heritage language and culture

The four parents who had Chinese-heritage background all thought that the Chinese DLI programs helped their children preserve their heritage language and culture. One parent said, 'My husband is a Mandarin speaker, and he is from Taiwan. So we thought it would be wonderful for her to be able to learn that language and also be part of the culture' (P17). Another parent described how knowing the Chinese language helped her children keep the connection with their family in China. She said,

Because my parents and my family are back in China and of course they don't speak English at all. In order for my girls to communicate with their grandparents and uncles and aunts, they have to speak Chinese and that is one reason...I don't want them to ever forget where they come from, and that was part of the culture I was not willing to give up. (P11)

The Chinese DLI programs were successful in preserving the Chinese root for the heritage students as the parents made comments such as 'I think it has helped them because I think they see who they are a little bit more' (P10), and 'He knew all the [Chinese cultural] things that we did and was very involved in the time we had with my grandparents' (P13).

Fast learning at a young age

Some of the parents believed that Americans started learning a second language too late and saw the Chinese DLI programs as a great opportunity for their children. One parent said, 'Every other country starts really young, teaching their kids another language, we are the only country where kids grow up with no second language because they only get two years in high school.' (P17). A couple parents mentioned their own language learning experiences as adults and believed that starting to learn a second language at a young age is advantageous. One parent said,

My husband and I had tried to learn Chinese as adults with some success but we found it very difficult, and we were in favor of any dual immersion program first of all, just because we feel the younger a student can learn a second language the faster they are going to pick it up. (P15)

It seems evident to some of the parents when they described how they were amazed by their children's quick learning speed. One parent said,

It has been so surprising to me that the kids could do it in such a short amount of time and just how quickly the kids progress like walking into their classroom and then just chatting it up like they are full on speakers and so it is just exciting, so to me it's just more surprising how quickly they can learn and how much they've learned. (P4)

The parents thought that the children were learning so much faster due to their young age that it became second nature for them to learn the second language.

Challenges Identified by the Parents

The parents identified a few challenges, mostly in regard to supporting their children's study in the DLI programs (see Table 3.3).

Lack of support

The parents identified several aspects of the programs lacking support. First, a parent noticed the lack of learning resources in the library. He said, 'There is no Chinese-English section in the school library. And that is the thing that I have been the most disappointed with' (P9). The same parent guessed that there could be a cost concern after knowing that the prices for Chinese-English bilingual books online were much higher than the same books in a single language. A different parent also pinpointed that the programs needed more resources and that more funding support is needed from the state. She said, 'If the state really wants to support bilingual learning, they need to come with a lot more money.

Table 3.3 Parents' perspectives on challenges encountered

Ranking	Challenges Identified by Parents	# of Parents
1	Lack of Support	4
2	Retaining Teachers	4
3	Divisions between DLI and Non-DLI Students and Parents	3
4	Difficulty in Supporting Their Children's Study	3
5	Difficulty in Learning the Specifics of the Children's Progress	2

I think they should offer an after school supplemental tutoring or supplemental program that is specific for all of the dual immersion kids' (P18).

Despite the lack of monetary support to get more learning resources and create supplemental programs, some of the parents also observed a lack of support from the school administration. One parent said,

> The feeling is that the administration doesn't want to be there, you know I don't think that they lobbied for it. It came to our school and so she's had it and had to make the best of it, but as far as really being on board and this is something that is valuable and this is good, no I don't think so. (P2)

The same parent also mentioned that the current school teachers' unwillingness to support the programs by being recruited as the English partner teachers. She said,

> You know they kind of have to force teachers to take on the job in the dual immersion, you either take it or you have to find a job elsewhere. And it felt that way every single year of this program. And it feels that way again next year. That is frustrating. (P2)

A different parent who was in district meetings noticed that not all board members in the district were supportive of the programs. She said, 'I know there's quite a few board members who disagree with even having the program. I don't feel like necessarily it gets all the resources or all of the help that it could receive because of these members that aren't supportive' (P14). In sum, the parents who identified the lack of program support were disappointed and were unsure how to get more program support.

Retaining teachers

Some parents felt that the high Chinese teacher replacement rate each year affected their children's learning. One parent expressed the view, 'I think that my fourth grader has been hindered by having new teachers every year' (P2). Another parent thought that this issue might have 'hurt the credibility of the program' (P3). One of the reasons for the low retention of the Chinese teachers is that some of these teachers were Hanban teachers, who could only temporarily work in the US for three years. The short amount of time they could stay in the programs did not have a positive effect on the programs, as one parent said, 'The Hanban teachers that come and then they aren't there for very long and that's hard because then the English teacher is working with a new teacher almost every year and that is a little bit difficult' (P16). The newness of the Hanban teachers was not seen as a positive trait for the parents as one parent explained,

> It takes them a couple months to get used to the school and the process and they are even finding housing, I mean they are so fresh into the U.S.

that naturally there is going to be a cultural integration period that is just going to take some time. (P3)

Divisions between DLI and Non-DLI students and parents

A few parents noticed that there was a separation between the Chinese DLI students and the students who were not in the Chinese DLI programs and thought that it brought negativity to the school. One parent commented, 'You have children who will say "oh they only do certain programs for the Chinese kids and they don't do anything special for us"' (P16). The division was not only observed between students, but also between parents. A parent noticed, 'Some of the parents of the Chinese program think that they're kind of better and so they kind of roll their eyes at the [non-DLI] parents, thinking that, "my child is better because they're in the Chinese program"' (P2).

Although the parents identified the divisions as a challenge, they also recognized that the school administration was attempting to ease the situation. One parent described that,

> I feel that they are very aware of it and they work very hard to try and bridge that gap and there are some really practical things that they do and there are things that they suggest parents do to try and help make sure that no one is feeling excluded. (P15)

The parents observed that the schools tried to create opportunities to mix DLI and non-DLI students so that there were more interactions between the two groups.

Difficulty in supporting their children's study at home

Most of the parents in the DLI programs were not Chinese speakers, and therefore they encountered difficulty helping with their children's Chinese homework at home. One parent described how,

> There are a lot of things that kids bring home and the Chinese teachers say they taught it in school, so they should be able to do it, but my child gets home and says 'I can't remember a thing' and I have no clue how to help them. (P19)

The same parent mentioned that to remedy this issue, the teacher started using an online tool for homework, but the parent still felt out of the loop on the child's progress. She said,

> I still don't know if my student is doing it correctly or not. They could just be getting on there, clicking buttons and just say 'Yup, I did my Chinese.', and I'm like, 'Great.' I have no idea. I can't tell. (P19)

Another parent encountered the same challenge and decided to hire a Chinese au pair to live with the family and help with the child's homework. She said,

> So that works for our family, but you know, not everyone is able to do that, so how you support that development in your kids is kind of the biggest downside to doing this if you are a family that doesn't speak Mandarin. (P3)

In sum, the parents believed that the programs were going to try to give them more support by offering tutoring and recruiting more Chinese-speaking volunteers, but at the same time they still recognized that this issue of not being able to help their children's Chinese will continue to be a struggle at home.

Difficulty in learning the specifics of the children's progress

A couple of parents felt that it was difficult to know their children's progress in Chinese learning. One parent described that,

> The Chinese teacher will tell me her scores, like her class scores but I wish there was you know like…She's like the lowest in class or she's the best in the class, or she's somewhere in the middle or you know, anything, I really feel like I don't know. (P4)

Another parent encountered the same challenge and thought that knowing the benchmark and where their children were on the benchmark would be helpful. She said,

> It's really hard to measure her progress, and I know they've started taking tests at the end of the year in the Chinese classes but because the state doesn't require those scores to be shared they're not sharing them and I don't think there is any ill intent there but it's hard information for me to get my hands on…I wish there was something…where it could say, here's the benchmark, this is where your kid is at. I would love to see that in her Chinese. (P6)

For the parents who did not know any Chinese, they felt the need for more feedback to give them a better understanding of how their children were doing.

Parents' Suggestions

The parents offered a couple of suggestions, one to the programs and the other one to themselves as parents (see Table 3.4).

Table 3.4 Parents' suggestions

Ranking	Parents' Suggestions	# of Parents
1	More Chinese Homework Assistance and Chinese After-School Activities	2
2	Parents' Long-Term Commitment	2

More Chinese homework assistance and Chinese after-school activities

One suggestion made by a couple parents was for schools to offer more Chinese homework assistance and Chinese after-school activities. One parent expressed, 'You know, it would be nice to have a Chinese mentor or someone that I could call or video chat and say "my kid doesn't know what this means on their homework" and have somebody read it to me or tell me what I need to do' (P19). The other parent said that for the purpose of better Chinese retention, Chinese after-school programs in addition to the regular class were needed. She stated, 'They could have more Chinese activities...because with language you really have to retain and use in order to master' (P11).

Parents' long-term commitment

A couple of parents mentioned that some of the DLI parents did not fully commit to the Chinese programs when they decided to enroll their children in the programs and that when the children of these parents encountered academic challenges, the parents pulled their children out of the programs. The parent interviewees wanted to warn future Chinese DLI parents that it was challenging to learn in a Chinese DLI program and suggested that parents should be committed to assisting their children throughout the years their children are in the programs. One parent said,

> If you want your child to be in this, then you have to commit to helping your child with that baseline education and not whine about doing homework and not whine about being there to help your child with reading and math concepts and helping them understand. (P1)

According to research, it takes many years for an individual to master a second language, let alone that in the DLI programs, the students need to study different content subjects through the target language. Hence, DLI parents' commitment and patience are crucial in supporting their children's education in the programs. One parent stated,

> Put in as much time as you can and, as parents, demonstrate an attitude of learning as well. I think it has meant a lot to our kids that we have

tried to learn with them as much as we can and I think that has helped them to face those challenges and not get discouraged because they can see that it is important to us, so there is value in it and then they're willing to work through that hard stuff. (P15)

Conclusion

Most of the findings in this chapter and the previous chapter (Chapter 2) regarding the views of the parents, teachers and administrators on the benefits of the Chinese DLI programs were aligned with the results of the majority of the previous studies. That is, the major benefits for studying in the DLI programs included future job opportunities, multilingualism, multiculturalism, fast language learning at a young age and intellectual stimulation for brain development.

However, this study did not align with a major finding in Howard and Loeb's (1998) study, in which the teacher participants identified education equality and fairness as a benefit for DLI programs. In Howard and Loeb's study, the teachers described how having both language majority and minority students in the same classroom created a space for language modeling and learning for both groups and that this learning space promoted equal learning opportunities. The fact that such a benefit was not mentioned in this study could be explained by the DLI model in Utah. The majority of the DLI programs in Utah are one-way programs, whose main purpose is for monolingual English speakers to learn a second language. The Utah DLI website spelled out clearly that the one-way programs serve 'a student population comprised of a predominant majority of native English language speakers with limited to no proficiency in the L2' (Utah Dual Language Immersion, 2017). Even though the design of the one-way programs was not geared toward heritage learners, similar to the findings of most of the previous studies, all four heritage parents in the current study strongly identified the preservation of their heritage language and culture as the major benefit for their children in DLI programs.

In addition, many parents in this study praised the benefits of the state DLI program for their children. These include having overseas Chinese teachers, which offered new cultural experiences to students and teachers; the strictly imposed Chinese-only rule in school (this policy is discussed more in Chapter 9), which created and reinforced the space for the target language environment; the statewide program consistency; and program improvements observed over the years. The parents and teachers in this study also identified a rarely mentioned benefit, which was the development of positive character traits such as curiosity, confidence and adaptability. The development of confidence could be attributed to the high level of difficulty of mastering the Chinese language. The parents and teachers frequently mentioned in the interviews that they observed that studying the difficult-to-learn language sent the message to their students that they were capable of 'doing hard things'. In addition, the diverse language and cultural learning in the DLI programs also increased their curiosity level. Moreover, having two teachers and receiving instruction in two languages daily trained the students to easily adapt to new situations. Finally, a unique benefit mentioned by the state director was the influence of the Utah model on other states. Despite the controversial issues regarding the Utah model mentioned in the current literature, Utah DLI programs are the fastest-growing and the largest in the nation, and the Utah model has attracted many other states to follow and implement DLI programs. According to Valdez *et al.* (2016a), Utah has influenced more than 30 states, with two states, Delaware and Georgia, echoing the Utah model.

In terms of challenges encountered in the Chinese DLI programs, the challenges identified were mostly diverse amongst the different interviewee groups, with some overlap. First, the parent interviewees mentioned a couple of challenges similar to the ones identified in Parkes and Ruth's (2011) study. They found it difficult to support their children's study at home and to learn the specifics of their children's progress. Parents not knowing the target language and inefficient communication between parents and teachers seemed to be the cause of such challenges. The parents in this study also mentioned their observation of the lack of support for the DLI programs at various levels as a challenge. They saw a lack of support for getting learning resources, and a lack of support from some of the teachers and board members in the districts. This challenge could be derived from a few causes. First, as the teachers described in the interviews, the extra work for them in the DLI programs was tremendous; however, the extra monetary return was at most a $1000 stipend. As a result, most current English teachers were not willing to teach in the DLI programs. Second, Utah has been a conservative state in terms of its view on bilingual education. In fact, Utah enacted an English-only bill in 2000, which prohibits the state from using languages other than English to conduct business or print information. In such a conservative state, it is reasonable to assume that some of the decisionmakers at the district level were skeptical toward the rapidly growing DLI programs in the state.

The next challenge identified by the parents in this study was also a challenge pinpointed by the teachers in Howard and Loeb's (1998) study, which is related to the tensions between DLI and non-DLI students and parents within the schools. This challenge was derived from the distribution of resources between DLI and non-DLI students and some of the DLI parents' apparent attitudes toward non-DLI parents. Fortunately, as the parents stated, the school administrators recognized the issue and were attempting to ease the divisions between the two groups.

The last challenge mentioned by the parents, retaining teachers, was mentioned also by the teachers and administrators in this study. This study found that all three groups of interviewees recognized that it was difficult to keep teachers in the programs. Several reasons contributed to this challenge. First, as the parent and school administrator interviewees mentioned, the English-speaking teachers were forced to take the teaching jobs in the DLI programs because no-one volunteered to take the jobs. The current DLI English teachers expressed frustration with being overworked and their desire to discontinue working in the DLI programs. Second, the Chinese-speaking teachers had a high turnover rate due to the majority of them being foreign nationals who were on a temporary work visa and had to leave the US after working for a couple of years. This issue was not stressed as much in the other studies, most of which had a focus on Spanish DLI programs. Compared to Spanish, the second most-spoken language in the US, there are fewer Chinese-speakers in the nation with an education background. Hence, the issue of not being able to find qualified Chinese-speaking teachers who could legally stay permanently in the US and having to look for temporary quality teachers overseas was severe in the Chinese DLI programs; as one parent noted, the Chinese teacher her child had each year was brand-new to the program. This issue is also related to other challenges mentioned by the teacher and administrator interviewees, such as communication between the Chinese and English teachers and Chinese–American cultural conflicts. The language and cultural barriers between the English teachers and the overseas Chinese teachers made their teaching tasks more stressful and the administrators' management more challenging. The fundamental culture and teaching differences between teachers from a Chinese-speaking country and America was discussed in Wu's (2017) study, which stressed that effective communication and teaching of the newly arrived Chinese teachers almost requires them to unlearn the training they received overseas.

Besides the challenges aforementioned, the teachers and the school administrators all identified DLI as a work-intensive program. The large class sizes, having to teach two classes of students daily, having to prepare for the curriculum that changed every year and time spent on making Chinese teaching materials all contributed to the challenge of work intensity. This finding is in support of the other DLI teacher study (Howard & Loeb, 1998), in which challenges such as finding time to make one's own teaching materials due to the lack of existing materials available in the target language and having to teach two classes with double the typical number of students were mentioned. Indeed, the DLI programs took a lot of continuous effort on the part of the teachers to overcome the shortage of teaching resources and compromises for teaching twice the normal number of students.

Finally, many Chinese teachers also mentioned the challenge of the gap between students. The Chinese teachers found that there was a small group of students who did not progress in Chinese language learning and were bored in class due to incomprehension. The gap between students grew bigger when the students reached higher grade levels and the teachers encountered great difficulty in helping to close the gap. This issue should be detected and addressed by the teachers and upper management early in the program before the gap becomes bigger. In addition, extra assistance should be offered to the already-busy Chinese teachers who have difficulty finding time to give extra help to the low-performing students. Moreover, more teaching training is needed to educate teachers in how to teach students with varying levels of learning abilities in the DLI context.

With respect to the suggestions made by the interviewees, two key elements often found in the interviews were being supportive and being flexible. From the parents' perspective, the DLI children's level of success depended largely on the commitment level of the parents in terms of how supportive they were toward the children's learning. On the other hand, the teachers asked for more flexibility and support from the school administrators and the state in terms of teaching methods applied in the classrooms and the amount of help offered in the form of teaching assistants. Moreover, they asked the state for more support in teaching by asking the state to offer more effective and appropriate teacher training sessions. The school administrators also made similar statements on having support from the state. In particular, they hoped the state would be more supportive by being more patient in explaining to the administrators and teachers the reasons certain program implementations could not be altered. Finally, the state director stressed that being highly supportive at the state-level coupled with highly supportive local school administrators were the keys to success in the DLI programs.

Discussion

In sum, the benefits of the Chinese DLI programs in Utah are mostly benefits associated with knowing a second language. None except the four heritage parent interviewees themselves mentioned that the DLI programs were beneficial for preserving their own heritage language and culture. This finding reflects the main objective of the one-way DLI program designed by the state, which is to enrich monolingual English-speaking students with multilingualism, rather than the preservation of one's heritage. This is evident as the Utah rule R277-488 Critical Languages Program defines the one-way program model as a program 'in which a student population consists of English language speakers with limited to no proficiency in the foreign immersion language. In such a model, less than 30 percent of the students have a native language other than English' (Utah Administrative Code, 2017). One may argue that the main reason the majority of the DLI programs offered in Utah are one-way rather than two-way is due to the low language minority population in the state; however, a study analyzing Utah's DLI policy in printed media conducted by Valdez *et al.* (2016a) pointed out that the discourses in the printed media from 2009–2015 shifted away from an equity/heritage framework to a global human capital framework, and that such a shift showed that 'marketability', which refers to 'a preoccupation with economically conceptualized language skills' (2016a: 854) overshadowed equity and heritage concerns. Their finding illustrates that the rapidly growing Utah one-way DLI programs, which set a 30% cap on heritage population, have an agenda of enriching English monolingual students in preparation for global competitiveness. It also shows the state's lack of concern and interest in maintaining minority students' heritage language.

According to the well-known DLI leading expert and researcher, Lindholm-Leary (2001), a very important factor separating dual language education from other types of immersion programs is student composition. DLI programs purposely include English as well as the target language speakers in the same classrooms to create opportunities for the two groups to develop bilingual competencies, academic achievement and cross-cultural understanding. In fact, many researchers (Alanís & Rodriguez, 2008; Lindholm-Leary, 2001; Lee & Jeong, 2013) strongly recommended DLI programs having 50% English-speakers and 50% language minority speakers, which are called 'two-way programs'. If such ideal percentages cannot be achieved, the researchers suggested that the minimum of 2:1 ratio should be met. In other words, the proportion of neither language group should be below 33%. Such a ratio promotes educational and linguistic equity in the classroom, cross-cultural interactions and program success. Findings in the Cantonese two-way DLI programs conducted by Yang *et al.* (2018) and Leung *et al.* (2018) illustrated that the majority of both heritage and non-heritage learners in the programs spoke positively regarding their education in the two-way model and believed that they gained the specific benefits they desired (e.g. heritage maintenance and future job opportunities). Based on the oversight of the benefit, preserving one's heritage, found in this study, and the education equity issue and the suggested optimal student composition (1:1 or 2:1) in DLI stated in the current literature, it is urgent that the state of Utah re-evaluates its current program policies and take educational equity into account. Given that the population of language minority groups other than Spanish-speakers are low in the state, active state efforts need to be made in promoting the maintenance of one's heritage as a major benefit of the DLI programs and reaching out to heritage families to recruit more heritage students for the programs, instead of setting an upper limit of 30% for heritage speakers to enroll in the one-way programs. Active attempts to reach the minimum of 33% heritage student population in the DLI programs will benefit the learning of not only the heritage students, but also the English-speakers, resulting in a win-win situation.

With respect to the challenges identified, despite the unique challenge of having to recruit Chinese teachers from overseas, which causes the challenge of communication barriers between teaching staff, the rest of the challenges were similar to other DLI programs in previous studies. As the interviewees in this study suggested, being supportive and flexible in these growing DLI programs at the developing stage was critical for overcoming the current challenges toward program success. Their suggestions echo most of the core criteria for successful DLI programs identified by Lindholm-Leary (2001), which include supportive administrators, teacher training, employing qualified teachers, meeting needs of all students from various backgrounds and offering a target-language environment. To close this chapter, it is important to point out again that as Utah DLI programs are the fastest-growing and the largest in the nation, its DLI implementation and practice attract great attention at the national level and its impact on the implementation of DLI programs in other states could be tremendous. Hence, the state of Utah servers as a role model, which carries the responsibility of demonstrating a DLI model that meets the criteria for success and is also one that supports educational equity. The findings on the benefits, challenges and suggestions mentioned by the Utah DLI parents, teachers and administrators hopefully have offered some food for thought for DLI decision makers to reflect upon for program re-evaluation in the future.

References

Alanís, I. and Rodriguez, M.A. (2008) Sustaining a dual language immersion program: Features of success. *Journal of Latinos and Education* 7 (4), 305–319.

Craig, B.A. (1996) Parental attitudes toward bilingualism in a local two-way immersion program. *Bilingual Research Journal* 20 (3–4), 383–410.

Howard, E.R. and Loeb, M. (1998) *In their own words: Two-way immersion teachers talk about their professional experiences.* Berkeley, CA: University of California Berkeley, Center for Research on Education, Diversity & Excellence. See http://escholarship. org/uc/item/9td4m00c (accessed 7 July 2017).

Lao, C. (2004) Parents' attitudes toward Chinese–English bilingual education and Chinese-language use. *Bilingual Research Journal* 28 (1), 99–121.

Lee, J.S. and Jeong, E. (2013) Korean–English dual language immersion: Perspectives of students, parents and teachers. *Language, Culture and Curriculum* 26 (1), 89–107.

Leung, G., Uchikoshi, Y. and Tong, R. (2018) 'Learning Cantonese will help us': Elementary school students' perceptions of dual language education. *Bilingual Research Journal* 41 (3), 238–252.

Lindholm-Leary, K.J. (2001) *Dual Language Education* (Vol. 28). Clevedon: Multilingual Matters.

Parkes, J. (2008) Who chooses dual language education for their children and why. *International Journal of Bilingual Education and Bilingualism* 11 (6), 635–660.

Parkes, J. and Ruth, T. (2011) How satisfied are parents of students in dual language education programs?: 'Me parece maravillosa la gran oportunidad que le están dando a estos niños'. *International Journal of Bilingual Education and Bilingualism* 14 (6), 701–718.

Utah Dual Language Immersion (2017) Why immersion? See http://utahdli.org/whyimmersion.html (accessed 9 July 2017).

Utah Administrative Code (2017) Utah rule R277-488 Critical Languages Program. See https://rules.utah.gov/publicat/code/r277/r277-488.htm (accessed 9 July 2017).

Valdez, V.E., Delavan, G. and Freire, J.A. (2016a) The marketing of dual language education policy in Utah print media. *Educational Policy* 30 (6), 849–883.

Valdez, V.E., Freire, J.A. and Delavan, M.G. (2016b) The gentrification of dual language education. *The Urban Review* 48 (4), 601–627.

Wu, M.-H. (2017) Examining Mandarin Chinese teachers' cultural knowledge in relation to their capacity as successful teachers in the United States. *Asian-Pacific Journal of Second and Foreign Language Education* 2 (11), 1–19. DOI: 10.1186/s40862-017-0034-y.

Yang, L., Leung, G., Tong, R. and Uchikoshi, Y. (2018) Student attitudes and Cantonese proficiency in a Cantonese dual immersion school. *Foreign Language Annals* 51, 596–616.

Young, R.L. and Tran, M.T. (1999) Vietnamese parent attitudes toward bilingual education. *Bilingual Research Journal* 23 (2–3), 225–233.

4 Exploring Chinese DLI Teachers' Identities

Teacher Identity

In different second language classroom contexts, the analysis of teacher identity is proven in the literature to be a powerful tool for understanding second language acquisition (Stranger-Johannessen & Norton, 2017). Researchers, such as Varghese *et al.* (2005), have stressed the importance of learning the multi-dimensional aspects of a teacher's identity:

> In order to understand language teaching and learning, we need to understand teachers; and in order to understand teachers, we need to have a clearer sense of who they are: the professional, cultural, political, and individual identities which they claim or which are assigned to them. (2005: 22)

Indeed, despite a teacher's professional identity, which includes the training received, their work motivation, beliefs about teaching and learning, teaching commitment and perceptions toward learners, colleagues and school administrators (Mutlu & Ortaçtepe, 2016), identities in other arenas, such as one's upbringing, friends and the media, are interwoven with and help shape a teacher's identity. Giovanelli (2015) explained that since teaching requires investing oneself and that a teacher's self-image affects how they view their teaching, personal and professional identities are tightly interrelated in a teacher's identity. Hence, when examining teacher identity, it is essential to take a holistic approach to include not only the professional, but also the analysis of the personal aspects, such as the teacher's previous experiences, family and sociocultural background, and influential people in his or her life. As a teacher's identity is so complex in nature, Meijer (2011) suggests that it should be viewed as 'simultaneously unitary and multiple, continuous and discontinuous, and individual and social' (2011: 315).

Poststructuralist View of Identity

This study takes Norton's (2013) poststructuralist view of identity as the theoretical framework for analysis and interpretations of the findings. Two key elements describe such a view. First, identities constitute one's beliefs and assumptions about local communities through in-person interactions and about global communities through social media. Norton called it one's relationship to the world. The relationship relates to both *people* and *social structures*. Taking the context of teaching as an example, learner (*people*) is considered an entity to which a teacher relates and with whom he or she has regular interactions in their local community, while national language policies (*social structures*) are seen as an entity at the macro level that depicts the tendency of the political and economic atmosphere of the nation. Through day-to-day social interactions with people, and with the influence of the particular social structures in which they are situated, individuals locate and position themselves within the context.

Second, identity is constructed across time and space. In other words, identity is formed across the past, present and imagined future, and across different spaces, including both physical and imagined metaphorical spaces. For example, Barkhuizen (2016) explained that for pre-service teachers, the imagined future membership in the teaching community influences their current expectation of their own education work and the present construction of their identities.

The fact that identity is constantly constructed within social relationships and structures in day-to-day life, and across time and space, implies that identity formation is a discursive event that is fluid and changeable (Barkhuizen, 2016). In order to examine such complex phenomena of teachers' identities, this study adopted the narrative inquiry approach, in particular short stories, as the analysis method (see the Narrative Inquiry section for more detail).

Studies of Second Language Teacher Identities

The existing literature utilizing the narrative inquiry approach in researching second language teacher identities had focused on the investigation of different factors that had an impact on a teacher's identity formation and reformation.

A few studies emphasized the impact of space shifting on language teacher identity. For instance, Mutlu and Ortaçtepe (2016) studied the teaching identities of Turkish teachers of English who relocated to the United States for a year teaching Turkish as exchange teachers. Through interviews and personal reflection journals, the researchers found that as the teachers moved overseas and their identities shifted from teaching English to Turkish, the past and current identities were blended. For example, they often referred to their past English teaching experiences in current teaching, and reflected on how their new Turkish teaching experiences in the United States would be useful when they taught English again after their return to Turkey. Mutlu and Ortaçtepe concluded that the constant interactions between the current and past teaching identities in the two different locations illustrated that teacher identity is multiple and blurred, and not fixed as the contexts changed from one to the other.

Huang's (2014) study also investigated teachers who moved away from where they were raised to teach English as a second language (ESL). Three secondary ESL teachers in the US from different non-English speaking countries participated in Huang's study. The findings illustrated that the participants possessed positive self-perceptions of being fluent English speakers and effective non-native ESL teachers. Huang explained that the positive identities were attributed to both their past upbringings and their current interactions with others. For instance, with respect to their childhood experiences, the participants were coming from middle-class backgrounds in their countries of origin and had access to opportunities such as learning standard English and travelling internationally. With regard to their current interactions with others, the teachers' English ability was validated and positively appraised by their colleagues, administrators and students. Huang stressed that a teacher's identity cannot be uncovered unless researchers consider the sociocultural and historical events in the teacher's life.

The results of Bukor's (2015) study were in support of Huang's claim. In searching for teacher identities through the narrative approach using in-depth interviews and reflexive autobiographical journaling, Bukor explored the identities of three experienced ESL teachers. Her findings suggested that the teachers' childhood histories were tightly connected to their instructional beliefs and practices, and ultimately the construction of their teacher identities. To be more specific, Bukor identified that the family environment and events, which are the foundations for cultivating the participants' core beliefs and perceptions, influenced the participants' self-development, career choice (of becoming a teacher) and ultimately the teaching traits they possessed. For example, one of the participants had a poor relationship with her mother in her childhood and realized that her choice of becoming a teacher might be connected to her searching for love from students due to the lack of love from her family.

Other existing studies were more focused on how one's professional role of being a second language teacher was institutionally, individually or culturally constructed. For instance, Farrell (2011) researched the professional identities of three tenured ESL college professors in Canada. The participants met 12 times over a two-year period as a group to verbalize their thoughts on their professional role identities. Among the many role identities mentioned in the group meetings, Farrell found that a teacher's professional role identities could be explained by creating a continuum, with one end being the institutionally created ready-made roles (e.g. teacher as vendor, which refers to teacher's role in student retention), and the other end being individually created or negotiated (e.g. teacher as motivator), in which individual teachers use unique ways to present the roles. Farrell concluded that teacher identity develops through daily experience and through 'communities of practice'; hence, an analysis of teachers' role identities provided reflective information from teachers on how and by what and whom they had been shaped during a teacher's career. This analysis is essential for teachers to realize whether any change is necessary.

Another study, Han's (2016) investigation of Korean pre-service ESL teachers' professional identity, also revealed similar findings in which certain role identities were institutionally created, while the others were influenced by the local culture where the teachers were raised. For example, although the pre-service teachers valued the communicative language teaching approaches influenced by western countries and adopted by the national English curriculum, they emphasized even more a teacher's holistic abilities, such as human education (e.g. the learning of compassion and respect) based on Confucian cultural influence. Another study (Ma & Gao, 2017) regarding Asian pre-service teachers' identities also reported the influence of the culture of Confucian thinking. The participants believed that a couple of important teacher identities, which emphasized the nurturing nature of a teacher, such as using the metaphorical terms of 'mother' and 'farmer' (e.g. mother taking care of children and farmer taking care of plants and flowers), are based on the Confucian belief that teachers are expected to not only convey knowledge, but also nurture and give life guidance to their students.

The previous studies on second language teacher identities have illustrated that many factors in different spaces and times could influence a teacher's identity construction. In the context of the Utah Chinese DLI programs, the teachers are from diverse sociocultural, political and language backgrounds. These teachers' identity formations probably would be very different both among themselves, and when compared to the participants studied in the existing literature, which mostly analyzed identities of ESL teachers of various backgrounds. Hence, it is necessary to conduct the current study to learn more about the thought processes and identity construction of the Chinese DLI teachers in hope to contribute more understanding of the Chinese DLI teachers' reasonings behind their teaching. The current study asks the following question: How do Chinese DLI teachers of various backgrounds construct their teacher identities through their personal and professional experiences?

Narrative Inquiry

This study used the qualitative method of narrative inquiry to investigate teachers' identities. Narrative inquiry 'is a way of doing research that focuses on the stories we tell about our lives' (Barkhuizen, 2016: 28). The specific type of narrative inquiry data used in this study is short stories extracted from interviews with the participants. Barkhuizen explained that short stories come from a bigger set of data (e.g. conversations, reflection journals and in-depth interviews), which are examined for their content (who, where and when), context (inner thoughts and emotions, inter-personal context and sociopolitical context) and how they relate to the narrator's other short stories. In this study, the short stories that were told in the two-hour one-on-one in-depth interviews with the participants helped the participants reflect on their past, connect the past with the present and envision the future.

The stories became narrative inquiry when there was an audience (the interviewer) and when the purpose of telling the stories was for research. The data assisted us in understanding the ways in which the participants positioned themselves as teachers in the particular contexts. The interview questions that prompted the participants' short story-telling touched upon their family and educational backgrounds, the reasons they became teachers, how they perceived themselves and how others perceived them as teachers, their teaching experiences, evaluations of their strengths and weaknesses, and their confidence level.

The interviews were transcribed and reviewed by us and checked against the audio recordings to ensure their accuracy. We read the transcriptions separately to identify the short stories and the three intersecting dimensions of the stories in content (who, where and when), and in context (inner thoughts, interpersonal context and sociopolitical context). After that, both of us came together to discuss whether we agreed with each other's coding and how these stories were interrelated to form the participants' teacher identities.

The Four Teacher Participants in the Utah Chinese DLI Programs

Four Chinese DLI teachers with varying teaching experiences and backgrounds volunteered to participate in this study. The four teachers represent four typical types of Chinese DLI teachers in Utah: (1) Chinese native speakers who received a degree in the US prior to teaching in DLI (Amy); (2) Chinese native speakers who have not studied in the US and reside in the US due to marriage (Linda); (3) Chinese native speakers who are sent to the US from China by the Confucius Institute (Cindy); and (4) English native speakers who speak Chinese as a second language fluently through an academic degree or immersion in Chinese language and culture overseas (Tony). Their background information is presented in Table 4.1 below.

Table 4.1 The teachers' background information

Pseudonym	Country of Origin	Education	Years of DLI Teaching
Tony	USA	M.A. in World Language Pedagogy	Seven years
Linda	Taiwan	B.A. in Early Childhood Education	Five years
Cindy	China	B.A. in Teaching Chinese as a Foreign Language	Three years
Amy	Taiwan	M.A. in Second Language Teaching	Six years

The Initial Formation of the Participants' Teacher Identities

The participants' past personal or professional experiences positively shaped the image of a teacher, and certain past events steered them to become teachers.

Tony

Tony's father ran an interior design company, and all of his siblings worked for his father. However, Tony's grandmother was a well-known vocal singer and teacher. Tony told the following short story about his grandmother.

> She was a vocal teacher, singing teacher. She was actually a famous sing-ing teacher. She taught classic opera, but she taught for like 65 years or something like that. She was really well-known. She's written books, and so I always knew her as a teacher. She had lots of students. She taught until she was 92 or 93 years old, and so she's taught the week before she died. She was a really passionate teacher and was really an amazing person. That could have been an influence on me.

Tony's story about his grandmother being a teacher was full of positive terms. Being 'well-known' and contributing books in her professional field and being 'passionate' and 'amazing' as a teacher and an individual helped Tony define how a teacher should be and inspired him as a child to become a teacher.

Later in Tony's life, an event which helped him decide to be a teacher was when he served as a Mormon missionary in Taiwan. Tony described,

> I think I really fell in love with teaching as a missionary. We taught English classes there (in Taiwan) and I can feel that I was a little bit better than other missionaries. It came more naturally and it seemed to me like I had a lot of people who wanted to come to my class. Maybe they enjoyed the way I taught. I was just able to be more engaging than some other people on site. That was the first time I thought maybe I

can do this, maybe I am good at that and I came back feeling excited about it.

Through his interactions with students in Taiwan, Tony recognized his ability to be a good teacher and has loved teaching ever since. In his story, he used 'better than others', 'more natural' and 'more engaging' to mark his teaching qualities. As he realized his teaching ability through the missionary event, Tony's inner feelings toward being a teacher grew strong and exciting.

Linda

None of Linda's family were teachers, but her interactions as a student in her childhood with her teachers made her feel that teachers were nice people.

> Since very early in my childhood I met teachers who treated me very well. I still remember the names of my teachers in elementary. I could feel that they all valued me as their student. So, by sixth grade, I thought about being a teacher because the teachers I met were all pretty good people.

The good qualities of Linda's teachers helped her develop a positive view of teachers as nice people and inspired her to be the same kind. However, it was not until one incident after many years of teaching that Linda found the real meaning of being a teacher.

> A few years ago, I taught a child who had special medical conditions and needed to take medicines daily. Due to the side-effects, the child's emotions and behaviors could be atypical sometimes. The mother was often worried about her child, but I was very patient with her and with the child. Many years after the child graduated from the program, I ran into him and his mother. His mother chatted with me for a while and put him on the back seat of the bike to leave. As the bike was going further and further away, the child kept his head turned back toward me as I saw them leave. His behavior made me feel that he remembered and missed me. In a common scenario, if you run into a student who graduated years ago, you greet each other briefly and say goodbye, but this student continued to look at me while they were leaving until they were too far away for me to clearly see them. I was moved by his behavior and this incident made me realize what a teacher is about. I feel as a teacher, everything you give will be remembered in the students' hearts. The extra efforts I make for my job are not wasted.

The student's action helped Linda confirm her belief that students would appreciate and would not forget a teacher's extra effort. Touched by her student's action, the warm feeling Linda experienced reassured her that it is worthwhile to be a teacher.

Cindy

Cindy, affiliated with the Confucius Institute, did not set her mind on being a teacher until she began teaching for a couple years.

> When I had to select what subject to major in college, I thought I was good at Chinese and English, and I like cultural things, I mean both languages and cultures are my favorite, so I chose to study Teaching Chinese as a Foreign Language. I didn't feel determined to be a teacher until I started working for a Singaporean bilingual school in Xiamen, China. My boss inspired me a lot. She took me step by step. When I did not understand something, she would explain and guide me without me pointing out my confusion. She would further help me find ways to solve the problems. I found that she was the same way with her students. I feel that she's got an organized personality and is willing to work hard. For example, she would ask me to write lesson plans every day in English. She would read them and give me systematic feedback and new teaching ideas. I learned a lot under her guidance.

Serving as a teacher role model, the supervisor at the Singaporean school guided Cindy on how to be a quality teacher. This positive work experience assisted Cindy to be able to more concretely define the qualities of a good language teacher in an authentic teaching environment and inspired Cindy to work toward obtaining those qualities.

Amy

Amy's decision to become a teacher was influenced by her mother and later by her professor's guidance.

> My mom always wanted to be a teacher, but my grandfather did not have enough money for her to go to a teacher training school, so she had to go to a vocational school and became an accountant later. She had been hoping that her daughter could go to a teacher training school, so I feel that now my mother had passed away, I am making her dream come true for her. The other thing that also inspired me was after I got into the training program of second language teaching, I was able to observe my professor's daily teaching. She gave me opportunities to write lesson plans and test out the plans in her language class. She also guided me step by step on how to plan or modify a lesson. During that time, I was thinking about making fun activities for the lesson plans even when I was asleep. I think this is the biggest turning point for my teaching career. I had no doubt that I wanted to be a language teacher.

Amy's idea to become a teacher was originally initiated by the goal of fulfilling her deceased mother's dream; however, once she started her training as a language teacher, similar to Cindy, it was the trainer who inspired her by offering professional knowledge and a space to practice teaching.

The Participants' Interpretations of Themselves as Teachers

When trying to define their roles as Chinese language teachers, the participants' past experience as students, their personal beliefs, their cultures and their professional knowledge all played a part in their stories.

Tony

Tony recalled how he was as a student and how it affected his belief in what a teacher should do.

> When I was little, I felt my teachers didn't like me. I was the type of student who spaced out and didn't pay attention to teachers. I didn't feel I was dumb, but what I was interested was not in school. So now I would spend time on developing a good relationship with students. I would learn their interests and try to understand them. I believe every student has their talents. I can attract most of the students and make them think this thing (Chinese) is very cool and interesting. Using this term might be a bit weird, but I like to see my students 'be addicted' to Chinese. This way they would improve more and be more confident.

Having a negative schooling experience as a student unmotivated in school subjects and having a distant relationship with his teachers, Tony saw how important teacher–student relationship-building and motivating students are. His own negative learning experience helped him reinforce his teacher role as a motivator that his former teachers lacked.

Linda

When Linda was asked to define her role as a language teacher, she said,

> I think my teaching role is 'a heavy responsibility and a long road'. I mean teachers are not just a tool for teaching, what you say and do are served as models your students follow, so I am very careful in these areas. If your words and behaviors do not go together, students would be confused. For example, I explain to my students that they can learn in a relaxed way such as doing fun activities like games, but that doesn't mean that there are no classroom rules. When they do activities, they need to consider their safety and respect others. When I give instruction,

they need to listen seriously. My students understand the rules very well and like my way of teaching.

Linda's definition of teacher role, 'a heavy responsibility and a long road' (任重道遠), originally comes from *The Analects of Confucius* (Confucius & Waley, 1938), a classical book which presents a collection of Confucius' sayings and ideas. Linda's short story about how she practiced the defined teacher role illustrates that the 'heavy responsibility' Linda referred to is not the teaching of subject knowledge, but human education (e.g. respect, compassion, empathy, etc.) also mentioned by the Korean teachers in Han's (2016) study. It seems that the teachers from East Asian background are heavily influenced by Confucian thinking.

Cindy

Cindy's definition of her teacher role was offering authenticity. She described how,

> My position is to make my best effort to increase my students' Chinese level and help them learn original Chinese. I feel that they can learn my language from me is one of the happiest things for me. I mean I feel so happy to see that they talk just like me, that they see from me what real Chinese is like. I think I have a lot of authentic experiences that shouldn't be wasted. I would bring some small items, small toys I used to play with in China. At first my students were being skeptical as they had never seen the toys before, but after they tried to play with the toys, they loved them. So, the most important thing is to open a door to a new world for them. When they grow up, they won't be so scared or close-minded.

As a Chinese native speaker who possessed Chinese language and cultural knowledge, Cindy saw herself as someone who could provide authentic resources and first-hand information to her students. The fact that she used the terms 'original' and 'real' to describe the Chinese language her students learned from her and herself as a 'real Chinese', indicates her thought of associating her native speaking status with originality and authenticity.

Amy

Amy's definition of herself as a language teacher seemed to be influenced by both her professional knowledge and the Confucian cultural thinking.

> In terms of language teaching, I am an assistant helping students be in contact with the Chinese language and culture, helping them plant the seed of Chinese for future learning. Moreover, my teaching is influenced

by my culture, which is different from the kind of education my students receive from adults at home or school. To them, I am from an outside culture, who brings the language of Chinese to their world, so I see myself as an important person who could influence the students' lives. You know a Chinese saying, 'Even if someone is your teacher for only a day, you should regard him like your father for the rest of your life'. I think this saying sums up my belief of my teaching role.

Amy's notion of language teacher as an assistant complies with the current language teaching approach, communicative language teaching (CLT), which encourages a student-centered approach where teachers act as monitors, supporters and assistants (Richards & Rodgers, 1986). On the contrary, the other role Amy defined using the old Chinese saying, 'Even if someone is your teacher for only a day, you should regard him like your father for the rest of your life' (一日為師, 終身為父), is based on Confucian thinking which positions teachers as highly important and respected people, who heavily influence students' thinking. Amy's definition of her teaching role interestingly shows the intersection of two distinct ideas from her culture and her profession.

The Participants' Teaching Identities as Chinese DLI Teachers

Some of the stories told by the participants with regard to their current teaching identities in the Chinese DLI programs were similar in the way that they all involved the renegotiation and reformation of their general teaching identities after becoming a Chinese DLI teacher in Utah. For example, the three Chinese native-speaking teachers all noticed the differences of student character between their countries and the United States, and tried to adjust their teaching styles and beliefs. As for the non-native-speaking teacher, Tony, he saw his non-native-speaking teacher identity as both an advantage and a disadvantage.

Tony

Tony elaborated,

When I first started teaching in the Chinese DLI program, I was very worried that my Chinese was not as good as my students' because I was assigned to teach fourth grade and was afraid that since they had been spending time with native speaking teachers for three years, their Chinese was probably very good. However, as a non-native speaking teacher, I had gone through what they are going through as a Chinese language student, so I am able to guide them on how to overcome language challenges and I have a lot of funny stories to tell them. For example, once I was describing a person in Chinese. I said, 'He is a good person and he is a Lùchī (a person with a terrible sense of direction on the road)'. Everyone started laughing because I was supposed to say Lǜshī (lawyer). I thought I said it right! So, telling my students my own stories about learning Chinese would show them how important it is to master the language.

Amy

Amy's story about her identity as a Chinese DLI teacher relates to her realization for identity adjustment based on her observations across space and time. She described,

> When I started teaching in the DLI program, one thing I noticed was that Taiwanese students I had in my country were much more obedient than students here in the States. In general, if you ask Taiwanese students to follow your step-by-step instruction to write characters, they would do it, but American children have more individual thoughts and opinions. They often ask you the 'why' questions, and sometimes I am not able to react to their questions instantly. So, after noticing the difference, I would think for the answers first, and explain why they need to do or learn certain things before I give them instruction.

In Chinese culture, where teachers are highly respected, it is considered rude to question a teacher's instruction. However, after learning that the students in the United States are more outspoken and individualistic, Amy renegotiated her teacher role, from a teacher who saw herself as the authority to a teacher who preached the importance of following her instructions.

Cindy

Cindy had a similar experience where she realized the cultural differences between the Chinese and American teaching contexts.

> My belief was that the role of a teacher was serious, so I was the serious kind of teacher. I thought if I criticize students to their faces in front of the class, they would feel embarrassed, which would stop them from misbehaving. This is the kind of education I received in my country, but I didn't know that doing that here would make the students feel very sad. When I did that, the students were like, 'Teacher, you can't be like this. This is bad'. I have been trying not to do that, but sometimes I can't help it.

Cindy recognized the different teaching beliefs and behaviors between where she was from and the current teaching context; however, the influence of her cultural background was so strong that, even though she intended to redefine appropriate teaching behaviors, sometimes she failed to do so.

Linda

Like Amy and Cindy, Linda also recognized the cultural conflicts and how they affect her teacher role.

> I have lived in the States for a long time, so I understand that in general Chinese people are more serious and the local people here are more relaxed. For example, if you don't turn in your homework on time, the Chinese way is punishing the student by deducting points, but here if you turn in homework, you get one point, and after so many points, you are offered a homework party. To Chinese, this is cultural conflict. Turning in homework is your responsibility. If you don't turn it in, you are not being responsible. But, since I started teaching here, I have changed my expectations. I don't pressure students here too hard.

Linda's story about the point deduction system in Chinese versus the point addition system in American classroom cultures illustrates the fundamental difference in education. Due to the context difference, regardless of her own belief, Linda redefined her role as a teacher who advocated the point addition system, as it is more acceptable to the students in the United States.

The Teachers' Interpretations of How Others See Them as Chinese DLI Teachers

Most of the stories which described how others see the participants as Chinese DLI teachers were not very positive.

Tony

Tony's story about how the non-DLI teachers at school perceived him as a Chinese DLI teacher were negative. Tony explained,

> I feel they [teachers outside the DLI program] probably think that I am a bit different. One thing is I know Chinese, which is a bit strange to them, and I am a male teacher, my attitude might be a bit different, and our hobbies are different, too, so they don't feel I belong to their group. My English partner teacher also has the same feeling. I just discovered about two months ago that they didn't feel that my partner and I belong to their group.

Tony pointed out that several of his teacher characteristics, such as being a male, speaking Chinese, and having different hobbies and attitude to the other teachers, possibly contributed to the distant relationship between him and the non-DLI teachers. However, he also mentioned that his English-partner teacher also felt the same way, suggesting that maybe the cause of the unfriendly relationship had to do with Tony and his partner being in a specialized program.

Cindy

The other teacher, Cindy, also felt isolated in the DLI program.

> I feel that the non-DLI teachers teaching the same grade level were closer together amongst themselves, but maybe it is my problem. I am not very outgoing and don't take the initiative to communicate with them. But sometimes I feel a bit weird that they would only communicate with my English-partner teacher, and not me. The parents also communicate and reply to my English partner more. This is probably because of the communication problem. They probably think that communication with me is not very smooth.

Cindy blamed her shy personality and perceived limited English ability for the distant relationship between her and the non-DLI teachers and parents.

Linda

The observation of the distant relationship between Chinese language teachers and the parents in the DLI programs was also mentioned by Linda. Linda stated that parents' preference of going to the English-partner teachers for communication seemed to be a common scene in the DLI programs.

> According to my and other Chinese DLI teachers' observations, it is common to see that when the students have issues, parents would go to the English-partner teachers first. In my first two years of teaching here, it was exactly like that, but slowly the parents discovered that I was a teacher who cared about students and was good at communicating with them. So, slowly they started to contact me for any issues.

It seems that the parents' preference of going to the English-partner teachers might indeed have to do with what Cindy pointed out; that the parents' perception toward Chinese teachers as having limited ability to communicate with them. Linda's story showed that once she proved herself to be a good communicator with English-speaking parents, the misperception of the parents was dismissed.

Amy

Amy's story about how she was perceived by others in school explains her rationale for the cold relationship between the Chinese DLI and non-DLI teachers at school.

I feel indistinctly that to non-DLI teachers at our school, we DLI teachers could be a threat to their positions. There are more and more DLI programs in Utah, so more language teachers are needed. Every district has a set number of teaching job openings, though. So, adding a Chinese DLI teacher equals taking a regular teacher out if the total number exceeds the limit. Some other districts have had this situation happen before and the regular teachers were forced to teach in a different district. So, one reason some non-DLI teachers are opposed to the DLI programs is because we might take away their jobs. Other than that, I think to them I am a trainer of future Mormon missionaries. I chatted with the non-DLI teachers before. I think because we are in Utah, and many of them are returned missionaries, they see me as a trainer who will prepare the children to spread the gospel overseas in the future.

Despite the non-DLI teachers' perception toward DLI teachers as job competitors, Amy was positive about her role as a trainer of future missionaries in her fellow non-DLI teachers' eyes.

The Teachers' Positions in Relation to Heritage Students in the Program

When asked about how they position themselves in relation to the students from different backgrounds, all four teachers noted the huge difference in number and characteristics between the Chinese heritage and the English-speaking students in their classes.

Cindy

Cindy described how,

Last year I didn't have any heritage students, but this year I have two. I expect more from them because their Chinese level is higher than others. Sometimes they can be my little assistants to help others. I feel that their presence brings good things to the class, as I can clearly see that the language level of the class this year is much higher than the one last year. The heritage students would say words that are not taught in the class and the other students would be curious about the meanings of the words and try to imitate saying the words. One time, a heritage student said the word 'slingshot' and other students were asking what it was, and the student started acting out the word to explain to the others. So, I think if I could have more heritage students, the level of the whole class would be increased.

Cindy positioned the heritage students in her class as her helpers due to their advanced language level. According to Cindy, they brought in authentic language not included in the textbook, which increased the other students' curiosity about the language. She also noted the low number of the heritage group in her class and how it would help the whole class if there were more of them.

Linda

Linda's story about heritage students was very similar to Cindy's. Linda said,

> Their Chinese level is good, so they usually become my little tutors, this way they feel they are valued. They have become role models in the class. Other students would think, 'Wow, their Chinese is so good,' and I would say to the class, 'Yours can be as good as theirs,' to encourage them.

Linda used the terms, 'little tutors', and 'role models' to describe her position in relation to the heritage students in class. In Linda's mind, the heritage students were a positive influence and encouraged the other students to be as good as them in Chinese.

Tony

Tony's story also mentioned the advantage of having heritage students in class; however, he also pointed out an issue. Tony noted,

> I feel some students with heritage background are very confident. This is the polite way to say it. I feel that they think they already know everything, so they don't need to listen. Once I had a student, he would raise his hand very often and say, 'I already knew'. My thought was, 'you had been speaking the language since you were born, this is not a special skill or talent you studied'. But at the same time, there are some heritage students who are nice and happy to help other students. This kind of student is good for the class. They can be the role models and little tutors for others. Sometimes it feels awkward to have two Americans speak in Chinese, so if you have Chinese children in the class, then the whole class would feel that speaking Chinese is natural. So, I think maybe having more Chinese students will help English-speaking students see that Chinese is needed and is natural.

Just like Cindy and Linda, Tony recognized the positive aspects of having heritage students in class such as being tutors and role models, and making the use of Chinese in class less awkward. Nonetheless, Tony also identified the negative attitude of some heritage students when they found that the knowledge taught in class was too easy for them and therefore they did not need to pay attention.

Amy

Tony was not the only participant who noted this issue – Amy also pointed out the distinct Chinese language level between heritage and non-heritage students as an issue. She said,

> One thing I am still puzzled about and not sure what to do is every year, almost all of my students are white English-speaking students except one or two students are from Chinese heritage background. After about a semester, I noticed that the Chinese students' Chinese level regressed. Because they were affected by the American students, so after they came to the program, they spoke more English. This regression also reflected on their written and oral tests. There was one time, to my surprise, a Chinese student started talking to me in English. I was thinking, 'if you know how to speak in Chinese, why don't you speak it with me?' So, my thought is what do we do if the heritage students come to our program and are affected by the English-speaking kids?

Amy's worry revealed the issues derived from the grossly disproportionate number of Chinese heritage students and English-speaking students. As all of the Chinese DLI programs in Utah are one-way immersion programs, which should consist of mostly English language speakers, and less than 30% of the students should have a native language other than English, the few heritage students in the classrooms were singled out. On the one hand, they were seen by the teachers as role models and helpers to other students; however, on the other hand, the instruction was not sufficiently balanced to accommodate both heritage and English-speaking students' language levels. As a result, their Chinese regressed and some of them who showed their boredom were being viewed as too proud or not paying attention.

Discussion

By adopting Norton's (2013) poststructuralist view of identity, this chapter examined how four Chinese-speaking DLI teachers in Utah positioned themselves in relation to the *people* (students, colleagues and parents) within Utah *social structures*, where the state government favored the rapid and expansive implementation of DLI programs. In light of the poststructuralist view of identity, the Chinese DLI teacher participants' short stories documented in this chapter revealed that their teaching identities were formed and continuously reshaped throughout their teaching career across different times and spaces. In concordance with the other study (Bukor, 2015), this chapter found that the participants' initial teaching identities were mostly cultivated by events which occurred in their childhood. For example, Tony's grandmother being a teacher demonstrated to Tony that a teacher needed to be passionate and amazing, and Linda's elementary teachers showed Linda that teachers treated others well. The experiences of their childhoods affected their career choices and the teaching traits they later had. As the participants decided to become teachers and started practicing teaching, their past learning experiences as students, their home cultures and their professional knowledge of language teaching all played a role in shaping their identities. As in other studies (Han, 2016; Ma & Gao, 2017), it was especially evident that the Chinese culture of the Chinese native-speaking teachers had a significant impact on their teaching identities, as two of the three (Amy and Linda) quoted Confucius as documented in *The Analects of Confucius* (Confucius & Waley, 1938). This finding, along with similar findings in the current literature (Wu, 2017) illustrate the long and heavy impact of the millennia-old Confucianism on current Chinese teachers' identities.

When reflecting on their specific teaching identities in the DLI programs, the three native-speaking teachers compared the different learning and teaching styles in their countries of origin and in the US, and how they tried to make efforts to modify their identities to fit the US context. This finding is very similar to Mutlu and Ortaçtepe's (2016) and Huang's (2014) studies, in which the teachers' identities were not fixed when the teaching contexts changed from one (home country) to the other (the US). On the other hand, when reflecting on how others (non-DLI colleagues and parents) perceived the participants as DLI teachers, negative terms were used. Two reasons contributed to such negativity. First, the non-DLI teachers viewed the participants as job competitors who could potentially cost traditional teachers their jobs in the district, as the state planned to implement more DLI programs in the future. Second, the DLI parents had a general perception of the Chinese native-speaking DLI teachers being inefficient in communication due to their limited English ability, which resulted in a preference for contacting the English-partner teachers in the DLI programs. This finding is in support of Huang's (2014) finding that how others perceive the teachers could possibly influence the teachers' identities (e.g. their confidence level as a teacher). For example, the non-native English-speaking teachers in Huang's study received praise from their colleagues regarding their English ability and had very positive self-perceptions of being effective English language teachers, whereas in this chapter, Cindy blamed her own shy personality and concluded that the parents probably thought her English level was low based on her interactions with non-DLI teachers and the parents of her DLI students.

A specific situation that other existing studies, which mostly emphasized the identities of English language teachers, would not find is the presence of heritage students in the classroom. As the Utah Chinese DLI programs consist of a small group of Chinese heritage students, how the teachers position themselves in relation to the heritage students is important to understand. This chapter found that the heritage students were often referred to as the teachers' 'little tutors' and were presented in class as role models due to their superior Chinese language level compared to their peers. However, one of the participants (Amy) expressed her worry of how to best maintain the heritage students' current level. It seems that due to the heritage students being the minority (usually only one to two heritage students in a class), their Chinese had regressed over time since they came to the program. As the teachers positioned the heritage students as assistants, Amy raised a valid concern regarding how Chinese DLI teachers can reshape their position in relation to the heritage students in order to improve their language level, and not only see them as classroom helpers.

Teachers' identities are multi-dimensional and are formed, not only based on their personality and talents, particular cultural values they adopted, and their affiliations with different groups, but are also influenced by the specific teaching context in which the individual is currently situated. Hence, teacher identity formation is an ongoing process, in which the individual continuously negotiates and renegotiates, defines and redefines his or her own position in relation to others. The findings reported in this chapter suggest the need to examine teachers' life experiences in both personal and professional arenas in order to identify the main influences on teaching identities. As Bukor (2015) suggested, once teaching identities are identified, it would be useful to hold teacher development programs to acknowledge and address the interconnectedness of the personal and the professional facets of being a teacher, which will assist the teachers in understanding more about themselves and how to better relate to their students, parents and colleagues.

References

Barkhuizen, G. (2016) Narrative approaches to exploring language, identity and power in language teacher education. *RELC Journal* 47 (1), 25–42.

Bukor, E. (2015) Exploring teacher identity from a holistic perspective: Reconstructing and reconnecting personal and professional selves. *Teachers and Teaching* 21 (3), 305–327.

Confucius and Waley, A. (1938) The analects of Confucius. New York, NY: Random House.

Farrell, T.S. (2011) Exploring the professional role identities of experienced ESL teachers through reflective practice. *System* 39 (1), 54–62.

Giovanelli, M. (2015) Becoming an English language teacher: linguistic knowledge, anxieties and the shifting sense of identity. *Language and Education* 29 (5), 416–429.

Han, I. (2016) (Re)conceptualisation of ELT professionals: academic high school English teachers' professional identity in Korea. *Teachers and Teaching* 22 (5), 586–609.

Huang, I.C. (2014) Contextualizing teacher identity of non-native-English speakers in US secondary ESL classrooms: A Bakhtinian perspective. *Linguistics and Education* 25, 119–128.

Ma, X. and Gao, X. (2017) Metaphors used by pre-service teachers of Chinese as an international language. *Journal of Education for Teaching* 43 (1), 71–83.

Meijer, P.C. (2011) The role of crisis in the development of student teachers' professional identity. In A. Lauriala, R. Rajala, H. Ruokamo and O. Ylitapio-Mäntylä (eds) *Navigating in Educational Contexts: Identities and Cultures in Dialogues* (pp. 41–54). Rotterdam: Sense Publishers.

Mutlu, S. and Ortaçtepe, D. (2016) The identity (re)construction of nonnative English teachers stepping into native Turkish teachers' shoes. *Language and Intercultural Communication* 16 (4), 552–569.

Norton, B. (2013) *Identity and Language Learning: Extending the Conversation* (2nd edn). Bristol: Multilingual Matters.

Richards, J.C. and Rodgers, T.S. (1986) *Approaches and Methods in Language Teaching.* New York, NY: Cambridge University Press.

Stranger-Johannessen, E. and Norton, B. (2017) The African storybook and language teacher identity in digital times. *The Modern Language Journal* 101 (S1), 45–60.

Varghese, M., Morgan, B., Johnston, B. and Johnson, K.A. (2005) Theorizing language teacher identity: Three perspectives and beyond. *Journal of Language, Identity, and Education* 4 (1), 21–44.

Wu, M.-H. (2017) Examining Mandarin Chinese teachers' cultural knowledge in relation to their capacity as successful teachers in the United States. *Asian-Pacific Journal of Second and Foreign Language Education* 2 (11). DOI: 10.1186/s40862-017-0034-y

5 Creating an Effective and Supportive Dual Language Classroom

The Problems

Scholars Perry and Stewart (2005) once stated, 'If a marriage doesn't go well, you don't want people watching. If a partnership doesn't go well, you don't want students watching' (2005: 563). Their statement stresses the importance of collaboration between teachers in team teaching. Team teaching takes many forms and has been used as an effective method in curricula at all school levels from pre-school to graduate school. The different types of team teaching can be placed on a continuum of collaboration from the type in which two or more instructors loosely share responsibilities for a group of students, to the type in which more than one instructor jointly plan, teach and evaluate a group of students (Sandholtz, 2000). Regardless of the types of team teaching on the continuum of collaboration, all types of team teaching involve 'a group of instructors working purposefully, regularly and cooperatively to help a group of students learn' (Buckley, 2000: 4).

In the Utah Chinese DLI context, the Chinese and English partner teachers teach independently in their own classrooms through different mediums of instruction (the Chinese-speaking teacher teaches in Chinese, and the English-speaking teacher teaches in English). However, they closely collaborate with each other at many levels, as they teach the same two groups of students daily. In terms of content, DLI teachers are expected to reinforce the knowledge taught by their partner teacher. For example, after a first-grade Chinese teacher teaches certain math concepts to a morning group, the English teacher needs to check their level of understanding of the math concepts, and reinforce the new knowledge through the English instructional medium.

Not only do the partner teachers share the responsibility of teaching to reach the learning objectives stated in the state standards, having the same groups of students daily also means that they encounter similar student issues (e.g. behavioral or academic) that they need to collaboratively think of tactics to address. Moreover, the partner teachers need to plan and execute events together, such as Chinese

New Year celebration, back-to-school-night, field trips and meetings with parents. For instance, in a meeting with parents where the student is also present, the Chinese teacher relies on the English teacher to explain the student's performance as the USOE encourage target language teachers not to speak English in front of their students. Since the partner teachers share many responsibilities in the partnership, and some of the teachers interviewed in Chapter 2 encountered difficulties in communication with their partner teachers, one focus of this chapter is to examine how formal and informal communication of the Chinese and English partner teachers can build not only a professional, but a friendly team relationship, which positively influences the program quality.

This chapter has a second focus and extends the meaning of 'partnership' from team teaching to the collaboration between teachers and parents, as assisting student learning is in the mutual interest of both parties. At home, parents support their children's performance and foster positive attitudes towards learning through scaffolding and reinforcement (Gao, 2012). Cunha *et al.*'s (2016) study on parents' conceptions of their involvement in elementary schools reported a positive view of parental involvement. The involvement fostered the children's autonomy, allowed them to exert control over their own learning and provided the children with encouragement when they had difficulties. However, Cunha *et al.* cautioned that good quality parental involvement is necessary to aid student development and urged parent–teacher collaboration to improve the quality of the parents' work. Indeed, studies (Bartram, 2006; Sénéchal & LeFevre, 2002) have shown that active parental involvement with collaboration with teachers offers children advantages in academic performance and in both first and second language acquisitions. In other words, effective parent–teacher communication and a positive teacher–family relationship benefit students. However, current literature revealed that teachers lack preparation for communication with parents, and often encountered challenges communicating with parents (Shartrand *et al.*, 1997). In the Utah Chinese DLI context, the parent–teacher communication and parental involvement can be even more challenging for both Chinese teachers and parents, as the majority of the parents do not understand the Chinese language and culture and rely heavily on the Chinese teachers' communication to support parental involvement. Evidence was found in the parents' interviews in Chapter 3 that due to a lack of knowledge of Chinese, some of them found it difficult to support their children's studies. Hence, the second focus of this chapter is to document the level of effectiveness of communication and assistance from Chinese DLI teachers to parents and to make parent–teacher communication suggestions for Chinese DLI teachers who have a majority of parents without Chinese competence.

Cultural-Historical Activity Theory

This chapter takes the Cultural-Historical Activity Theory (CHAT) approach in examining the collaboration phenomena between Chinese DLI partner teachers and between a Chinese teacher and her students' parents. CHAT, originally founded by the Russian scholar, Vygotsky (1978), and further developed by Engeström (1987), believes that human activities that occur in any point in time must take into account their historical and cultural contexts as humans' actions are shaped by their cultural knowledge, which is grounded in history (Foot, 2014). CHAT sees collaboration as an activity system, which has six core components: subject, object, tools, community, rules, and division of labor. 'Subject' refers to the actor (may be an individual or a group) in action. 'Object' is the motive or desired outcome in the activity. 'Tools' are the instruments used by the subject to reach the object. 'Community' refers to the social group which shares a common interest with the subject for reaching the object. 'Rules' are regulations the subject refers to when making actions toward the object. 'Division of labor' refers to the task assignments involved in the activity. All six core components are seen as mediators that affect and lead to an outcome for each other (Engeström, 1993).

From the perspective of CHAT, human collaboration often triggers tensions, which could potentially alter the nature of the subject's activity participation or cause the activity to collapse and make the subject fail to achieve the object. The success of human collaboration requires harmony among the six core components. By drawing upon the CHAT perspective, this chapter seeks to discuss the nature and dynamics of teacher–teacher and parent–teacher collaborations by analyzing the interplay of the six core components in the activity system and how the interactions of the components yield successful results.

Team Teaching

In current literature, team teaching is found to be beneficial to students. First, having more than one teacher exposes students to different views, experiences, and sources of information (Garner & Thillen, 1977). Second, team teachers presenting multiple perspectives to the class invites students to join the conversation, which increases student participation (Hertzog & Lieble, 1994). Third, having more than one teacher to evaluate the quality of students' work and their learning progress is more efficient and reliable (Reynolds, 1985). Although team teaching has been widely researched in many contexts, there is a lack of research in the dual language context where target language and English-speaking teachers work together.

A recent study conducted by Perry and Stewart (2005), which investigated language and content teachers' collaboration, can somewhat represent the DLI context where students learn content subjects through a second language medium. Perry and Stewart examined the views of team teaching of seven pairs of teaching partners in a Japanese tertiary institution, where many classes were co-taught by language and content faculty. In this English-medium college with 80% of professors from out of the country, Japanese students learned content areas from a discipline professor in English, while an ESOL specialist supported the students' English language. The partner teachers took turns to take the lead and support roles as deemed necessary. For example, when they thought that a language point needed to be reinforced, the ESOL teacher would start the class in the lead role while the content teacher supported the instruction. On the other hand, when the content teacher took the lead, the ESOL teacher assisted with comprehension difficulties. In their findings, Perry and Stewart reported that teachers' beliefs about teaching and an understanding of teaching roles and expectations were key elements for an effective teaching partnership. Although the learning situation in Perry and Stewart's study is similar to the DLI context in which students learn through a second language, the distinct education levels of the students (tertiary vs. elementary) and the team teaching structures (both teachers in one classroom vs. one teacher in each classroom) could make the dynamics of the teacher partnership different. Therefore, teacher collaboration research done specifically in the DLI context such as the one in this chapter is needed.

Parent-Teacher Collaboration

A bridge is connected between home and school when parents are invited by teachers as partners to jointly support their children's learning development. As the parent–teacher collaboration is highly valued in education, a few DLI empirical studies documented how parent–teacher collaboration was formed in particular DLI programs. For example, in Sawyer et al.'s (2016) study of the Teachers and Parents as Partners (TAPP) project, the English monolingual teachers and the Spanish preschool DLI parents met bi-monthly to build their relationship, learn about language development of dual language learners, experiment with the use of technology (e.g. iPad games) for home and school learning activities and generate Spanish key phrases that can be used with dual language students for English teachers. After the project, Sawyer et al. (2016) interviewed the participants and found that they spoke highly about the project. For the Spanish DLI parents, the negative perception they received from others regarding their Spanish-accented English was lowered; instead, they valued their home language more as an asset and their bilingualism as a positive trait. For the English teachers, their knowledge about Spanish and the Latino culture increased, their negative views about Latino families were dispelled and they saw the

Spanish-speaking parents as a valuable resource. Most importantly, the project made the parent–teacher relationships closer.

In another study by the same group of researchers (Sawyer *et al.*, 2017), the beliefs of pre-school DLI parents and teachers about their collaboration were examined. First, the study reported that both parents and teachers believed that positive collaborations should be built on trust and respect. Second, both parents and teachers encountered difficulties in collaboration, including logistics and a clear view of parents' roles and responsibilities. Many parents in the study suggested that their Spanish language knowledge should be utilized in parent–teacher collaboration, which indicated that the parents recognized their Spanish language expertise as their 'funds of knowledge'. However, Sawyer *et al.* (2017) pointed out that the parents overlooked their expert knowledge in the area of their culture. In addition, parents lacked ideas on how to collaborate with teachers. The study therefore suggested that professional training for teachers on ways to collaborate with parents would be beneficial.

The context in current literature regarding DLI parent–teacher collaboration was very different from the context of the Chinese DLI. In the studies discussed above, the majority of the students in the DLI programs spoke the minority language, Spanish; hence, the discussion of collaboration centered around how English teachers could better understand the language and culture of the minority students and how the parents could be a valuable asset to provide help. In contrast, in the Chinese DLI, the parents were English-speakers who had difficulties providing help to aid their children's Chinese development, and the Chinese teachers were seen as a linguistic and cultural resource for both students and parents. Therefore, how the Chinese teachers use their expertise to collaborate with parents is crucial. Since research in the Chinese DLI context where most parents are English-speaking is lacking, this chapter includes such research to close the gap.

To be specific, this chapter investigates (1) how Chinese DLI partner teachers collaborate and communicate to effectively manage their classes, and (2) how a Chinese DLI teacher thought of ways to collaborate with and support non-Chinese-speaking parents to aid their children's Chinese as a second language development.

Participants

Two pairs of female Chinese-English partner teachers in two different Chinese DLI programs in Utah volunteered to participate in the team teacher collaboration study in this chapter. Table 5.1 below shows their educational background and teaching experiences.

The table illustrates that all four teachers held degrees in education with different focuses (e.g. early childhood, language teaching, special education and elementary education). The differences in educational

Table 5.1 Team teachers' educational background and teaching experiences

Teacher ID	Education	Past Experiences	Current Experiences
C1	B.A. in early childhood education	Preschool: 4 years	Chinese DLI (2nd grade): 2 years
E1	B.A. in teaching with ESL endorsement	Elementary: 8 years	Chinese DLI (2nd grade): 2 years
C2	M.A. in second language teaching. B.A. in special education.	Special education: 6 years	Chinese DLI (1st grade): 4 years
E2	B.A. in special education and elementary education	Middle school: 3 years Preschool: 7 years Special education: 1 year Elementary: 1 year	Chinese DLI (1st grade): 1 year

specialty amongst each pair of the teachers could be seen as an advantage to allow them to supplement each other and enhance each other's knowledge. In addition, all four teachers had spent many years (ranging from six to 13 years) teaching in various learning contexts, which brought significant experience, knowledge and resources to their teams.

With regard to the participants in the parent–teacher collaboration, the second author is the teacher participant in the parent–teacher collaboration study (see Chapter 1 for details regarding the second author as a teacher participant). The parents were from both classes in cohort one (see the focal teacher and student participants section in Chapter 1 for the cohort one participants' demographic background information).

Procedures

This study of teacher–teacher and parent–teacher collaborations was a 15-week long project in the fall semester. With respect to the team teaching collaboration, data collection included the team teachers' weekly meeting records, each teacher's bi-weekly self-reflection notes and an interview with each teacher at the end of the semester. The partner teachers utilized the sheet, *Collaboration Protocol for Dual Language Immersion K–3*, provided by the state as a guide for their weekly formal meetings. The sheet consists of five parts. Part I, task progress, is a follow-up on previously assigned tasks. Part II, curriculum collaboration, identifies the concept and academic vocabulary taught in the target language and concept and academic vocabulary to be reinforced in English in each of the content areas (Math, Social Studies, Science, Literacy/Language Arts). Part III, communication and public relations, documents any communications from the teachers to the parents (e.g. newsletters, emails, phone calls). Part IV, student monitoring, describes particular students' academic or behavioral issues and the interventions the teachers plan to take to remedy the problems. Part V, team problem-solving, records any questions or problems the teachers need to address to students or parents. Part VI, communication with administration, reports any news to celebrate and things to know. The meeting records were used as supporting data, which offered discussion information regarding the collaboration, while the self-reflection notes and the interviews provided information on the nature and dynamics of the collaborations. In the reflections and interviews, the participants were asked to reflect on the content of their communication and elaborate on their perception of the quality and effectiveness of the collaborations. The interviews were transcribed and we read the reflections and the transcriptions of the interviews separately to look for themes within the data. After that, the themes were categorized and the participants' quotations which represent the ideas of the themes were listed. Next, we compared our analyses and resolved any disagreements on the categorizations. The inter-rater reliability before the discussion was 96%.

As for the parent–teacher collaboration, surveys that the teacher used as tools to reach out to communicate with the parents were collected as data. The first survey was a parents' pre-survey, which inquired about the types of assistance parents thought their teacher needed to provide in order for parents to assist their children's study after class. The survey items were on a six-point scale ranging from 'not interested at all' to 'very interested'. The second survey was a parents' post-survey, which asked the parents open-ended questions to indicate which support tools were beneficial to them.

The Team Teachers' Formal Weekly Meetings

An examination of the partner teachers' meeting records showed that three topics occupied most of their meeting time. First, they spent time updating each other on the concepts taught in their classes and how well their classes as a whole grasped the concepts, and identifying concepts which needed reinforcement. In the interview, E1 elaborated, 'We did a whole chicken unit on the life-cycle of a chicken, and so we would talk about that and make sure they understand the vocabulary and they learned it in Chinese as well' (Interview).

Second, the teachers spent time identifying individual students who lagged behind in different content areas and discussing strategies for intervention. Both pairs of teachers identified math as the content area frequently being the focus of discussion. For example, C1 mentioned 'a significant amount of time was spent on identifying the students who still needed help, especially in the content area of math' (Interview). The math instruction in the Chinese DLI programs in Utah is taught by the Chinese teacher and reinforced by the English teacher in K–3 grades. According to the teachers, it was sometimes hard for certain students to grasp math concepts in a second language. C1 said,

I would analyze their math test results and identify the concepts each low performing student lacked and together we would make a plan on how my partner and I could provide extra help to the individual low performing students. (Reflection)

The third main topic in the meetings was the students' behavioral issues. C2 gave an example of how she and her partner dealt with a student with behavioral issues. At the beginning of the semester, both C2 and E2 observed the behavioral problems of the student (e.g. not paying attention in class, often having conflicts with peers, making disruptive noises in class and low academic performance). They discussed it in a meeting and asked the parents for their support on using a reward system specifically designed for the student to use both in school and at home. Both teachers closely monitored the effectiveness of the reward system and when they observed that the student's behavior was not improving, they came up with a different reward system in the formal meeting.

The Team Teachers' Informal Talk

The data from the self-reflection notes and the interviews showed that in addition to formal meetings, the teacher pairs often had daily informal conversations multiple times a day (e.g. at lunch time, when students line up to leave, in the copy room, in the hallway, or texting). Some informal conversations were work-related, while others were personal. The work-related conversations were mostly quick updates on certain students' behaviors. For example, C2 stated that 'it's about what's happening in my partner's classroom, or what's happening in my classroom' (Interview). C2's partner, E2 elaborated, 'Just little behavioral things like Annie is not wanting to do anything, or Thomas has a bad day... that really helps' (Interview). On the other hand, the personal conversations usually had the purpose of showing care and affection toward their partners. For instance, C1 described, 'Sometimes we talked about our lives, like I told her about my family sometimes, and she told me about her family' (Reflection).

The Team Teachers' Perspectives Towards Collaborating

A few themes emerged from the teachers' self-reflection notes and interview data regarding their perceptions toward their collaborations, which are discussed below.

Learning new skills

The pairs learned new skills from each other. For example, C2 stated, 'I learned a lot from my partner because she showed me how to better communicate with parents. I feel that after I adopted her way to talk to parents, they could understand more what's happening'. The specific way that C2 learned from E2 for communicating with parents was described by E2 as being positive with parents, but to not candy-coat any issues. In E2's own words, it is 'like making things not as a big deal, like no, this is happening, we still love them'. This serious, but amiable, communication style with parents is distinct from that of the traditional Chinese educator, who is usually seen by parents and students as the authority, and their words should always be taken seriously without question and with respect. However, C2 found that the new communication method was a better fit in the DLI context, as the majority of parents were American. The other pair of teachers, C1 and E1 also mentioned the learning of new skills from each other. For example, C1 noted that E1 was much more technology–savvy than she was and E1 taught C1 how to more effectively utilize it. C1 said, 'Once I wanted to print out students' name tags with their birthdate information on them. I didn't know that I could print them out by their birthdate sequence. After E1 taught me how to do it, it made organizing the tags easier and faster'.

Better student performance

All four teachers stated that frequent communication from both the formal and informal conversations paid off and was reflected in their students' improved academic performance. C1 said, 'I noticed that after we regularly worked together to identify the weakness of our students in math and how to remedy it, their math performance had been going up'. In addition, the teachers also felt that the daily quick updates on students' behaviors helped the students realize that they could not get away with bad behavior, even after switching to a different classroom with a different teacher in the middle of the day. For example, E1 described, 'I would tell my students that I would tell Ms. C1 that you already have two warnings this morning, so when you go to her class this afternoon and get a third warning, you will receive "think time" [a punishment]'.

Multiple-channel communication

All four teachers mentioned the effectiveness of using multiple means to communicate. In addition to the in-person communication in the formal meetings, often the teachers used phone, email, text, and written notes to communicate with each other. They especially liked texting, as it was instant and was not restricted to where one was, as long as the individual carried a technology device. E2 said, 'So many times I'll think of something at night and then I text my partner and she can just text back, and I think that's so helpful' (Interview). C1 wrote, 'We texted to each other whenever we got a chance. This helped us to be able to communicate the things that we still needed to take care of when we were busy' (Reflection). C2 also made a similar comment that she felt that 'it is good to have this way to communicate when we cannot talk face to face' (Reflection). Through multi-channel communication, the teachers developed not only professional relationships, but close friendships, which enhanced their teaching efficiency. This was evident when C1 stated, 'I like that we don't only talk about school items but also care about each other's life. No matter if it is physical or emotional concerns, we try to listen and care for each other. That makes us a better partnership' (Interview). E2 also stressed that the informal conversations about their personal lives expanded their relationship to the friendship domain, which helped with their teaching. E2 stated, 'I think if you are friends, you're going to be a better team. If you don't really get along, you are not going to be a good team to be working together'.

Support, affection and personality

The teachers identified a few key elements as important for the success of collaborations. First, the partners need to support each other. E2 noted, 'This year I feel like C2 and I are a great team. She supports me and I support her. Even with parents. Last year, I felt like I always had to be the bad guy. This year is going so much better' (Reflection). E2 did not have a very positive collaboration experience with a different Chinese partner teacher the year before the study was conducted and recognized how important being supportive to the partner was. E2's partner, C2, felt the mutual support from her partner as she described, 'My partner responds to parents' texts all the time and I know she covers many things for me when parents ask her questions. I am so grateful that we have a good relationship to work together' (Reflection). The supportive attitude toward their work extends to their personal lives and was shown as their affection and care toward their partners. For example, both pairs of partners celebrated each other's birthdays. They also texted or phoned their partners when they were sick. When one had personal issues, the other would show their support. For instance, C2 stated how she was touched by her partner's full support when her partner learned that the school district might not agree to help C2 get permanent residency in the United States. She said,

> My partner even got tears…She even said that she can write a letter of support for me if needed. I really appreciate that! Maybe the possibility of applying for a green card is very little, but my partner's support means a lot to me! (Reflection)

In addition, all of the teachers complimented their partners' personalities and how their personalities helped with team work. For example, E1 mentioned, 'I do enjoy working with C1. She has a lovely and positive personality which makes her easier to work with even when this is only our first year working together' (Interview). C2 also mentioned, 'I can feel she is pretty open-minded to share everything with me. I am really happy to work with her and her personality having characteristics of a mom' (Reflection). The key personality traits identified by the teachers, which are being positive, lovely, open-minded and caring, strengthened the partnerships and made the collaborations enjoyable.

In sum, the partner teachers recognized the importance of their partnership and how much it would affect the level of success of the program, as E2 elaborated,

> This year I have a totally different feeling about the Chinese program in general. Last year I honestly felt like it was not a good program. I would not have put my own child in the program if I had had to make that decision. This year, because of C2, my whole perspective of the program has changed. If I knew all the teachers were like C2, I would put my child in. I think the whole program will succeed or fail, depending on the teachers they hire. (Interview)

Parent–Teacher Collaboration

At the parent–teacher night before the school year began, the Chinese teacher stressed the importance of the parent–teacher collaboration and the concept of teacher and parents as partners supporting the students' studies. She handed out a pre-survey to the parents with a list of support options that she could provide to parents, and asked for the parents' feedback. The definition of each support option is described in Table 5.2. The different kinds of support tools covered the various needs of the students and parents. For example, Quizlet enabled the students to do practice activities at home. The Teacher's Blog listed learning resources students could use to expand their level of contact with the target language. The weekly newsletter assisted parents with helping students preview and review materials. Chinese lessons enabled parents to gain basic knowledge of the Chinese language and culture. Games and activities suggested ideas for parents to help the students practice Chinese in a fun way. A total of 40 parents returned the completed pre-survey. Table 5.2 below illustrates the 40 parents' level of interest in using the tools to communicate with the teacher and to help their children with the study of Chinese.

Table 5.2 illustrates that the majority of the parents expressed interest in trying almost all of the tools listed, except for the item 'Chinese lessons'; a third of the parents were neutral about that tool. In the survey, some of the parents explained that their families had a busy schedule and it would be difficult for them to make time to attend the Chinese lessons for parents, otherwise, it would be a great idea to help their children. In addition to the list of tools suggested by the teacher, a couple of parents suggested that the teacher could help the families create opportunities

Table 5.2 Parents' pre-survey results

List of Tools for Parent–Teacher Collaboration	1..5 (Not interested at all)......(very interested)				
Quizlet: A website in which the teacher can make and share digital flashcards. Parents and students can download the flashcard lists to practice at home.	0	2	2	18	18
Teacher's Blog: A website made by the teacher, through which Chinese videos, songs, and language learning resources can be posted.	0	0	3	8	29
Weekly Newsletter: The teacher can send home a weekly letter that provides an overview for the Chinese that will be studied in class. Parents can use this to help students prepare for new material or review previous material.	0	0	1	12	27
Weekly Test Preview: Along with the newsletter, the teacher can send home practice tests for students and instructions for parents to help students prepare for upcoming tests.	0	1	2	12	25
Chinese Lessons: The teacher can provide regular hour-long Chinese language training sessions to parents.	1	1	14	11	13
Games and Activities: The teacher can send out weekly online games or activities that parents can do at home with their children to help them learn Chinese.	0	2	4	16	18

to be immersed in the target language, such as helping with organizing Chinese-English language exchange. This suggestion prompted the teacher to recruit Chinese-speaking international students at the nearby university who were interested in practicing Chinese with English-speaking American families.

As the parents responded positively toward the idea of the teacher using multiple tools to support them and their children's education, the teacher tried all of the tools listed in the survey and added the language exchange program (called Chinese-English Language Friends) to the list as well. At the end of the semester, the parents were asked to complete the post-survey, which inquired about their opinions regarding the effectiveness of each tool. They circled the particular support tools deemed useful to them and explained their reasons in the comments areas. A total of 45 parents turned in the completed post-surveys (see Table 5.3).

In the comments area, the parents explained the reasons they thought each tool was or was not useful to them. The reasons are summarized below.

Quizlet

More than one third of the parents thought positively about Quizlet. They thought that it was 'a nice review' (survey#5) and that it was a tool that the children could use to review Chinese 'without parents' help' (survey#3). A few parents also mentioned how much their children enjoyed using Quizlet. They stated that the children 'loved

Table 5.3 Tools that parents thought were particularly helpful or unhelpful

Support Tools	Helpful
1. Quizlet	17 (38%)
2. Teacher's Blog	26 (58%)
3. Weekly Newsletter	23 (51%)
4. Chinese Lessons	9 (20%)
5. Games and Activities	3 (7%)
6. Weekly Test Preview	30 (67%)
7. Chinese-English Language Friends	5 (100%)*

*Only five families joined the Language Friends program.

quizlets' (survey#7) and thought that 'it's a treat' (survey#13) for the children. On the other hand, a few parents did not think Quizlet worked for them. A couple parents encountered technical issues as they stated in the survey that they 'struggle getting it to open' (survey#24) while another parent thought that 'using Quizlet was frustrating' (survey#34) because it did not provide enough explanation in regard to the errors made by the child and the parent did not know Chinese and could not explain to the child.

Teacher's blog

The teacher's blog was useful for more than half of the parents who answered the survey. The blog was useful in many ways. First, it 'gives links and sources that are helpful and fun to use' (survey#29). Second, the list of weekly events posted on the blog 'is good as a secondary confirmation' (survey#7). Third, the informative blog content made parents feel connected as they commented that 'It's always nice to have communication with teachers' (survey#15).

Weekly newsletter

Approximately half of the survey respondents expressed the view that the newsletter was useful. The newsletter informed parents of the key concepts taught that week and suggested ways to help students review for the concepts. The parents stated that it had 'given great insight into what's going on in the classroom' (survey#4), helped the parents know 'exactly what and where the child should be' (survey#7), the parents 'didn't feel lost' (survey#33) and the children were 'better prepared for the tests' (survey#24). However, one parent suggested that the newsletter could be even more helpful if it was given earlier during the week. She stated, 'I like reviewing the newsletter but feel like it would be more useful to see what they will be learning at the beginning of the week rather than when it's over' (survey#34).

Chinese lessons

Although the Chinese lessons were offered free to parents every Friday afternoon, due to the parents' work schedules or other obligations (e.g. 'I have little kids at home, so I cannot go' (survey#18)), only an average of five parents showed up to the weekly lessons. The parents who had attended the lessons spoke highly about them. One parent commented that the lessons 'allowed us to see exactly what our children are learning' (survey#15). According to the parents, their children liked that their parents knew some Chinese as well, as one parent said, 'I've been able to review some Chinese words and phrases with my child and they have liked when I am able to do that' (survey#39), and the other said, 'It was great to learn a little bit of Chinese. My son loved quizzing me on what I learned' (survey#40). The parents appreciated the teacher's effort in offering the lessons and stated that 'Every Friday she was ready with a lesson to help parents with the vocabulary the students learned. She was always happy to answer any questions we had on the homework' (survey#17). As a result, a parent felt that the lessons 'helped boost my confidence to help my son and learn with him' (survey#29).

Games and activities

Only three parents indicated that the online games and activities were useful. Two reasons explain why the parents rated them low. First, some of the families did not have sufficient technology tools to use the online activities. One parent described, 'The activities on the computer are great, but I have four kids using the computer and my husband is on it a lot. It is difficult to get much computer time when he is home' (survey#39). Second, the parents felt that they did not have time to try all of the support tools offered. One parent said, 'I'm really busy with my four children and all their activities, music, church, and other things in life. I just haven't taken the time to do the extra things—if their daily homework is done, I call it good' (survey#31).

Weekly test preview

The weekly test preview gave practice questions and guides for parents to help students review for Chinese tests. The parents appreciated that the preview 'helps us know what they are learning each week and the best ways to help them' (survey#5). It 'helped me to help my child in areas she might be weak' (survey#33), 'helped with understanding some of the homework, especially in regards to writing Chinese' (survey#23) and 'was helpful to review the concepts' (survey#43). In some of the parents' opinions, the preview was 'by far the best resource' (survey#7) and it was 'fun to see how much she was understanding' (survey#8). However, the preview did not work out so well with a couple of parents.

One parent complained that 'some pictures were unclear as far as what they were' (survey#19) and did not understand the term regarding the component 'radical' in Chinese characters. The other parent felt that the preview only 'made my daughter nervous' and 'felt pressured and terrified' (survey#21).

Chinese-English language friends

The teacher paired up families in her classes with international Chinese-speaking students from the nearby university and encouraged them to meet regularly and casually for Chinese-English language practice. Many parents expressed their interest in the program; however, the teacher was only able to find five Chinese college students to pair them up. The five families who signed up were very pleased with the program. One parent mentioned that 'the Language Friends has been the best program to be a part of' (survey#35). Another parent 'highly recommended it' (survey#40), as it offered several benefits such as 'having somebody to text or call about Chinese questions and test review' (survey#24), 'expanding their use of the language and understanding' and 'helping them love China and be more excited about learning a language' (survey#3).

At the end of the survey, the parents were asked if they tried all of the support tools and the reasons they did not try some of them. Except one parent who stated that she thought the few tools she tried were sufficient to support her child (survey#36), and one parent who felt 'overwhelmed' to have so many support tools (survey#30), the rest of the parents who did not try all of the tools (29 out of 45 parents) indicated time constraints as the reason. For example, one parent said, 'We don't always take advantage of all the support items mainly just because we are so busy and don't have enough time' (survey#35). However, the parents recognized the usefulness of using the tools and hoped that they could make time to use them more frequently. One parent stated, 'I need to develop a better system at home to remind him and myself to get online and do his Chinese' (survey#35), and the other parent said, 'I need to take more advantage of the support and resources that have been shared with me' (survey#12).

In sum, the parents' survey responses showed that the majority of the parents recognized and appreciated the support offered by the teacher. The teacher received so many positive responses at the end of the survey such as 'You are doing an amazing job!' (survey#41), 'My son's teacher is amazing this year. She has provided so much support' (survey#12), 'The support offered by the teacher has been exceptional' (survey#16), 'the support has gained my confidence' (survey#24), 'I am very pleased with our introduction to Chinese because of our teacher. I hope our future years in Chinese will be this good' (survey#33), 'All of the supports were very helpful in increasing my confidence and ability to help my child at home' (survey#40) and 'you have gone so far above and beyond to help us as parents and I truly appreciate everything that you do!' (survey#40). In addition to the positive comments made in the post-survey, the parents admired the teacher's effort so much that they sent letters to the district to nominate the teacher for the district's Hats Off Award, and the teacher won the award.

Conclusion and Discussion

Viewing the DLI teacher–teacher and parent–teacher collaboration phenomena through the theoretical lens of CHAT, the collaboration activity system can be analyzed using the six core components (subject, object, tools, community, rules and division of labor) as follows. First, the subjects (teachers and parents) had the common object of helping DLI students perform well academically and behaviorally. In order for the subjects to reach the object, many tools were utilized. For example, in the case of the team teachers' collaboration, they used multiple channels for communication and the guidelines provided by the state for formal meetings. In addition, their positive personality traits could also be seen as useful tools to make the partnership tight-knit and successful. In the case of parent–teacher collaboration, the teacher offered a wide variety of support tools (e.g. newsletter, blog, language exchange program) for parent–teacher communication and for parents to help their children with Chinese study after school. Although the fourth component, community (individuals who share the common interest with the subject for reaching the object), was not the focus of the investigation in this study, occasionally it could be seen in the results. For example, when the teachers collaborated to develop a reward system for the student with behavioral issues, they gained the parent's support to also use it at home. In terms of the fifth component, rules, in the team teacher collaboration, one can see that one rule the teachers attempted to follow was using different means to ensure that their collaboration was effective. For example, the teachers found that texting was the quickest way to be in touch with their partners and it became a tool they frequently used. Moreover, it was observed that the subjects' rules might change over time due to being in a different cultural context and working with a partner. For instance, C2, originally from a Chinese culture overseas, stated that she learned from her partner how to more effectively communicate with American parents. Her rules for communicating with parents apparently changed due to the collaboration with her partner.

In terms of parent–teacher collaboration, it was obvious to note that the parents followed their own rules in deciding which support tools provided by the teacher they wanted to use and how much time they invested in using the tools. Parents' rules for making the decisions seemed to be affected by their lifestyle, habits and values. For example, some parents 'called it good' as long as the children finished their homework, some were busy with different agendas (e.g. church, music, sports), while others took the time to try all of the support tools. The sixth component, division of labor, was observed to be fairly shared by the team teachers in their collaboration, as all four teachers seemed to be deeply involved in the collaboration and equally committed to ensure their students' success. With regard to parent–teacher collaboration, the individual parents took on different amounts of labor, as some reported not having time to help their children and some fully utilized the support from the teacher.

The team teachers involved in this study demonstrated how the harmony of the six core components led to a positive collaboration outcome. In one of the teachers' (E2) own words, she believed that her team was 'ahead of everyone' (Reflection). On the other hand, in the parent–teacher collaboration, although the teacher's effort in initiating communication and offering support to the parents was highly recognized by the parents, the level of involvement in the collaboration was different amongst parents. This result was due to the difference in the parents' beliefs and values. This implies that in order to promote effective collaboration between teachers and parents, teachers will need to think of ways to educate the parents of the importance of parental involvement in children's education. In addition, teachers can think of different tactics to encourage parents to try the support offered by the teachers. For example, instead of introducing all support tools to parents at once, teachers can invite parents to try one to two tools each week and decide on which tools are most effective to them to keep using. Moreover, the parent–teacher collaboration investigated in this study illustrated that in a DLI program, which had no, or a very low number of, language minority students, the teacher was the only expert in the collaboration and carried a heavy load in assisting parents to help their children with Chinese study after school. If more language minority students, who usually have parents that speak the target language, are enrolled in the DLI program, the teacher could utilize the parents' target language expertise in helping other parents and students. In the case of the parent–teacher collaboration studied in this chapter, the teacher could only find five Chinese college students who wanted to join the Language Friends program. If the teacher's classes had more heritage-speakers, she could have paired up heritage-speaking with English-speaking families. The teacher could have also created opportunities (e.g. online community, play days) to promote interactions between heritage- and English-speaking families, which would enhance the students' target language learning. The lack of heritage students in this study definitely weakened the parent-teacher supportive system.

References

Bartram, B. (2006) An examination of perceptions of parental influence on attitudes to language learning. *Educational Research* 48 (2), 211–221.

Buckley, F.J. (2000) *Team Teaching: What, Why and How.* Thousand Oaks, CA: Sage Publications Inc.

Cunha Jr, F.D., van Oers, B. and Kontopodis, M. (2016) Collaborating on Facebook: Teachers exchanging experiences through social networking sites. *Cultural-Historical Psychology* 12 (3), 290–309.

Engeström, Y. (1987) *Learning by Expanding: An Activity-Theoretical Approach to Developmental Research.* Helsinki: Orienta-Konsultit Oy.

Engeström, Y. (1993) Developmental studies of work as a testbench of activity theory: The case of primary care medical practice. In S. Chaiklin and J. Lave (eds) *Understanding Practice: Perspectives on Activity and Context* (pp. 64–103). Cambridge: Cambridge University Press.

Foot, K.A. (2014) Cultural-historical activity theory: Exploring a theory to inform practice and research. *Journal of Human Behavior in the Social Environment* 24 (3), 329–347.

Gao, X. (2012) Parental strategies in supporting Chinese children's learning of English vocabulary. *Research Papers in Education* 27 (5), 581–595.

Garner, A. E. and Thillen, C. (1977) Is your school of nursing ready to implement interdisciplinary team teaching? *Journal of Nursing Education* 16 (7), 27–30.

Hertzog, C.J. and Lieble, C. (1994) Arts and Science/School of Education: A Cooperative Approach to the Teaching of Introductory Geography. Proceedings of the National Conference on Successful College Teaching, Orlando, FL. (ERIC Document Reproduction Service No. ED 390 470).

Perry, B. and Stewart, T. (2005) Insights into effective partnership in interdisciplinary team teaching. *System* 33 (4), 563–573.

Reynolds, J. (1985) *Teaching Writing in an Interdisciplinary Context: One Experiment.* Commerce, TX: Texas A&M University Commerce. (ERIC Document Reproduction Service No. ED 307 603)

Sandholtz, J.H. (2000) Interdisciplinary team teaching as a form of professional development. *Teacher Education Quarterly* 27 (3), 39–54.

Sawyer, B.E., Manz, P.H., Martin, K.A., Hammond, T.C. and Garrigan, S. (2016) Family involvement in early education and child care teachers and parents as partners: Developing a community of practice to support Latino preschool dual language learners. *Advances in Early Education and Day Care* 20, 159–186.

Sawyer, B.E., Manz, P.H. and Martin, K.A. (2017) Supporting preschool dual language learners: Parents' and teachers' beliefs about language development and collaboration. *Early Child Development and Care* 187 (3–4), 707–726.

Sénéchal, M. and LeFevre, J.A. (2002) Parental involvement in the development of children's reading skill: A five-year longitudinal study. *Child Development* 73 (2), 445–460.

Shartrand, A.M., Weiss, H.B., Kreider, H.M. and Lopez, M.E. (1997) *New Skills for New Schools: Preparing Teachers in Family Involvement.* Cambridge, MA: Harvard Family Research Project (HFRP).

Vygotsky, L.S. (1978) *Mind in Society: The Development of Higher Mental Process.* Cambridge, MA: Harvard University Press.

6 Language Teaching and Learning Strategies Employed in a First-Year Chinese Dual Language Immersion Classroom

Introduction

Strategy is defined as 'any organized, purposeful and regulated line of action chosen by an individual to carry out a task which he or she sets for himself or herself or with which he or she is confronted' (Council of Europe, 2002: 10). According to Oxford (1990), the term 'strategy' carries the characteristics of 'planning, conscious manipulation, and movement toward a goal' (1990: 7). Hence, the purpose of strategy use is to assist the user to optimize processing for the intended task. In applying the concept of strategy in second language acquisition in the classroom setting, language teaching and learning strategies are two sides of the same coin, both of which aim to maximize the learners' language performance. 'Language teaching strategies (LTS)', which refers to 'techniques, methods, and skills teachers employ in the language teaching and learning process' (Onovughe, 2012: 79), are used by teachers to facilitate dynamic, efficient and diversified learning in the classroom. According to Oxford, teachers who abandon the traditional role as authoritative figures and who employ strategies to take on the new roles as 'facilitators', 'helpers', 'coordinators', 'guides' and 'co-communicators' (1990: 10), foster highly independent learners who know how to utilize strategies to learn. Indeed, results from research in the second language acquisition field have demonstrated that teachers who use relevant strategies to guide students, or who implicitly or explicitly demonstrate appropriate strategy use to their learners, create successful learners in classroom settings (Alabsi, 2016; Hashemi & Ghalkhani, 2016; Izadpanah & Ghafournia, 2016; Ngo, 2016; Rido et al., 2016; Sabbah, 2016; Saeidi & Farshchi, 2015; Shih & Reynolds, 2015). On the other hand, 'language learning strategies (LLS)', a term which is defined as 'specific actions, behaviors, steps, or techniques that students use to improve their own progress in developing skills in a second or foreign language' (Oxford, 1993: 8), allows learners to become self-directed, confident and successful learners. Research has shown that when relevant language learning strategies were applied by learners, language learning became efficient (Ehrman & Oxford, 1995; Oxford, 2011).

There is no doubt that language teaching and learning strategies both play crucial roles in second language acquisition, and have been researched extensively in different learning contexts. However, most of the previous studies had a tendency to focus on the study of alphabetical languages and involved only adult learners (see more discussions regarding the shortages of research in the sections on Language Teaching Strategies and Chinese Language Learning Strategies). Studies with young learners learning a non-alphabetical language such as Chinese are needed. Hence, this study attempted to lessen the research gap by investigating language teaching and learning strategies employed in a first-year Chinese language class in a dual language program.

Oxford's Taxonomy of Strategies

Strategies used in second language classrooms have been identified and strategy categorizations have been discussed by many researchers, among which Oxford's (1990) taxonomy of strategies is the most comprehensive and has been widely used by scholars in the field. Hence, the current study adopted Oxford's classifications of strategies as the framework for analyzing teacher and learner strategy use in the Chinese dual language classroom. According to Oxford, strategy use plays an essential role in language learning and can be grouped into two major classes – direct and indirect strategies. Direct strategies refer to strategies that directly involve the use of the target language and require learners to mentally process the language. Three groups of direct strategies (memory, cognitive and compensation) are identified by Oxford, each of which processes the target language differently and for a different purpose. First, memory strategies help organize the language to make it meaningful for learners. Grouping words into meaningful units, for instance, is a kind of memory strategy, which makes the vocabulary words easier to remember. Second, cognitive strategies involve manipulating the target language in order to understand or produce the language. For instance, underlining or color-coding words or phrases in a passage is a type of cognitive strategy, which assists learners to focus on important information. Third, compensation strategies are used by learners for efficient communication, even when they do not have thorough knowledge about the target language. For example, learners can use linguistic or other clues to guess for meaning to facilitate communication with others.

The second major class of strategies, indirect strategies, also consists of three groups (metacognitive, affective and social) of strategies. They are distinct from direct strategies as they do not directly involve the target language, but support and help manage the learning of the language. The first type of indirect strategy is metacognitive, which assists learners to coordinate their learning process by using actions such as setting goals, planning for a language task and evaluating one's learning. The second type of indirect strategy, affective, refers to the positive reinforcement of learners' emotions, motivations and attitudes while learning a target language. Strategies such as encouraging oneself and using different means to lower one's anxiety are considered affective strategies. The third type of indirect strategy is social, which helps learners acquire the target language through interaction with others, such as asking for language help and developing target cultural understanding.

Direct and indirect strategies are interconnected in that one strategy group can assist other groups. For example, when a learner is in the process of using the compensation strategy of guessing to interpret the meaning of a target utterance, reasoning (a cognitive strategy) and sociocultural knowledge (a social strategy) are required (Oxford, 1990). Hence, these strategies do not work independently from each other; on the contrary, they work hand-in-hand to aid the development of second language acquisition. This study utilized Oxford's classifications of strategies in capturing and analyzing language teaching and learning strategies employed in a dual language classroom setting.

Language Teaching Strategies (LTS)

The role of a language teacher in the classroom is of paramount significance. In order to maximize learners' language performance, language teachers not only need to possess high level competency in all four language skills (listening, speaking, reading and writing) in the target language, but also need to be capable of implementing appropriate LTS suitable for their learners to ensure that learning and teaching progress smoothly and comply with class objectives. Hence, knowing about how teachers employ LTS in the classroom is important in research. Current literature on LTS tried to investigate the LTS phenomenon from different angles. A few studies gained more understanding of the LTS phenomenon by identifying different types of LTS language teachers used in classroom contexts. For example, Chen (2016) used a questionnaire to investigate primary in-service teachers' pronunciation strategies in ESL classrooms and found that teachers frequently used pronunciation-related adjustment strategies such as speech rate modification, repetition and sentence stress emphasis, to ensure learners' understanding of their speech. The exploration of the pronunciation LTS used in the classroom contributed useful information for ESL teachers to become more self-aware of the LTS they used and helped explore ways in integrating pronunciation instruction in second language teaching. Another LTS study, which used the method of observation to examine the use of LTS in a vocational English classroom in Indonesia, was conducted by Rido *et al.* (2016). The study found that the teachers used a variety of strategies, such as scaffolding, discussion, games, drawing, presentation and individual task, which were positively perceived by the students. While some of the LTS studies found positive results in which the teachers used theoretically sound strategies, or a wide range of strategies, which their students appreciated, results reported in other LTS studies were not so positive. For instance, Onovughe (2012) surveyed 160 primary ESL students and teachers and reported that some of the LTS used by the teachers were outdated. In a different study, Göçer (2008) observed four teachers in Turkish as a foreign language (TFL) classrooms and found that due to a lack of training in teaching TFL, the teachers employed mostly traditional techniques in teaching, and that only certain aspects of the language (e.g. grammar) were emphasized in their teaching. Similar results were described in Kara's (2015) study, which looked into ESL pre-service teachers' LTS with a focus on reading. By analyzing their lesson plans and actual teaching, Kara noted that the teachers had only few attempts to teach the reading strategies.

While some of the LTS studies attempted to capture the use of LTS in a natural classroom setting, other studies emphasized seeking LTS that were efficient by conducting experiments in a controlled classroom setting. The LTS experimental studies usually focused on the LTS for a particular language aspect, such as reading (Sabbah, 2016; Shih & Reynolds, 2015), vocabulary (Alabsi, 2016; Izadpanah & Ghafournia, 2016), spelling (Hashemi & Ghalkhani, 2016; Nahari & Alfadda, 2016), listening (Ngo, 2016) and speaking (Saeidi & Farshchi, 2015; Zarandi & Rahbar, 2016). Most of these studies identified certain LTS that were more effective than traditional LTS. For example, Shih and Reynolds integrated the teaching of think-pair-share as a reading strategy in a traditional EFL reading class and reported increased student motivation. Saeidi and Farshchi found positive results after experimenting with communication strategy teaching on junior high EFL learners' speaking skills. Sabbah tested the jigsaw strategy in aiding Qatar ESL students' learning of reading and also found positive results.

The existing LTS studies provided information on the phenomenon of LTS in terms of how they were used in authentic classroom settings, and which particular LTS were efficient in the study contexts. However, these studies only focused on the learning of alphabetical languages, with the majority being English as a second or foreign language. Non-alphabetical scripts being left out of research poses a major issue in the LTS research field, as the appropriate use of LTS depends on many factors and the target language structure is one of them (Cohen, 2014).

Therefore, in order to lessen the research gap, this study emphasized a non-alphabetical script, Chinese, as the language of study.

Chinese Language Learning Strategies (LLS)

Most of the existing LLS studies emphasized the learning of alpha-betical languages (Akbari & Hosseini, 2008; Hong-Nam & Leavell, 2006, 2007; Nisbet *et al.*, 2005) and only a few in the current literature examined the Chinese language; however, the results of the Chinese LLS studies contributed valuable information in the field and helped pinpoint directions for the current study. A summary of the major findings from the previous Chinese LLS studies follows.

Several Chinese LLS studies used the strategy inventory for language learning (SILL) survey developed by Oxford (1990) to investigate Chinese as a foreign language (CFL) students' strategy use. For example, Cáceres-Lorenzo (2015) surveyed 61 teenage Spanish CFL students and identified social as the most, and memory as the least, frequently used strategies. Srisupha (2012) surveyed 746 Thai college CFL students and the survey results illustrated that the students used compensation, metacognitive and social strategies with high frequency, while the use of memory, affec-tive and cognitive strategies were used with medium frequency. These different frequencies of strategy use reported in different studies could be explained by the different learning contexts where the studies were conducted. For example, previous LLS research (Green & Oxford, 1995; Oxford, 2011) had revealed that learners' current language level could be a factor influencing frequency use of strategies. Advanced learners are likely to concentrate their strategy use within a small group of strate-gies that most efficiently assist them to cope with the complexities of advanced learning.

In terms of Chinese language learning, one crucial factor which may alter learners' frequency and types of strategy use is the language struc-ture. This claim is evident in some of the Chinese LLS study findings. For instance, by employing the methods of think aloud and retelling protocols, Lee-Thompson's (2008) study of reading strategies used by American college advanced CFL students found that many of the LLS were unique to the learning of the Chinese language. The participants frequently marked the text by drawing lines or boxes to segment words and phrases. This strategy use was to accommodate the lack of word boundary in Chinese script. Another example of the use of a unique strategy for reading Chinese found in the study was writing Pinyin, the romanization Chinese phonetic system, around the characters to mark their pronunciation. The need for such strategy use is attributed to the unclear connection between Chinese script and pronunciation. The results of a different study conducted by Grenfell and Harris (2015), which also used the think-aloud protocols to investigate adolescent learners' strategies in learning Chinese as a foreign language, were aligned with Lee-Thompson's study. In order to accommodate the learning of the unique features in Chinese script, despite the use of memory strategies that are common to learning a second language, the learners in Grenfell and Harris's study also employed newly developed memory strategies. Some of the Mandarin Chinese-specific strategies identified in the study include 'I try to spot any characters I already know', 'I look at where the slashes in the character go', 'I think of pictures to connect the shape to the meaning', 'I write the characters out lots of times with the correct stroke order' and 'I group similar characters into categories' (2015: 7). The list of examples of the Chinese-specific LLS have illustrated that when learners encounter particular challenges of a target language, especially one with distinct features from their native language, unique strategies to aid the development of the target language emerge. Thus, it is essential for research to not only look into one category of languages (e.g. alphabetical languages), but also other languages which are structurally different, such as Chinese.

Although a few LLS studies had investigated the Chinese language, such as the aforementioned ones, more are needed to confirm their findings. Moreover, the review of the current literature above showed that there is a lack of LLS research with a focus on young learners, especially those of elementary school age. The studies reviewed in this section included either adolescent or college CFL learners, but younger learners were absent. According to Le Pichon *et al.* (2013), individuals do not fully develop self-autonomy until age 12. Young language learners evolve toward self-regulation after many years of language learning, and such evolution only occurs with the support of parents, teachers and the community (Muñoz, 2014). Hence, it is imperative to understand how teachers use strategies to guide young learners whose strategy use is still at a developing stage, and how teachers suggest strategies for younger learners to use in achieving second language acquisition.

Considering the shortages (e.g. lack of focus on Chinese and young learners) identified in the previous research, this chapter investigated a first-grade Chinese dual language teacher's LTS, and LLS that the teacher suggested her six-year-old students use in the classroom.

The Study Context

The current study involved the second author as the teacher participant and one of the classes in cohort one, which had the heritage speaker, Alice (see the focal teacher and student participants section in Chapter 1). This study focused on the LTS and LLS employed during the daily 50 minutes of Chinese language instruction. The major teaching and learning that occurred during the Chinese language instruction included the introduction of target Chinese characters (e.g. meanings, radicals, stroke orders and pronunciations), sentence patterns, grammar and communication-based activities which helped review the materials taught in all four language skills.

Data Collection and Analysis

Many of the previous LTS and LLS researchers had attempted to capture language learning and teaching strategy use by utilizing the methods of questionnaires and/or interviews to gather information. Such methods rely on the teacher and learner participants' recall of their strategy use and pose the possible issue of participants making inaccurate reports on strategy use and use frequencies. As Cohen (2014) explained, once individuals move away from instances of language learning or teaching behavior, they might not be accurate about their actual strategy behavior. Research methods other than questionnaires and interviews need to be employed in studies in order to confirm findings in previous studies. Therefore, this study used classroom observation as the data collection method in examining classroom strategy use. The observations were twice a week on average during an eight-week period in the fall semester, which was the learner participants' first semester in the program. A trained research assistant (RA) was sent to observe the class. When the RA observed the class, he used Oxford's (1990) taxonomy of strategies as the guidelines to help identify LTS and LLS used in the class. The guidelines included a total of 62 individual strategies in the six groups of strategies: memory, cognitive, compensation, social, metacognitive and affective. During observations, the RA added two more strategies that the teacher used which were not indicated in the 62 strategies. They are the cognitive strategies of *analyzing characters* and *distinguishing characters, radicals, sounds or tones*.

When the RA observed a strategy employed by the teacher, he would record the use of the particular strategy on the sheet of guidelines for the teacher. On the other hand, when the RA observed a strategy that the teacher directed the learners to use, he would record the use of the particular strategy on the sheet of guidelines for the learners. After observing all of the sessions, the RA tallied the incidents of strategy use. The observation sessions were audio-recorded for our review for the purpose of ensuring that the RA captured all of the LTS and LLS in the sessions. Both the observation notes and the audio recordings were used as data collection tools to increase data reliability. During the eight-week study, data collection of a total of 16 observation sessions were obtained, which resulted in approximately 800 minutes of audio-recording data. We individually listened to the recordings and read the RA's tallies and notes. The inter-rater reliability between us was 97%. Due to limited space, only the more frequently used LTS and LLS in the form of excerpts are shown in the results section.

The Teacher's Use of LTS

The results from the classroom observations illustrated that a total of 280 incidents of the use of LTS were identified, which comprised 15 strategies. Of those 15 strategies, six were memory, five were cognitive, three were affective and one was compensation. Among the LTS identified, the top three most frequently used strategies, which were used more than 10% of the instructional time, were the memory strategy of *using imagery*, the affective strategy of *using music*, and the memory strategy of *using physical response or sensation* (see Table 6.1).

The strategy of using imagery was used far more often than any other LTS in the classroom. The results of the classroom observations showed that the teacher frequently used the strategy when she tried to review or introduce new Chinese characters or words to the students. Excerpt 1 is a typical example of how the LTS of using imagery was employed. In the

Table 6.1 LTS employed in the classroom

Frequency Ranking	Strategy	Strategy Type	# (%) of strategy incidences
1	Using imagery	Memory	55 (20%)
2	Using music	Affective	35 (13%)
3	Using physical response or sensation	Memory	34 (12%)
4	Formally practicing with sounds and writing systems	Cognitive	25 (9%)
5	Analyzing characters	Cognitive	23 (8%)
6	Structured reviewing	Memory	20 (7%)
7	Distinguishing characters, radicals, sounds and tones	Cognitive	20 (7%)
8	Associating/elaborating	Memory	17 (6%)
9	Translating	Cognitive	13 (5%)
10	Recognizing and using formulas and patterns	Cognitive	10 (3%)
11	Making positive statements	Affective	10 (3%)
12	Using mime or gesture	Compensation	8 (3%)
13	Placing new words into a context	Memory	5 (2%)
14	Rewarding yourself	Affective	3 (1%)
15	Grouping	Memory	2 (1%)

excerpt, the teacher tried to review the character '里' (inside), the body part, '肚子' (stomach) and a few food items.

Excerpt 1

Teacher:　　蔡老師畫一個男生。他有一個大肚子。他的肚子裡有…?
　　　　　　[Teacher Tsai is drawing a boy. He has a big stomach. Inside his stomach there are …?]

Page:　　　糖果、冰淇淋。
　　　　　　[Candy, ice cream]

Harrison:　蘋果。
　　　　　　[Apple.]

Emma:　　　漢堡, 跟…
　　　　　　[Hamburger, and …]

Teacher:　　餅乾。
　　　　　　[Cookie.]

Emma:　　　跟餅乾。
　　　　　　[And cookie.]

Oxford (1990) stated that visual supports such as drawings assist learners to make new vocabulary by making the mental images more concrete for remembering. The teacher in this study adopted this strategy for both the introduction and review of new words. It is evident in Excerpt 1 that several students were able to successfully recall the target words by looking at the drawings.

The second most commonly used LTS in the class was the affective strategy of *using music*. This strategy was sometimes accompanied by the use of the third frequently used strategy, *using physical response or sensation*, a memory strategy. Excerpt 2 illustrated how the two strategies were utilized by the teacher.

Excerpt 2

Teacher:　　這是 '頭', '耳朵', '肩膀', '膝', '腳趾', '眼睛', '鼻子', '口'。
　　　　　　[This is 'head', 'ear', 'shoulders', 'knees', 'toes', 'eyes', 'nose', 'mouth']

(The teacher was pointing to her body parts when she said them aloud to the students.)

Students:　　'頭', '耳朵', '肩膀', '膝', '腳趾'。
　　　　　　['Head', 'ear', 'shoulders', 'knees', 'toes']

(Some of the students spontaneously repeated and pointed to their body parts.)

Teacher:　　好, 每個人跟蔡老師一起唱。
　　　　　　[OK, everybody, sing together with Teacher Tsai.]

(The teacher and the students all sang the song of body parts using gestures.)

Using music was categorized as one of the affective strategies, which lower learners' anxiety (Oxford, 1990). For example, for some people, listening to calm music makes them feel more relaxed before a stressful language study session. However, this strategy was used in a different way in the observed classroom. Music was used as a teaching tool. The lyrics of the song were the target words that the students needed to learn. Accompanied by the gestures, the song singing not only made the students feel pleasant, but also reinforced their learning.

In addition to employing the third commonly used LTS, *using physical response*, in song singing, the strategy was also often used in a game similar to Simon Says to review vocabulary or expressions. Excerpt 3 shows an example.

Excerpt 3

Teacher: 每個人站起來, 我們來玩老師說。
[Stand up, everybody. Let's play Teacher Says.]
(The students all stood up.)

Students: 我可以是老師嗎?
[Can I be the teacher?]
(Some of the students asked if they could be the teacher.)

Teacher: 蔡老師先當好嗎?等下可以換你們。
[Teacher Tsai does it first, OK? You will take turns to be the teacher later.]

Teacher: 老師說: '頭' 。
[Teacher says, 'head'.]
(The students quietly pointed to their heads.)

Teacher: 老師說: '腳趾' 。
[Teacher says, 'toes'.]
The students quietly pointed to their toes.

Teacher: 膝蓋。
['knees'.]
(Some of the students pointed to their knees.)

Teacher: 啊! 蔡老師有沒有說 '老師說' ?
[Ah! Did Teacher Tsai say, 'Teacher says'?]

Students: 沒有。
[No.]

Teacher: 那有的人要坐下囉, 對不起。
[Then some of you need to sit down. Sorry.]

The game described in Excerpt 3 is referred to as Total Physical Response (TPR), which is based on the belief that physical movements help store new information in memory. It was evident from the observations that this strategy was especially efficient for young learners as they tended to have a shorter attention span than adults. By using TPR, the teacher was able to tightly engage learners in the learning activity.

Unlike the three most commonly used strategies discussed above, the remaining 12 strategies were more sparsely used. The majority of them were either cognitive (five) or memory (four) strategies. Three of the five cognitive strategies: *formally practicing with sounds and writing systems, analyzing characters* and *distinguishing characters, radicals, sounds and tones*, were solely used when the teaching of Chinese characters was involved. These strategies emphasized different components of individual characters (e.g. pronunciations, radicals, meanings and stroke orders), and comparisons of characters that have similar or the same parts of the features (e.g. same tones, same radicals or similar stroke orders). The fourth cognitive strategy, *translating*, was used when the learners spoke in English, which was discouraged in the program, and the teacher translated their utterance into Chinese. The fifth cognitive strategy, *recognizing and using formulas and patterns*, was used in class to review sentence patterns such as '我愛我的爸爸' (I love my dad.) and 我愛我的媽媽' (I love my mom.). Sometimes when the teacher taught sentence patterns, she would also incorporate the memory strategy of *placing new words into a context*. For example, using the sentence pattern already taught, '我愛我的＿＿＿' (I love my ＿＿＿.), the teacher demonstrated how to insert new words, such as '爺爺' (grandfather), '奶奶' (grandmother), and '貓' (cat). The other memory strategy, *structured reviewing*, was employed when the teacher periodically incorporated old materials into new lessons, such as using new words in an old sentence pattern as described earlier. According to Oxford (1990), this strategy, which keeps 'spiraling back' to the old materials while learning new ones, offers learners the opportunities of 'overlearning' (1990: 43). When students overlearn the same material many times, the target language will eventually become natural to them. Another memory strategy, *associating/elaborating*, was used when the teacher tried to associate characters with objects or people that represent the characters. For example, the teacher associated '大' (big) with big objects and adults in the classroom, while '小' (small) was associated with small objects and kids in the classroom. The last memory strategy, *grouping*, was applied when the teacher demonstrated how to group together words which contained the same character in them (e.g. '你好' (hello) and '你們' (plural you) both contain the character '你' (singular you)).

In addition to the use of the direct strategies (memory and cognitive), the teacher also applied a few indirect strategies; however, these strategies were seldom used. Two affective strategies, *making positive statements* and *rewarding yourself*, were employed when the students performed or behaved well. For example, the teacher would verbally praise the students by saying, '你好棒!' (You are excellent!), and allow them to move their popsicle stick up a list as a reward. According to Oxford (1990), affective strategies, which assist learners to take control of their emotions and motivations, 'can make language learning far more effective and enjoyable' (1990: 140). Even though affective strategies do not directly involve studying the target language, teachers should not overlook such strategies as powerful learning tools.

Lastly, the compensation strategy of *using mime or gesture* was occasionally used to aid the teacher's communication with her students. For example, the teacher pointed at the target locations when asking the students to move to different areas of the class while saying the names of the locations (e.g. '地毯' (rug) or '桌子' (table)) aloud. Oxford (1990) stated that compensation strategies are especially important for beginning learners, as they enhance learners' understanding and overcome their limitations in both target language perception and production. More frequent use of compensation LTS would demonstrate to learners the usefulness of such strategies.

LLS the Teacher Directed Her Students to Use

A total of 453 incidents of the use of LLS which the teacher directed her students to use were identified. There were 21 strategies, of which eight were memory, six were cognitive, three were affective, two were metacognitive, one was social and one was compensation. Among the LLS identified, the top three most frequently used strategies, which were used more than 10% of the instructional time, were the cognitive strategies of *repeating* and *analyzing characters*, and the compensation strategy of *using mime or gesture* (see Table 6.2).

Similar to the findings in the use of LTS in which three strategies were identified as being used for more than 10% of instructional time each, there were also three LLS that were more frequently used. The top most commonly used LLS was the cognitive strategy of *repeating*. The teacher often asked her learners to repeat characters or new words after her, or to write the stroke orders in the air or on a piece of paper after she demonstrated them on the board. The strategy of *repeating* used in these exercises is common in Chinese language learning. First, there is little connection between Chinese characters and their sounds; therefore, a typical way to memorize the pronunciations of characters is repeating the sounds after the teacher, while looking at the characters or words. Second, in order to write Chinese characters, learners need to remember the stroke orders of each character; hence, writing the characters with the correct stroke orders over and over is a common practice. In the classroom observed in this study, the teacher often directed the students to use the *repeating* strategy to remember how to read or write Chinese words and over time the students had developed the habit of repeating after the teacher when they heard something new. Excerpt 4 illustrated

Table 6.2 LLS used in the classroom

Frequency Ranking	Strategy	Strategy Type	# (%) of strategy incidences
1	Repeating	Cognitive	80 (18%)
2	Analyzing characters	Cognitive	55 (12%)
3	Using mime or gesture	Compensation	51 (11%)
4	Structured reviewing	Memory	29 (6%)
5	Using physical response or sensation	Memory	27 (6%)
6	Distinguishing characters/radicals/sounds/tones	Cognitive	25 (6%)
7	Recognizing and using formulas and patterns	Cognitive	24 (5%)
8	Using music	Affective	24 (5%)
9	Cooperating with peers	Social	24 (5%)
10	Placing new words into a context	Memory	19 (4%)
11	Using imagery	Memory	18 (4%)
12	Formally practicing with sounds and writing systems	Cognitive	18 (4%)
13	Associating/elaborating	Memory	14 (3%)
14	Grouping	Memory	13 (3%)
15	Representing sounds in memory	Memory	11 (2%)
16	Paying attention	Metacognitive	4 (1%)
17	Self-monitoring	Metacognitive	4 (1%)
18	Making positive statements	Affective	4 (1%)
19	Using mechanical techniques	Memory	3 (1%)
20	Rewarding yourself	Affective	3 (1%)
21	Practicing naturalistically	Cognitive	3 (1%)

an example of such a moment. In the excerpt, the teacher tried to demonstrate how to write the new character, '你' (singular you), by writing it stroke by stroke on the board. The students not only followed the teacher by writing the strokes on their papers, but also repeated every stroke name the teacher said without the teacher requesting them to do so.

Excerpt 4

Teacher: 我們來寫 '你'。
            [Let's write 'you'.]
Students: 你。
            [You.]
Teacher: 好,一撇。
            [OK, a left leg stroke.]
(The teacher is writing on the board.)

Students: 一撇。
             [A left leg stroke.]
Teacher: 再來, 一豎。
             [Next, a down stroke.]
Students: 一豎。
             [A down stroke.]
Teacher: 再來, 一撇。
             [Next, a left leg stroke.]
Students: 一撇。
             [A left leg stroke.]
Teacher: 然後, 橫鉤。
             [And then, a right hook stroke.]
Students: 橫鉤。
             [A right hook stroke.]
Teacher: 橫鉤。
             [A down hook stroke.]
Students: 橫鉤。
             [A down hook stroke.]
Teacher: 一撇。
             [A left leg stroke.]
Students: 一撇。
             [A left leg stroke.]
Teacher: 一點。
             [A dot stroke.]
Students: 一點。
             [A dot stroke.]
Teacher: 好, 這是什麼字?
             [OK, what character is this?]

(The teacher pointed at the character just written when asking the question.)

Students: 你。
             [You.]
Teacher: 你。
             [You.]
Students: 你。
             [You.]

Although the repeating strategy may not sound exciting or creative, it is actually an essential strategy for all language skills (Oxford, 1990). Imitating native speakers' oral or written language productions helps learners improve their pronunciation and target language use (e.g. vocabulary, structures and gestures). When learning a tonal and ideographic language like Chinese, the repeating strategy also can help improve learners' tones and remember the correct stroke orders for characters.

The second most frequently used LLS was the cognitive strategy of *analyzing characters*. This strategy was often used after the teacher taught new characters and would like to help her students review and, at the same time, assess her students' level of understanding. The use of *analyzing characters* included examining the pronunciations, tones, radicals, stroke orders and meanings of the target characters. For example, the teacher often asked her students to work in pairs or small groups to identify the radicals and say the meanings of the radicals for the target characters. It was also common to observe the teacher asking her students to use different colors of markers to collaboratively write the correct stroke orders for the new characters on the board. Moreover, sometimes after teaching how to write a character, the teacher would deliberately write the character with a wrong kind of stroke in it and tried to guide the students to observe and point out the writing error. Excerpt 5 shows such a teaching moment.

Excerpt 5

Teacher: 好, 每個人看蔡老師寫對不對。
            [OK, everybody, look and see if Teacher Tsai writes it correctly.]
(The teacher is writing the target character, 'meal', with a wrong stroke in it.)

Teacher: 這個對不對?
            [Is this correct?]
(The teacher circled the stroke that was wrong.)

Students: 不對!
            [Incorrect!]
Teacher: 為什麼不對?
            [Why is it incorrect?]
Students: 因為....不是這個。
            [Because...it is not this one.]
(Some of the students tried to explain by writing the incorrect stroke in the air.)

Students: 應該這樣。
            [Should be like this.]
(Some other students were writing the correct stroke in the air.)

Teacher: 對! 是豎提, 不是豎鉤。
            [Yes! It should be a down tick stroke, not a down hook stroke.]
Jennifer: 差一點點 '你'
            [A little different from 'you'.]

(Jennifer *pointed out that the correct stroke, down tick, is very similar to a stroke order she saw in the character 'you'.*)

Teacher:　很像 '你', 但是不一樣
　　　　　[Very similar to 'you', but it is different.]

Students:　我寫對。
　　　　　[I wrote it correctly!]

(*Some of the students shouted out that they wrote it right.*)

Teacher:　那很棒!
　　　　　[Then that is excellent!]

The use of the *analyzing characters* strategy found in this study was aligned with the findings in the previous Chinese LLS studies (Grenfell & Harris, 2015; Lee-Thompson, 2008), both of which identified unique strategies in learning the Chinese language, especially in the area of character learning. In addition, some of the ways to analyze characters found in the previous studies were similar to the ones reported in this study. For example, strategies such as looking at the direction of ticks in a character and identifying radical(s) in a character mentioned in Grenfell and Harris's (2015) study were often used in the classroom under this study as well.

The third most frequently used strategy was the compensation strategy of *using mime or gesture*. This strategy was frequently used when the students did not know how to express themselves in Chinese and tried to use gestures to convey their meanings. A reason this compensation strategy was used often could be attributed to the program's No English rule. The students and the teacher were not allowed to speak any English in the Chinese classroom. Excerpt 6 illustrated how the student, Helen, used gestures to communicate the event she wanted to describe to her teacher.

Excerpt 6

Helen:　蔡老師。
　　　　[Teacher Tsai.]

Teacher:　什麼事?
　　　　　[How can I help you?]

Helen:　我...
　　　　[I...]

(*Helen stood up wanting to talk to the teacher, but did not know how to say what she wanted to say in Chinese.*)

Denny:　你可以這個。
　　　　[You can do this.]

(*Another student suggested that Helen use gestures by waiving his hands.*)

Helen:	我...
	[I ...]
Teacher:	想上廁所?
	[Want to go to the bathroom?]
Helen:	沒有。
	[No.]
Teacher:	那你比給我看, 好嗎?
	[Then you make gestures to show me, OK?]
Helen:	我的媽媽。
	[My mother.]

(Helen is making gestures.)

Teacher:	喔! 你的媽媽有小寶寶?
	[Ah! Your mother had a baby?]
Helen:	對!
	[Yes!]
Teacher:	喔!非常棒!
	[Ah! That is excellent!]
Helen:	對!
	[Yes!]

Helen smiles.

| Teacher: | Helen的媽媽昨天生小寶寶! |
| | [Helen's mother had a baby yesterday!] |

Although the use of LLS in the classroom was more diverse, incorporating all six groups of strategies, just like the LTS, the majority of the LLS used were either cognitive or memory. In addition to the two cognitive strategies already discussed in the top three frequency rankings, the other four cognitive strategies observed were all used to practice newly learned knowledge, and to integrate new knowledge into their existing Chinese language repertoire. For example, the strategy of *distinguishing characters, radicals, sounds and tones*, was employed when the teacher asked the students to group flash cards consisting of new and already learned characters that shared the same radicals. Sometimes the students were confused with two distinctive characters that share the same sound and tone; hence, one activity asked them to match each character with the word which incorporates the character. The other cognitive strategy, *recognizing and using formulas and patterns*, was used by the students when the teacher assigned them into pairs and asked them to use the sentence patterns learned to question each other. In addition, when the teacher wanted to focus on the practice of pronunciations or character writing, the strategy of *formally practicing with sounds and writing systems*, was used. The other cognitive strategy, *practicing naturalistically*, was used only three times. It is reasonable to assume that due to the novice level of the learners in Chinese, it was difficult to ask them to practice the language naturalistically, as they simply did not have a large enough repertoire in the target language.

This study observed eight memory LLS used by the students, which helped internalize new knowledge into their memory by different means (Oxford, 1990). For example, the strategy of *structured reviewing* was usually used by the students at the end of a lesson when the teacher wanted them to demonstrate their level of understanding. Activities such as counting together from one to 100 as a class, or making sentences using the characters written on the board, are examples of *structured reviewing*. A few other memory strategies used attempted to help the students make the new language learned more meaningful. For example, the strategy of *using physical response* helped the students to remember body parts and animal names. The strategy of *using imagery* was used when the students were asked to draw pictures that represent the target characters or words. This strategy strengthened the vocabulary's mental image in the students' minds and helped them for future recall. The strategy of *placing new words into a context* was used when the teacher asked the learners to test the use of new words by placing them in learned sentence patterns or in a short conversation. The strategy of *associating/elaborating* was used when the teacher tried to stress the meanings of the target characters by linking them to the real objects. For example, when teaching the characters '昨' (yesterday), '今' (today) and '明' (tomorrow), she gave her students character flash cards and asked them to pin the three characters on the appropriate dates on the calendar based on their meanings. The strategy of *grouping* was mostly used when the teacher asked the students to sort characters by their radicals or sounds. The strategy, *representing sounds in memory*, was used to remember the names of certain animals. For example, in Chinese, the sound of a cat is similar to the word for 'cat'. Hence, asking the students to imitate the sound of a cat was efficient to help them recall how to say 'cat' in Chinese. Next, the strategy, *using mechanical techniques*, was seldom used. It was used only three times in a telephone game where the students passed a piece of paper with a character on it and were asked to read aloud the character before they could pass it on. As the paper was passed, the students said the character loudly and at the end everyone learned the pronunciation of the character.

In addition to the direct strategies described above, a few indirect strategies were used by the students, among which three were affective. First, *using music* was employed after the teacher taught the class how to sing a song involving target words in the lyrics. The students were often asked to sing as a group. The other two affective strategies, *making positive statements* and *rewarding yourself*, were rarely used. This could be because the students saw the teacher as an authoritative figure and believed that positive statements and rewards should come from the teacher. This is evident, as these two strategies had more counts in the use of LTS.

The use of another group of indirect strategies, metacognitive, was identified in the observations, though they were seldom used by the students. The teacher suggested the use of the metacognitive strategy *paying attention* when she requested the students to put down their pencils and observe how she wrote the characters on the board. The other metacognitive strategy, *self-monitoring*, was suggested by the teacher when she asked the students to reflect on their learning. Questions such as, 'were you careful when you tried to write characters with the correct stroke orders?', and 'Did you check if your characters looked correct when you finished writing?' were offered by the teacher for the students' reflection. Metacognitive strategies involve focusing, planning and evaluating one's learning. Such strategies require well-developed self-regulation skills, which refers to the ability to recognize and control emotions, and maintain focus (Gillespie & Seibel, 2006). The low use of the metacognitive strategies in the classroom could be attributed to the young age of the learners, whose self-regulation ability was still at a developing stage. However, although the metacognitive strategies were rarely used, the teachers' encouragement of such strategy use will likely help the learners to develop the skills necessary for utilizing the metacognitive strategies in the future.

Lastly, the indirect social strategy of *cooperating with peers*, was used in the class. It was mostly used when the teacher assigned her students into pairs or small groups for interactive activities. For example, the teacher asked the students to show a drawing of their families to their activity partners and describe who each member was. *Cooperating with peers* promotes students' ability to work together with others with a common goal while practicing different target language skills. This strategy is deemed essential according to Oxford (1990), which implies that teachers should frequently create opportunities for students to work in interactive group activities to encourage the use of this strategy.

LLS the Heritage Learner Used

Considering that the language level of the heritage learner, Alice, was more advanced compared to the rest of the class and she might have a different pattern of strategy use, Alice's strategy use data was analyzed separately from the class. The observation of Alice's strategy use excluded the teacher-directed strategy use already mentioned above and only focused on strategy use initiated by Alice herself.

Table 6.3 illustrated that a total of 59 incidents of the use of LLS were identified, which comprised 14 strategies. Amongst the 14 strategies, Alice frequently used the compensation strategy of *getting help*,

Table 6.3 LLS used by Alice in the classroom

Frequency Ranking	Strategy	Strategy Type	# (%) of strategy incidences
1	Getting help	Compensation	22 (38%)
3	Self-monitoring	Metacognitive	10 (17%)
4	Cooperating with peers	Social	9 (15%)
5	Recognizing and using formulas and patterns	Cognitive	4 (7%)
	Using a circumlocution or synonym	Cognitive	3 (5%)
6	Cooperating with proficient users of the new language	Social	3 (5%)
7	Placing new words into a context	Memory	1 (1.6%)
8	Using imagery	Memory	1 (1.6%)
9	Using physical response or sensation	Memory	1 (1.6%)
10	Summarizing	Cognitive	1 (1.6%)
11	Avoiding communication partially or totally	Compensation	1 (1.6%)
12	Coining words	Compensation	1 (1.6%)
13	Overviewing and linking with already known material	Metacognitive	1 (1.6%)
14	Asking for clarification or verification	Social	1 (1.6%)

the metacognitive strategy of *self-monitoring*, and the social strategy of *cooperating with peers*.

Alice was much more verbally fluent in Chinese than others in class, and often reached out to her teacher for help when she could not express herself in Chinese. In Excerpt 7, Alice thought of a sentence she could write for her composition but did not know how to write it. She asked her teacher for help.

Excerpt 7

Alice: 我覺得二年級會很棒。
            [I think the second grade will be excellent.]
Teacher: 我覺得二年級會很棒, 可以。
            ['I think the second grade will be excellent', OK.]
Alice: 你可以寫嗎?
            [Can you write it?]
Teacher: 可以, 我等一下寫給你, 好嗎?
            [Yes, I will write it for you in a moment, OK?]

The strategy, getting help, assists learners to learn new knowledge about the language. According to Oxford (1990), learners who know to use this compensation strategy can communicate more efficiently.

While Alice could produce more language than others, she also was able to use the *self-monitoring* strategy to maintain the quality of her language production with the teacher's hints. In Excerpt 8, Alice and a peer were chatting. The teacher heard a sentence Alice said which contained an adjective that was not the best fit for the sentence and repeated it to Alice. The repetition prompted Alice to select a different adjective and produce a more native-like sentence.

Excerpt 8

Tom:	為什麼你跟你爸爸喜歡吃麵?
	[Why do you and your father like to eat noodles?]
Alice:	因為麵很棒 。
	[Because noodles are excellent.]
Teacher:	因為麵很棒...
	[Because noodles are excellent...]
Alice:	因為麵很好吃。
	[Because noodles are delicious.]

Self-monitoring helped Alice track the error she made in her speaking and eliminate such error.

The third frequently used strategy, *cooperating with peers*, is a social strategy to verbally practice the language. In addition to the assigned in-class conversation practice, Alice was observed to chat with her peers regularly. In Excerpt 9, the class was ending before lunch time, Alice asked her peer if he wanted to share some carrots with her.

Excerpt 9

Alice:	你想和我一起吃蘿蔔嗎？
	[Do you want to eat carrots with me?]
Ken:	我不想和你一起吃蘿蔔。
	[I don't want to eat carrots with you.]
Alice:	為什麼你不想和我一起吃蘿蔔?
	[Why don't you want to eat carrots with me?]
Ken:	因為我不愛蘿蔔。
	[Because I don't like carrots.]

Oxford (1990) stated that 'Because language in all its aspects is a social act, cooperating with other people is essential' (1990: 170). It was observed that Alice was comfortable using the social strategy to practice oral communication with others.

Conclusion

This study utilized the research methods of classroom observations and field notes to examine the LTS and LLS employed in a first-grade Chinese dual language immersion classroom during Chinese language instruction. The study results illustrated that among the use of 280 LTS incidents observed, the majority of them (224 incidents) were cognitive and memory strategies, both of which were direct strategies that required mental processing of the target language. This finding is not in support of some previous LTS studies (Chen, 2016; Rido *et al.*, 2016). For example, in Chen's study of primary teachers' LTS in ESL classrooms, compensation strategies such as speech rate modification and sentence stress emphasis, were used heavily to effectively communicate with the learners. In Rido *et al.*'s study, the use of social strategies, such as discussion and games, dominated the LTS for teaching vocabulary. Heavy use of the cognitive and memory LTS in this study could be attributed to learning two aspects of the Chinese language: (1) the complex structure of the Chinese writing system, and (2) the disconnection between the phonetic and writing systems in Chinese. Both language aspects are considered to have a high cognitive and memory demand for learners to master (Wang *et al.*, 2014). A closer look at the use of the LTS in this study illustrated that in addition to using strategies to teach different language skills that teachers of other languages with an alphabetic script would use, the teacher in this study very frequently employed LTS for the purpose of teaching Chinese characters. Hence, using cognitive LTS to demonstrate how to manipulate Chinese characters and using memory LTS to model how to make the Chinese characters meaningful for easy recall in the future were two key teaching purposes found in the teaching activities in this study. For example, the three most frequently used cognitive strategies, *formally practicing with sounds and writing systems*, *analyzing characters* and *distinguishing characters, radicals, sounds and tones*, which assisted the learners to internalize the character knowledge, made up 24% of the LTS use. On the other hand, the two most frequently used memory strategies, *using imagery* and *using physical response*, which helped the learners to remember characters or vocabulary composed of characters, made up of 32% of LTS use.

It was observed that compared to the use of LTS, cognitive and memory strategies made up even more of the LLS use. Among the 453 incidents of LLS use, 205 (45%) of them were cognitive and 134 of them (30%) were memory strategies. This finding illustrated how the teacher thought her learners need these two types of strategies for learning Chinese. For example, the most frequently used LLS, the cognitive strategy of *repeating*, was so commonly suggested by the teacher to her students that after a while this strategy use became automatic by the learners and made up 18% of the LLS use. A close analysis of the use of LLS showed again that these strategies were mostly for learning Chinese characters. This finding is aligned with some of the previous studies (Grenfell & Harris, 2015; Lee-Thompson, 2008; Wang, 1998), all of which reported heavy cognitive and memory strategy use for the learning of characters. The learners in Wang's study often used the cognitive strategy of *repeating* to read aloud or write characters. Lee-Thompson's study reported the learners using many Chinese-specific memory strategies to learn characters. One example was the use of the memory strategy of *associating* by writing Pinyin, the romanization of the Chinese phonetic system, next to the characters to remember their pronunciation. Grenfell and Harris's learners reported heavy use of memory strategies to learn all aspects of the characters.

On the other hand, the heritage learner, Alice, used a distinct set of strategies compared to the rest of the class. Alice used compensation, metacognitive and social strategies more often than cognitive, memory and affective strategies. A couple of studies (Cáceres-Lorenzo, 2015; Srisupha, 2012) were aligned with these results. For example, Cáceres-Lorenzo identified memory as the least used strategy for the teenage Spanish CFL participants and Srisupha reported that the Thai college CFL participants only used memory and cognitive strategies with medium frequency. Both studies with a low to medium cognitive and memory strategy use involved CFL learners at a more advanced level. This may imply that as learners are more knowledgeable about the structure of the Chinese language and are more familiar with the components of characters – like the heritage learner in this chapter – learning the language is no longer as cognitive and memory-demanding as at the beginning learning stage. However, this implication needs to be confirmed through rigorous research in the future. This finding also suggests that learners at different language levels seem to use distinct strategies and might have different strategy needs to continue developing their target language. How much of the cognitive and memory LTS and teacher-directed LLS found in this chapter are suitable for heritage learners at more advanced language levels needs more investigation.

Pedagogical Implications

The findings in this study, along with similar findings in other studies, have demonstrated that, at the beginning stage of Chinese language learning, regardless of the age of the learners, cognitive and memory strategies take essential roles in aiding acquisition, especially in the learning of Chinese characters. A teaching implication based on the findings is that, since beginners are not familiar with the language system, their teachers can help identify the cognitive and memory strategies that are especially useful for learning different aspects of Chinese characters (e.g. use *grouping* to help remember radicals, use *repeating* to recognize a character's sound) and systematically plan and explicitly teach learners how to use the strategies. The explicit teaching of strategies would be particularly helpful for young learners such as the ones in this study, who have not fully developed their life skills, let alone the ability to use strategies effectively. However, as Grenfell and Harris (2015) mentioned, focusing instruction solely on the learning of Chinese components might make young learners become bored with the lessons. Hence, another pedagogical suggestion would be that when teaching a language such as Chinese, which requires learners' high level of cognitive and memory capacity, integrating other types of LTS to aid teaching will increase young learners' motivation and attention. For example, the teacher in this study often used the affective strategy of *using music* in addition to the memory strategy of *using physical response* to teach Chinese words. This suggestion is supported by Oxford (1990) as she stated that different groups of strategies are linked and support each other. Lastly, since Chinese is seen as a challenging language to learn, teachers should consider using more indirect strategies to help learners feel at ease, even though these strategies do not directly involve the learning of the target language. For example, more positive statements can be made to boost learners' confidence and ensure that they feel good about learning the language.

In terms of the teaching implications regarding heritage learners, since heritage learners are often at a more advanced language level with different needs for strategy use, DLI teachers need to explore and encourage heritage learners to try diverse types of strategies in order to identify the most effective ones for them. Moreover, teachers in one-way DLI programs need to constantly remind themselves that, although the majority of the student population they serve is English-speaking, the fact that there is a heritage student in their class deserves their attention. Hence, while teachers utilize strategies that are suitable to lead the learning of the English-speaking students, they also need to spend time developing and executing strategies that help heritage learners.

References

Akbari, R. and Hosseini, K. (2008) Multiple intelligences and language learning strategies: Investigating Possible Relations. *An International Journal of Educational Technology and Applied Linguistics* 36 (2), 141–155.

Alabsi, T.A. (2016) The effectiveness of role play strategy in teaching vocabulary. *Theory and Practice in Language Studies* 6 (2), 227–234.

Cáceres-Lorenzo, M. (2015) Teenagers learning Chinese as a foreign language in a European Confucius Institute: the relationship between language learner strategies and successful learning factors. *Language Awareness* 24 (3), 255–272.

Chen, H.C. (2016) In-service teachers' intelligibility and pronunciation adjustment strategies in English language classrooms. *English Language Teaching* 9 (4), 30–53.

Cohen, A.D. (2014) *Strategies in Learning and Using a Second Language.* New York, NY: Routledge.

Council of Europe (2002) *Common European Framework of Reference for Languages: Learning, Teaching, Assessment*. Strasbourg: Cambridge University Press.

Ehrman, M.E. and Oxford, R.L. (1995) Cognition plus: Correlates of language learning success. *Modern Language Journal* 79, 67–89.

Gillespie, L.G. and Seibel, N.L. (2006) Self-regulation: A cornerstone of early childhood development. *YC Young Children* 61 (4), 1–6.

Göçer, A. (2008) Teaching strategies and class practices of the teachers who teach Turkish as a foreign language (A qualitative research). *Online Submission* 4 (4), 288–298.

Green, J.M. and Oxford, R. (1995) A closer look at learning strategies, L2 proficiency, and gender. *TESOL Quarterly* 29 (2), 261–297.

Grenfell, M. and Harris, V. (2015) Memorisation strategies and the adolescent learner of Mandarin Chinese as a foreign language. *Linguistics and Education* 31, 1–13.

Hashemi, A. and Ghalkhani, O. (2016) The impact of different teaching strategies on teaching spelling to kindergarten children. *Journal of Language Teaching and Research* 7 (4), 730–737.

Hong-Nam, K. and Leavell, A.G. (2006) Language learning strategy use of ESL students in an intensive English learning context. *An International Journal of Educational Technology and Applied Linguistics* 34 (3), 399–415.

Hong-Nam, K. and Leavell, A.G. (2007) A comparative study of language learning strategy use in an EFL context: Monolingual Korean and bilingual Korean-Chinese university students. *Asia Pacific Education Review* 8 (1), 71–88.

Izadpanah, E. and Ghafournia, N. (2016) The effectiveness of strategy-based vocabulary instruction on Iranian EFL learners' recall. *Theory and Practice in Language Studies* 6 (3), 603–609.

Kara, S. (2015) Reading strategies: Prospective teachers and their teaching practices. *Journal of Educational & Instructional Studies in the World* 5 (3), 20–28.

Le Pichon, E., De Swart, H., Vorstman, J.A. and Van Den Bergh, H. (2013) Emergence of patterns of strategic competence in young plurilingual children involved in French international schools. *International Journal of Bilingual Education and Bilingualism* 16 (1), 42–63.

Lee-Thompson, L.C. (2008) An investigation of reading strategies applied by American learners of Chinese as a foreign language. *Foreign Language Annals* 41 (4), 702–721.

Muñoz, C. (2014) Exploring young learners' foreign language learning awareness. *Language Awareness* 23 (1–2), 24–40.

Nahari, A.A. and Alfadda, H.A. (2016) From memorising to visualising: The effect of using visualisation strategies to improve students' spelling skills. *English Language Teaching* 9 (6), 1–18.

Ngo, N.T.H. (2016) The impact of listening strategy instruction on listening comprehension: A study in an English as a foreign language context. *Electronic Journal of Foreign Language Teaching* 13 (2), 245–259.

Nisbet, D.L., Tindall, E.R. and Arroyo, A.A. (2005) Language learning strategies and English proficiency of Chinese university students. *Foreign Language Annals* 38 (1), 100–107.

Onovughe, O.G. (2012) Instructional strategies and resource utility in language teaching among basic educators in 21st century Nigeria. *English Language Teaching* 5 (5), 79–84.

Oxford, R.L. (1990) *Language Learning Strategies*. New York, NY: Newbury House.

Oxford, R.L. (1993) Language learning strategies in a nutshell: Update and ESL suggestions. *TESOL Journal* 2 (2), 18–22.

Oxford, R. L. (2011) *Teaching and Researching Language Learning Strategies*. Upper Saddle River, NJ: Longman, Pearson ESL.

Rido, A., Nambiar, R.M. and Ibrahim, N. (2016) Teaching and classroom management strategies of Indonesian master teachers: Investigating a vocational English classroom. *3L-Language, Linguistics, Literature-The Southeast Asian Journal of English Language Studies* 22 (3), 93–109.

Sabbah, S.S. (2016) The Effect of Jigsaw Strategy on ESL Students' Reading Achievement. *Arab World English Journal (AWEJ)* 7 (1), 445–458.

Saeidi, M. and Farshchi, E.E. (2015) The effect of communication strategy teaching on EFL learners' oral production in content-based courses. *Theory and Practice in Language Studies* 5 (1), 71–78.

Shih, Y.C. and Reynolds, B.L. (2015) Teaching adolescents EFL by integrating think-pair-share and reading strategy instruction: A quasi-experimental study. *RELC Journal* 46 (3), 221–235.

Srisupha, R. (2012) Thai students' language learning strategies. *Quarterly Journal of Chinese Studies* 2 (2), 53–67.

Wang, S. (1998) A study on the learning and teaching of Hanzi-Chinese characters. *Working Papers in Educational Linguistics* 14 (1), 69–101.

Wang, Y., McBride-Chang, C. and Chan, S.F. (2014) Correlates of Chinese kindergarteners' word reading and writing: The unique role of copying skills? *Reading and Writing* 27 (7), 1281–1302.

Zarandi, S.Z.A. and Rahbar, B. (2016) Enhancing speaking ability through intervening scaffolding strategies. *Theory and Practice in Language Studies* 6 (11), 2191–2195.

7 Applying the Concept of Chunking in Teaching and Learning Chinese Characters

Introduction

China has been the world's fastest-growing major economy in recent years and the largest trading nation in the world. The official language of China, Mandarin Chinese, is now seen as one of the most important languages to learn. Despite the fact that Mandarin Chinese is deemed an essential language in the world, the language is considered one of the most challenging to learn by native English speakers. The Foreign Service Institute (FSI) placed languages into five categories to show the time an English-speaker needs to master a specific language. Mandarin Chinese, along with Cantonese, Arabic, Japanese and Korean are ranked as the most difficult languages to learn in Category V (Effective Language Learning, 2017). Compared to languages in Category I, such as Spanish, French and Portuguese, which only require 575–600 hours to reach a general professional proficiency, Category V languages require 2200 hours, almost quadruple the time investment.

The difference in difficulty levels among the categories of languages is due to the languages coming from different roots. Unlike English, Spanish or French, which share the same roots in the Indo-European language family, Mandarin Chinese belongs to the Sino-Tibetan language family (Padilla *et al.*, 2013). One of the most challenging tasks in learning Chinese is mastering the morphosyllabic writing system (DeFrancis, 1989). In Chinese writing, the basic orthographic units are characters, which are 'complex visual-spatial configurations that consist of any or all of eight basic strokes interwoven in patterns to form component radicals in a two-dimensional square' (Cao *et al.*, 2013: 441). Each character represents a morpheme and is monosyllabic. However, the characters have an absence of systematic correspondence between grapheme and phoneme (Xu *et al.*, 2014). In other words, the pronunciation and the orthography are independent of each other. Due to this nature, and the large number of complex orthographic symbols in Chinese, learning characters is difficult for second language learners. Moreover, Chinese has a significant number of homophones (Wong *et al.*, 2009). It is common to find characters with different meanings sharing the same sound, increasing the difficulty of accurately recalling characters (Sung, 2012). According to Liu *et al.* (1990), out of 1290 common characters, approximately 70% have homophones, with an average of 4.4 homophones per character. Hence, learning Chinese script is much more cognitively demanding than learning an alphabetic script, due to the structural complexity of Chinese characters and the arbitrary visual-phonological connections (Wang *et al.*, 2014).

Considering that the Chinese orthographic system consists of distinct aspects of linguistic complexity that are absent in learning French or Spanish as a second language, it is important to find effective methods for teaching and learning the system. This is especially essential to investigate in the Chinese DLI setting, as an objective of DLI programs is to produce highly proficient bilinguals in not only oral skills, but also literacy skills. Hence, this chapter intended to examine the effect of a recently proposed Chinese-character teaching method, chunking, on character acquisition in a first-grade Chinese DLI class.

Chinese Character Learning by Native-Speaking Children

The current literature on how Chinese children become literate in Chinese identified several key factors such as orthographic knowledge, phonemic awareness, rapid automatized naming (RAN) and morphological awareness (McBride & Wang, 2015). Amongst all of the factors, morphological awareness has been pinpointed as an important factor that accounts for the unique variance in reading and writing Chinese (Lo *et al.*, 2016). Morphological awareness in Chinese is the ability to be aware of a radical and its meaning, and how it is positioned in a character. Radical position and meaning in characters offer clues to children, which assist them in recalling characters learned and remembering new ones. A few studies reported the important role of positional and functional knowledge of radicals in young children's Chinese literacy development (Ho & Bryant, 1997; Packard *et al.*, 2006; Shu & Anderson, 1997; Yeung *et al.*, 2016), and a few experimental studies (Wang & McBride, 2015; Wu *et al.*, 2009) have shown that training children's morphological awareness improved their Chinese reading and writing skills.

In addition to morphological awareness, researchers have also found that strokes in characters are important units that readers must process in order to recognize characters (Zhang, 1992). Researchers have reported that stroke-sequence knowledge (e.g. one must write from top to bottom and left to right) aids character learning. For example, Giovanni's (1994) study found that knowing the temporal order of strokes facilitates character recognition, as the accurate identification of the sequential order of strokes helps readers recall the correct character and recall it quickly.

The last unique factor, which influences Chinese children's literacy development, is visual chunking. The concept of chunking initially derived from what the cognitive psychology field refers to as an information-processing mechanism. A chunk is defined as a number of pieces of information in a meaningful unit. Miller (1956) argued that a human being's memory capacity is limited; hence, the chunking mechanism helped people break information into smaller chunks for easier processing and remembering. Researchers in the language acquisition field have proposed to apply the concept of chunking to learning Chinese, calling the method visual chunking (Cao *et al.*, 2013; Chang *et al.*, 2014) or bujian jiaoxuefa (the chunking method) (Chu, 2009).

Chunks identified in a Chinese character are defined as units 'separated by a visible diminutive space from other units' (Shen & Ke, 2007: 99). In some cases, chunks can be whole characters, or radicals, which are 'the smallest orthographic units within a character that have semantic or phonetic functions' (Xu *et al.*, 2014: 774). However, some radicals may, themselves, be decomposed into smaller chunks. For example, the character, 筷 (chopsticks), has 快 as the phonetic radical, which can be further decomposed into two chunks, 忄 and 夬. Taft and Forster (1975) stated that the use of chunking is a decomposition procedure which saves learners' memory storage. To remember characters, learners only need to memorize chunks instead of each stroke in the chunks. According to Cao *et al.* (2013), a character contains 10.15 strokes on average; however, 98% of characters consist of only five or fewer chunks. If one can encode the chunks in characters when learning, it will greatly reduce their memory load (Chang *et al.*, 2014).

Several studies have shown that when reading, Chinese readers combine strokes into bigger chunks, such as radicals, and children as young as first-grade were aware of the internal structure of characters, such as encoding characters into chunks (Anderson *et al.*, 2002; Chua, 1999; Wu *et al.*, 1999). In sum, the current literature on Chinese children's literacy development pinpoint three unique factors: morphological knowledge, stroke-sequence knowledge and the chunking method, and suggests that in order to effectively utilize the chunking method, strong morphological and stroke-sequence knowledge might be needed to help decompose and locate chunk positions in characters.

Chinese Character Learning by Second Language Learners

In the teaching Chinese as a second language (CSL) field, radical knowledge has long been identified by researchers (Jackson *et al.*, 2003; Liu *et al.*, 2010; Shen, 2000, 2005; Shen & Ke, 2007; Taft & Chung, 1999) as a key factor when learning characters. For example, Jackson *et al.* observed that learners used a variety of radical knowledge to facilitate the learning of new characters. Shen (2005) identified learning strategies used by US college learners of Chinese and reported that the majority of the strategies were orthographic knowledge-based strategies, which included three types of radical knowledge (graphemics, semantics and phonetics). In a different study, Shen (2000) found that US learners of Chinese who acquired good radical knowledge performed much better on character recognition tests than those less knowledgeable in radicals. Furthermore, a different study found that radical knowledge not only facilitated character recognition, but also positively correlated with word reading ability (Shen & Ke, 2007).

More recently, the chunking method was proposed by a small group of researchers in the second language acquisition setting (Chang *et al.*, 2014; Chen *et al.*, 2013; Xu *et al.*, 2014; Xu & Padilla, 2013). Researchers believe that not only for native speakers, but also for second language learners, perceiving characters as composed of chunks instead of individual strokes is more efficient for processing Chinese orthography (Xu *et al.*, 2014). The effectiveness of the chunking method in character learning has been tested in a few studies. One is Xu and Padilla's (2013) study, which employed the method of meaningful interpretation and chunking (MIC) to teach high school learners of Chinese at various levels and learning backgrounds (e.g. heritage vs. non-heritage). The features of the MIC method included the introduction of the origin and types of Chinese characters, radical knowledge, definitions and examples of transparent and opaque characters (note: characters are considered transparent when their radicals carry meaning directly related to the characters.), and the use of the chunking strategy to read and write characters. Compared to the control group, which received the traditional stroke-order rote memorization method, the treatment group, which received the MIC method, performed significantly better on immediate character tests. However, the results of the delayed test two months after the instruction showed that the MIC method did not have a long-term effect on the learners. These results were independent of language level and learning background.

In another chunking study, Chang *et al.* (2014) compared the chunking method with other methods, such as passive reading, in a tightly-controlled first-year Chinese classroom setting in a university. The results of the participants' post-tests illustrated the effectiveness of the chunking method over the other methods. In addition, based on the chunking concept, the researchers grouped characters which shared the same radicals and introduced them in groups to the learners. The study results showed that the grouped method better assisted the learners' character production. Xu *et al.*'s (2014) study also tested the effect of the chunking concept on grouping characters which shared the same radicals. The researchers found that for adult beginning learners, the grouped method led to better learning performances, such as better recall and better radical generalization.

In sum, current studies on the effect of the chunking method in character learning, though mostly positive, are scarce and limited. For instance, the aforementioned chunking studies all had a focus on older learners. Younger CSL learners need to be investigated. More importantly, no current study looked into the effect of the chunking method in an immersion setting, such as Chinese DLI programs, where the target language is not taught as a subject, but used daily as a functional language. Considering the limitations of the previous studies, this chapter tested the chunking method with first-grade CSL beginning learners in a DLI setting. To be specific, this chapter aimed to learn whether applying the concept of chunking facilitated first-grade CSL students' character learning, and if any effect is immediate and long-term.

The Study Context

This study was conducted during the daily Chinese Language Literacy class period. For the class, the state-required Chinese textbook for the Chinese programs, *Mandarin Matrix*, which was designed specifically for young CSL learners, was used. The Chinese language learning goal set by the state for first-graders was that they were expected to learn approximately 100 characters when they finished the first year. When this study was conducted, the participants were in their first semester in the program. By the end of the semester, the instructor taught four lessons, within which a total of 49 characters were introduced to the participants. The instructor spent 30 minutes daily on the learning of characters. When teaching characters, the teaching of their pronunciations using pinyin, a romanization of Mandarin Chinese phonetics, using English letters and tone marks, was omitted. The state, at the Annual Utah Dual Language Institutes meeting, requested that the teaching of pinyin be postponed until the third grade, after the students had finished learning the English alphabet. This request was due to the fact that letters in pinyin are pronounced differently than in English.

Procedure

This study examined the effect of the chunking method on character learning during the daily 30-minute character instruction time for a semester. This study involved the cohort two students (see the focal teacher and student participants section in Chapter 1) in the fall semester. Before the study began, a pre-character recognition test, which contained 114 target characters the participants were going to learn in the academic year, was administered. The test results showed that no one except the Chinese heritage speaker, had prior knowledge of Chinese characters. Hence, the heritage speaker was excluded from this study. In sum, a total of 50 signed consent forms were obtained from the students' parents before the study began. Among the 50 monolingual English-speaking participants, half of them were male and the other half were female.

This study had a quasi-experimental design in which one first-grade class was randomly selected as the experimental group (hereafter called the chunking group) and the other as the control group. During character learning time, the chunking group was taught the following:

(1) radical knowledge: The teacher taught the meanings and positions of the semantic radicals in target characters, and used picture drawings to help students connect the meanings and the forms of radicals.
(2) grouping characters with the same radicals: Based on the chunking concept, alongside the target character, the teacher showed the students a group of characters, which shared the same radical in the fixed position as the target character. For example, when teaching the character, '好' (good), '妈' (mother) and '她' (she) were shown next to the target character as they all share the radical, '女' (female) in the same position in the characters. Grouping similar characters with the target characters could strengthen the learners' awareness of the radicals' positions and functions (Xu *et al.*, 2014).
(3) stroke sequence: When teaching how to write characters, the teacher demonstrated on the board how to sequentially write the strokes of a character while calling aloud each stroke's name. Figure 7.1 below is an example of the correct stroke sequence of the character, '你' (you).
(4) character structure: When a new character was introduced, the teacher would show the structural configuration of the character. Among the approximately 6000 frequently used common characters, 439 chunks and 11 structural configurations have been found (Chen *et al.*, 2011). As any random combination of chunks could produce nonexistent characters (Chang, *et al.*, 2014), showing the 11 structural configurations of characters would help learners realize that chunks are constrained to certain positions within a certain configurations.
(5) chunking activity: At the end of each lesson, the teacher handed pairs of students a bag in which printed lesson target characters were cut into chunks. The students were to put the chunks back together to make characters.

On the other hand, the control group did not receive any teaching of radical knowledge, stroke sequence knowledge, character structures

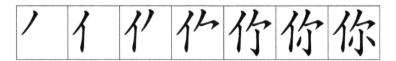

Figure 7.1 Correct stroke sequence of '你'

or the chunking exercise. Instead, the group focused on recognizing a character as a single unit. For example, the students were asked to repeat the pronunciations of the target characters after the teacher, read aloud characters listed on the wall or put characters in the right sentences listed in the worksheets. Both groups spent a similar amount of time reading their Chinese textbook in small groups and practicing writing characters.

Data Collection and Analysis

After the classes completed a lesson, the learners immediately took a character test. Each test contained five questions in each of seven sections, and each question was worth one point:

Section 1 (Radical Knowledge): The students were shown five characters, and three character components adjacent to each character. The students were asked to identify the semantic radical of the character by circling one of the three components.

Section 2 (Radical Meaning): The students were shown five radicals, and three pictures next to each radical. They were asked to identify the radical meanings by circling the appropriate picture.

Section 3 (Character Recognition by Listening): The students were presented with five two-character words, each with a character missing. The teacher wrote single characters from the lesson randomly on the board and read each of the five words one by one aloud. The students were asked to find the character that completed each word, and write it on their test. For example, the second character, '狗' [dog], in the word, '小狗' [puppy] was missing on the test. After the teacher read aloud the word, '小狗' [puppy], the students needed to find the missing character, '狗' [dog], on the board and copy it by handwriting it next to '小' [small] in the test.

Section 4 (Character Recognition Using Pictures): The students were shown five vocabulary words and five pictures. They were asked to draw a line between the corresponding words and pictures.

Section 5 (Stroke-Sequence Knowledge): The students were shown five characters and were asked to write the characters with accurate sequential stroke order in the boxes next to the characters. For example, in the first box, the student was supposed to write only the first stroke of the character. In the second box, they were supposed to write the first and second strokes just like the stroke sequence demonstration in Figure 7.1.

Section 6 (Structural Knowledge): The students were shown five sentences, each with one erroneous character. The erroneous character might have a wrong, missing, or extra radical or chunk. They were told to detect the characters with a wrong structure by circling them and write the correct characters next to the sentences. For example, in the sentence, '称好嗎?' [How are you?], the students needed to circle the first character, '称' [to call], and write '你' [you] next to the sentence.

Figure 7.2 '我' with missing parts

Section 7 (Stroke and Chunk Knowledge): The students were presented five characters with missing parts. The missing parts could be as small as one or two strokes, or as big as a chunk (or a radical). They were asked to complete the missing parts correctly. For example, seeing the character with missing parts in Figure 7.2, the students were supposed to complete the missing parts to produce the character shown in Figure 7.3.

In addition to the four lesson character tests, a comprehensive delayed test was given to the students a month after the fourth lesson was taught to check the level of character retention. The delayed test contained the same sections and numbers of questions as the other tests, except that the content of the test covered materials from all four lessons. The results of the lesson tests and the delayed test were used as language performance data to illustrate the level of effectiveness of the chunking instruction. Mixed Repeated-Measures ANOVAs were run to see whether there were any significant simple main effects of the method used in learning characters and the time spent using the method, and if there was any interactional effect between time and method. In other words, in this study, the within-subjects factor was time, and the between-subjects factor was method.

Figure 7.3 Correct form of '我'

Results

None of the Mauchly's sphericity tests run in each of the ANOVA tests was significant (p > .05). Therefore, it is reasonable to conclude that the variances of differences were roughly equal and the condition of sphericity had been met.

Radical knowledge

There was a significant difference across the factor of time, $F(4, 192) = 9.338$, $p = 0.000$. The results of the post-hoc tests illustrated that the main difference occurred in the chunking group only. The means of the tests showed that the chunking group did significantly better on tests 2 and 4 compared to tests 1 and 3. A close look at the test contents revealed that the difference between performances at different times in the chunking group could be due to the different levels of character transparency in each lesson. In lessons 2 and 4, more transparent characters were introduced. For example, in lesson four, the radical of the character, 牛(cow), is the same as the character; hence, it is easier to remember its radical than one in an opaque character, such as the radical, (to walk slowly) in the character, 很(very) in lesson one. By looking at Figure 7.4 below, one can see that the chunking group did better on tests 4 and 5 compared to the control group; however, the difference was not significant. There was no significant difference between the teaching methods, and no interaction effect between method and time.

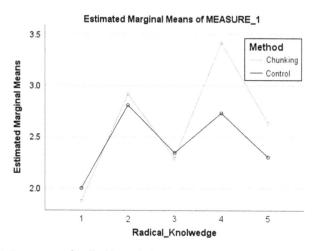

Figure 7.4 Test scores of radical knowledge

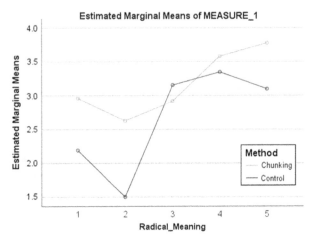

Figure 7.5 Test scores of radical meaning

Radical meaning

The main effect of time was significant, $F(4, 192) = 14.421$, $p = 0.000$. The post-hoc tests showed that the chunking group did significantly better on the delayed test compared to tests 2 and 3. The control group also did significantly better after test 2. Moreover, the main effect of method was also significant, $F(1, 48) = 4.898$, $p = 0.032$, meaning that one method was better than the other. The plot in Figure 7.5 revealed that the chunking group tended to do better four out of five times. In addition, the interaction of the time and method factors was also significant, $F(4, 192) = 2.786$, $p = 0.028$. The plot in Figure 7.5 revealed that over time both groups scored higher, but the chunking group was ahead of the control group most of the time. More importantly, the chunking group tended to have stronger retention than the control group.

Character recognition by listening

The main effect of time was significant, $F(4, 188) = 13.738$, $p = 0.000$. The results of the post-hoc tests showed that the chunking group did significantly better after test 1. Similarly, the control group did significantly better in the delayed test compared to test 1. Despite the similar trend within each group, this study found a significant main effect of method, $F(1, 47) = 4.139$, $p = 0.048$. The plot in Figure 7.6 illustrated that the control group did significantly better than the chunking group on four out of the five tests. In addition, a significant effect of interaction between time and method was found, $F(4, 188) = 6.287$, $p = 0.000$. This study concludes that over time both groups made improvements, but the control group had been ahead of the chunking group most of the time.

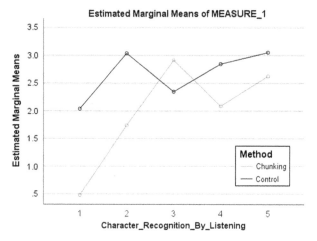

Figure 7.6 Test scores of character recognition by listening

Character recognition using pictures

The main effect of time was significant, $F(4, 192) = 17.878$, $p = 0.000$. The post-hoc tests illustrated that the chunking group did significantly worse in tests 2 and 3 compared to other tests (see Figure 7.7). A similar trend was found with the control group, who did significantly worse in test 3 compared to test 1 and did better again in tests 4 and 5. However, there was no significant difference between the teaching methods, and no inter-action effect between methods and time. A close look at the contents of the tests revealed that when the words tested were more concrete in meaning, such as family titles in lesson 1 and animal names in lesson 4, the learners scored higher, whereas when the vocabulary involved abstract concepts such as directions in lessons 2 and 3, the learners scored lower.

Stroke-sequence knowledge

The main effect of time was significant, $F(4, 192) = 18.813$, $p = 0.000$. The results of the post-hoc tests showed that both the chunking and the control groups did significantly worse on test 3 and significantly better on test 4. This result could be attributed to the characters tested in the section being more complex with more unfamiliar strokes in lesson 3 (e.g. '她' [she], '要'[want]) and simpler characters tested in lesson 4 (e.g. '什' [what], '五'[five]). Nevertheless, the retention of the stroke-sequence knowledge was not optimal for both groups as the scores of the delayed test were almost as low as their worst test, test 3. In addition, a significant main effect of method was found, $F(1.48) = 9.817$, $p = 0.003$. The plot in Figure 7.8 clearly showed that the chunking group did better on all tests compared to the control group. However, there was no interaction effect between time and method.

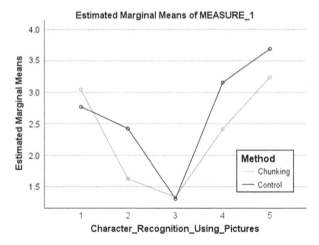

Figure 7.7 Test scores of character recognition using pictures

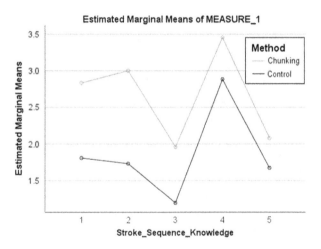

Figure 7.8 Test scores of stroke sequence knowledge

Structural knowledge

The main effect of time was significant, $F(4, 192) = 9.774$, $p = 0.000$. The results of the post-hoc tests showed that the significance was found in the chunking group, which did much better after test 2. In addition, there was a significant interaction between time and method, $F(4, 192) = 4.841$, $p = 0.000$. The plot in Figure 7.9 shows a trend of the chunking group doing much better than the control group over time, while the scores of the control group slowly decreased. The results seem to suggest that the chunking method, when used for an extended period of time, had a positive effect on helping learners identify erroneous structures in characters.

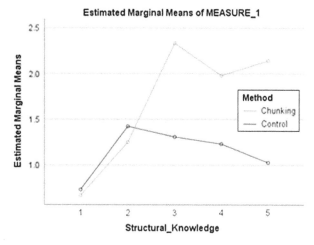

Figure 7.9 Test scores of structural knowledge

Stroke and chunk knowledge

The main effect of time was significant, $F(4, 192) = 5.843$, $p = 0.000$. The significance was found in the control group, which did much better on the delayed test compared to the other tests. The main effect of method was also significant, $F(1, 48)=21.162$, $p = 0.000$. The plot in Figure 7.10 illustrates that the chunking group did better every time compared to the control group. In addition, there was a significant effect of interaction between time and method, $F(4, 192)=2.780$, $p = 0.028$, which showed that although the control group did better at the end, the scores

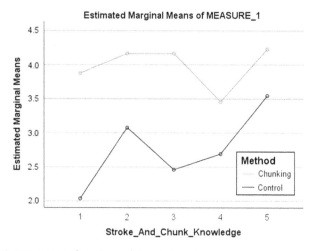

Figure 7.10 Test scores of stroke and chunk knowledge

of the chunking group were still significantly higher than the control group over time.

Discussion

This study investigated the effectiveness of the chunking method in character learning of true beginners in a Chinese DLI context. To answer whether the chunking method, or the duration of time the method was taught had an effect on the learners' character learning, and whether there was an interaction effect of time and method, mixed repeated-measures ANOVAs were run. The test results showed that the chunking group performed significantly better than the control group on radical meaning, stroke-sequence knowledge, structural knowledge and stroke and chunk knowledge. These findings are in support of other studies in which CSL participants who received the instruction of chunking performed significantly better on stroke knowledge (Chang et al., 2014), radical knowledge (Chen et al., 2013; Shen, 2000), and structural and chunk knowledge (Xu & Padilla, 2013) than those who did not receive the teaching of chunking, regardless of the learners' age. Chang et al. explained that when learners were taught chunking concepts, such as grouping characters with shared radicals, their recall of character knowledge was better. This is because the repetitive presentations of the same radicals (chunks) in the groups of characters strengthened the learners' generalization of radical and character knowledge. In the current study, not only was the grouping method of teaching characters employed, each character's structural configuration, which illustrates how chunks are constrained to certain positions, along with stroke and radical knowledge, were taught. Since the learners remembered characters as being made up of meaningful sub-components in fixed positions instead of individual strokes, it not only gave the learners deeper understanding of the internal structures of characters, but also freed up more memory space for them to remember the correct stroke sequencing. Moreover, making the correct stroke sequence for a character requires that the writer remembers not only the stroke sequencing, but also knows the correct positions of the sub-components of the character. It is possible that when trying to recognize or write characters, the participants, who had been taught chunking, already had a mental representation of the character configuration in mind, making their performances on the character tests more successful than learners who did not receive chunking instruction.

The superior scores of the chunking group compared to the control group on the four sections of the test demonstrates that the chunking group knew more about the meanings of radicals, knew better how to write characters with correct stroke sequence, could better recall missing components in characters and were more able to detect character errors when reading at sentence-level. All of the skills described were predictive factors of young children's Chinese literacy development found in current literature (Anderson *et al.*, 2013; Chua, 1999; Giovanni, 1994; Shu & Anderson, 1997; Yeung *et al.*, 2016). In conclusion, the test results revealed that the chunking method used in this chapter was fairly successful in developing character knowledge, including stroke-sequence, morphological awareness and chunking knowledge, necessary for future Chinese reading and writing. In addition, amongst the four types of knowledge, all except the stroke-sequence knowledge were well-retained by the chunking group after a month. The reason the stroke-sequence knowledge was not well-retained could be attributed to the lack of writing practice during winter break before the delayed test was administered. According to Cao *et al.* (2013), handwriting practice helped learners decompose the structures of characters, directing learners' attention to form, which includes stroke-sequence. In addition, neuroimaging studies (James & Gauthier, 2006; Longcamp *et al.*, 2003) have illustrated that there is an interaction between perception and action; therefore, motor memories from handwriting could strengthen character knowledge. This is probably especially true with stroke-sequence knowledge, as this chapter found that the lack of handwriting practice during break affected the retention of the knowledge.

On the other hand, the control group outperformed the chunking group on the section of character recognition by listening. The control group scored higher on almost all tests and also retained the knowledge better than the chunking group in the delayed test. The chunking method received by the chunking group did not seem to be effective. This could be attributed to the different amount of time the two groups had to hear the pronunciations of the characters. While the chunking group spent time on doing the chunking activities and the learning of stroke, radical, and chunk knowledge, the control group spent time on recognizing the characters displayed on the classroom wall by reading aloud. Therefore, in the character recognition by listening section, the teacher reading aloud the characters may have been helpful hints for the control group to find the right characters on the board, whereas for the chunking group, the pronunciation information did not assist them as much, as they did not practice making connections between pronunciations and characters the same way the control group did. This finding is supported by the current literature, which stated that phonological awareness is a universal factor of learning to read (McBride & Wang, 2015). Although the current literature recognizes phonological awareness as a factor predicting future literacy skills, more attention has been paid to the factors unique to Chinese learning (e.g. stroke-sequence, morphological awareness, chunking). However, phonological awareness is especially crucial with young beginners, as Song *et al.* (2015) found in their study; phonological awareness was the factor that could predict the future reading skills of pre-school five-year-old Chinese children before their other cognitive skills, such as morphological awareness, were developed at school. This implies that for beginning Chinese DLI learners without any Chinese language knowledge before entering school, developing their phonological awareness is urgent. The test results of this study have shown that the group which practiced making connections between characters and their sounds could recognize the characters better when they heard them. An implication of this research result is to teach beginning Chinese DLI learners the phonetic system early and not postpone it until third grade as required by the state of Utah. Without teaching any phonetic system, the learners could still learn the pronunciations by listening to the teachers and reading aloud; however, the use of a phonetic system ensures pronunciation accuracy. The teachers could use the zhuyin system (also called 'bopomofo') instead of the pinyin system to ease the state's worry regarding alphabet confusion in first graders. The zhuyin system represents Mandarin Chinese pronunciations, but it uses symbols derived from Chinese characters instead of English letters.

There were two sections that had no significant main effect of method or interaction effect between time and method. One was radical knowledge. In the radical knowledge section, the test results showed that when the tested characters were more transparent, the chunking group did significantly better in the test compared to the other tests. This finding implies that the chunking method might be more effective to beginners when learning transparent instead of opaque characters. However, the level of character transparency did not seem to affect the control group, as there was no significant performance difference found among their tests over time. This could be due to the fact that the control group did not receive any radical knowledge training and only used their observations when learning characters to answer questions. The teacher observed that, even though she did not point out that each character had a radical that had meaning, some of the learners in the control group would mention their observation to the teacher pointing out that the characters they learned before shared the same component as the new character being learned. This component awareness through observation might be the reason no significant difference was detected between the two groups.

The other section that had no significant main effect of method or interaction effect between time and method was character recognition using pictures. Both groups seemed to perform similarly. When the test contained more words with concrete meanings, both groups scored higher. In contrast, when the test contained more words with abstract ideas, both groups scored lower. This result is aligned with Shu and Anderson's (1997) study of the role of radical awareness and word acquisition of Chinese children. The researchers found that when the characters were not conceptually easy, even if the radical was familiar and provided meaning, children had a difficult time deriving the characters. This could explain the reason the chunking group did not perform better than the control group, as at least two of the four tests used Chinese words with abstract concepts.

Limitations

The current study provided new pieces of useful information on the use of the chunking instruction, namely, how the chunking method affects first-grade Chinese DLI true beginners' character learning over the course of a semester. However, this study has a few limitations. First, although the length of the study is longer than other studies, an even lengthier longitudinal study might be needed to detect the effect. This is particularly needed with true beginning learners who might start slowly with learning a target language structurally distinctive from their native language. In addition, many of the characters taught to true beginners are basic characters much simpler in structure than common characters. For example, the characters in this study only had an average of 5.57 strokes and 1.88 chunks per character, while commonly used characters have an average of 10.15 strokes and five or fewer chunks per character (Chang *et al.*, 2014). Although this chapter found the effectiveness of the chunking method in most parts of the test, it is possible that the chunking instruction did not exert its full effect, as the target characters were simpler characters with fewer strokes and chunks. According to Miller (1956), most people's working memory can only hold between five and nine (7 ± 2) pieces of information. Using the chunking method to learn more complex characters which have more than nine strokes might yield a better effect than for simpler characters.

Second, this study had to include the teaching of only the characters in the state-required textbook and could not control the type of characters taught to the learners. As some parts of the test results seem to suggest that the level of difficulty of the characters (transparent or opaque; abstract or concrete in meaning) might be factors influencing the effectiveness of the chunking method, future studies need to investigate the chunking method on the teaching of transparent vs. opaque characters, and characters with abstract vs. concrete concepts, and with an account of the learners' ages to see whether there is a significant effect of cognitive development.

Finally, this chapter is a small pioneer study, which focused on the effectiveness of the chunking method in a rarely investigated context, the Chinese DLI program. The results from this small number of learners ($N = 50$) need to be confirmed by similar studies. Moreover, future studies need to involve different types of Chinese DLI programs such as two-way programs or heritage programs, which consist of bigger groups of heritage learners. Even though there was a heritage speaker in the research site, who scored higher than other learners in the program, with a quasi-experimental research design and no other heritage speakers, it was difficult to study her performance against the monolingual English-speaking students in the current chapter and make inferences from the results.

References

Anderson, R.C., Ku, Y.M., Li, W., Chen, X., Wu, X. and Shu, H. (2013) Learning to see the patterns in Chinese characters. *Scientific Studies of Reading* 17 (1), 41–56.

Cao, F., Vu, M., Chan, L., Ho, D., Lawrence, J.M., Harris, L.N., Guan, Q., Xu, Y. and Perfetti, C.A. (2013) Writing affects the brain network of reading in Chinese: A functional magnetic resonance imaging study. *Human Brain Mapping* 34 (7), 1670–1684. doi:10.1002/hbm.22017

Chang, L.Y., Xu, Y., Perfetti, C.A., Zhang, J. and Chen, H.C. (2014) Supporting orthographic learning at the beginning stage of learning to read Chinese as a second language. *International Journal of Disability, Development and Education* 61 (3), 288–305.

Chen, H.C., Chang, L.Y., Chiou, Y.S., Sung, Y.T. and Chang, K.E. (2011) Construction of Chinese orthographic database for Chinese character instruction. *Bulletin of Educational Psychology* 43, 269–290.

Chen, H.C., Hsu, C.C., Chang, L.Y., Lin, Y.C., Chang, K.E. and Sung, Y.T. (2013) Using a radical-derived character E-learning platform to increase knowledge of Chinese characters. *Language Learning and Technology* 17 (1), 89–106.

Chu, C. (2009) The component-oriented net-weaving approach to character teaching: Rationale and application. Paper presented at the 2nd International Conference on Chinese Language Pedagogy, University of California–Berkeley.

Chua, F.K. (1999) Visual perception of the Chinese character: Configural or separable processing? *Psychologia* 42 (4), 209–221.

DeFrancis, J. (1989) *Visible Speech: The Diverse Oneness of Writing Systems*. Honolulu, HI: University of Hawaii Press.

Effective Language Learning (2017) Language difficulty ranking. See www.effectivela nguagelearning.com/language-guide/language-difficulty (accessed 21 April 2017).

Giovanni, F.B.D.A. (1994) Order of strokes writing as a cue for retrieval in reading Chinese characters. *European Journal of Cognitive Psychology* 6 (4), 337–355.

Ho, C.S.H. and Bryant, P. (1997) Phonological skills are important in learning to read Chinese. *Developmental Psychology* 33 (6), 946–951.

Jackson, N.E., Everson, M.E. and Ke, C. (2003) Beginning readers' awareness of the orthographic structure of semantic-phonetic compounds: Lessons from a study of learners of Chinese as a foreign language. In C. McBride-Chang and H.C. Chen (eds) *Reading Development in Chinese Children* (pp. 141–153). London: Praeger Publishers.

James, K.H. and Gauthier, I. (2006) Letter processing automatically recruits a sensory–motor brain network. *Neuropsychologia* 44 (14), 2937–2949.

Liu, P.D., Chung, K.K., McBride-Chang, C. and Tong, X. (2010) Holistic versus analytic processing: Evidence for a different approach to processing of Chinese at the word and character levels in Chinese children. *Journal of Experimental Child Psychology* 107 (4), 466–478.

Liu, Y., Liang, N., Wang, D., Zhang, S., Yang, T., Jie, C. and Sun, W. (1990) *Dictionary of Usage Frequency of Modern Chinese Words*. Beijing: Yuhang Press.

Lo, L.Y., Yeung, P.S., Ho, C.S.H., Chan, D.W.O. and Chung, K. (2016) The role of stroke knowledge in reading and spelling in Chinese. *Journal of Research in Reading* 39 (4), 367–388.

Longcamp, M., Anton, J.L., Roth, M. and Velay, J.L. (2003) Visual presentation of single letters activates a premotor area involved in writing. *Neuroimage* 19 (4), 1492–1500.

McBride, C. and Wang, Y. (2015) Learning to read Chinese: Universal and unique cognitive cores. *Child Development Perspectives* 9 (3), 196–200.

Miller, G.A. (1956) The magical number seven, plus or minus two: some limits on our capacity for processing information. *Psychological Review* 63 (2), 81–97.

Packard, J.L., Chen, X., Li, W., Wu, X., Gaffney, J.S., Li, H. and Anderson, R.C. (2006) Explicit instruction in orthographic structure and word morphology helps Chinese children learn to write characters. *Reading and Writing* 19 (5), 457–487.

Padilla, A.M., Fan, L., Xu, X. and Silva, D. (2013) A Mandarin/English two-way immersion program: Language proficiency and academic achievement. *Foreign Language Annals* 46 (4), 661–679.

Shen, H.H. (2000) Radical knowledge and character learning among learners of Chinese as a foreign language. *Linguistic Studies* 6, 85–93.

Shen, H.H. (2005) An investigation of Chinese-character learning strategies among non-native speakers of Chinese. *System* 33 (1), 49–68.

Shen, H.H. and Ke, C. (2007) Radical awareness and word acquisition among nonnative learners of Chinese. *The Modern Language Journal* 91 (1), 97–111.

Shu, H. and Anderson, R.C. (1997) Role of radical awareness in the character and word acquisition of Chinese children. *Reading Research Quarterly* 32 (1), 78–89.

Song, S., Su, M., Kang, C., Liu, H., Zhang, Y., McBride-Chang, C., Tardif, T., Li, H., Liang, W., Zhang, Z. and Shu, H. (2015) Tracing children's vocabulary development from preschool through the school-age years: An 8-year longitudinal study. *Developmental Science* 18 (1), 119–131.

Sung, K.Y. (2012) A study on Chinese-character learning strategies and character learning performance among American learners of Chinese. *Chinese as a Second Language Research* 1 (2), 193–210.

Taft, M. and Forster, K.I. (1975) Lexical storage and retrieval of prefixed words. *Journal of Verbal Learning and Verbal Behavior* 14 (6), 638–647.

Taft, M. and Chung, K. (1999) Using radicals in teaching Chinese characters to second language learners. *Psychologia* 42 (4), 243–251.

Wang, Y. and McBride, C. (2015) Character reading and word reading in Chinese: Unique correlates for Chinese kindergarteners. *Applied Psycholinguistics* 37 (2) 371–386.

Wang, Y., McBride-Chang, C. and Chan, S.F. (2014) Correlates of Chinese kindergarteners' word reading and writing: The unique role of copying skills? *Reading and Writing* 27 (7), 1281–1302.

Wong, K.F., Li, W., Xu, R. and Zhang, Z.S. (2009) Introduction to Chinese natural language processing. *Synthesis Lectures on Human Language Technologies* 2 (1), 1–148.

Wu, X., Anderson, R.C., Li, W., Wu, X., Li, H., Zhang, J., Zheng, Q., Zhu, J., Shu, H., Jiang, W. and Chen, X. (2009) Morphological awareness and Chinese children's literacy development: An intervention study. *Scientific Studies of Reading* 13 (1), 26–52.

Wu, N., Zhou, X. and Shu, H. (1999) Sublexical processing in reading Chinese: A development study. *Language and Cognitive Processes* 14 (5–6), 503–524.

Xu, X. and Padilla, A.M. (2013) Using meaningful interpretation and chunking to enhance memory: The case of Chinese character learning. *Foreign Language Annals* 46 (3), 402–422.

Xu, Y., Chang, L.Y. and Perfetti, C.A. (2014) The effect of radical-based grouping in character learning in Chinese as a foreign language. *The Modern Language Journal* 98 (3), 773–793.

Yeung, P.S., Ho, C.S.H., Chan, D.W.O. and Chung, K.K.H. (2016) Orthographic skills important to Chinese literacy development: the role of radical representation and orthographic memory of radicals. *Reading and Writing* 29 (9), 1935–1958.

Zhang, W. (1992) A study on the unit of processing in recognition of Chinese characters. *Acta Psychologica Sinica* 24 (04), 45–51.

8 Oral Interactions Between Teacher and Students: Corrective Feedback, Learner-Uptake and Learner-Repair

Corrective Feedback (CF)

In general learning, feedback is beneficial to learners. It motivates learners, reinforces learning and provides more information (Annett, 1969). In applying the concept of feedback in the context of second language learning, feedback is seen as language input. According to Gass (1997), positive input exposes language learners to well-formed utterances, while negative input prompts learners to notice their erroneous utterances. The negative input often comes in the form of corrective feedback (CF). For example, in the classroom setting, a teacher's oral corrective feedback refers to the teacher's oral responses to learners' non-native-like oral language production. Oral CF can 'consist of an indication of an error, provision of the correct target language form, or metalinguistic information about the nature of the error, or any combination of these' (Choi & Li, 2012: 332). There has been growing research interest in the role of CF in language learning, which is attributed to the long-term debate on the topic of error-correction. Some researchers, such as Krashen (1981) and Schwartz (1993), believe that error-corrections might impede rather than assist language acquisition. However, scholars who view language learning from the interactionist perspective claim that negative input offered in teacher-student interactions facilitates the learner to recognize errors and make attempts to correct the errors. Since the influential work on CF by Lyster and Ranta (1997), who established the taxonomy of CF for language classroom research, CF has been examined for its role in developing second language acquisition in various contexts from a variety of perspectives. Li (2010) conducted a meta-analysis of CF and concluded that CF has been generally reported as being advantageous in second language learning; however, Li also pointed out that some of the findings in CF studies varied depending on the learning situations. For example, Li noted that the frequencies of subsequent student responses after receiving teachers' CF varied depending on the learning contexts. Nassaji (2016) further identified that variables such as the class structure and organization, the themes of the lessons and the learning activities may all influence the use of, and student responses to, CF. Thus, in order to provide better teaching implications to Chinese DLI teachers and shed more light on the nature of CF in the particular immersion setting, it is essential to conduct studies such as the one in this chapter, which focused on the investigation of the DLI teacher's CF and the DLI students' subsequent responses to the CF.

Social Interactionist Theory

This chapter applies the view of the social interactionist theory in analyzing the interactions between the Chinese DLI teacher and her students. The social interactionist theory builds on the sociocultural theory, which emphasizes the crucial role of social interaction in child development. The seminal scholar Lev Vygotsky (1978), who contributed the foundation work of the sociocultural theory, explained that child development is two-layered – it first occurs through interactions with other people and then is internalized on the individual level. Vygotsky proposed the concept of the zone of proximal development (ZPD) to further explain a person's learning process. ZPD is defined as 'the distance between the actual developmental level as determined by independent problem solving and the level of potential development as determined through problem solving under adult guidance, or in collaboration with more capable peers' (1978: 86). In other words, skills too difficult to develop on one's own can be mastered with the appropriate form of assistance through social-mediated interactions with more knowledgeable individuals such as adults or peers. In applying the interactionist perspective in language learning, social interactions involve meaning negotiations, which aids language acquisition. Nassaji (2016) pointed out that the current literature has documented the ways in which meaning negotiations during interactions can assist language learning. For example, meaning negotiations made the input more comprehensible, highlighted linguistic problems and offered opportunities to provide CF. Scholars (Gass, 1997; Long, 1996) stated that feedback such as CF is particularly beneficial during interactions, as it directs the language learner's attention to form when the learner tries to convey meaning. This process of helping the learner map form and meaning is an essential skill for second language acquisition. Moreover, CF offered in negotiated interactions supplies space for the learner to attempt to produce comprehensible output, which involves the learner testing the language hypothesis and internalizing the linguistic knowledge (Swain, 1995). Through the lens of the interactionist view, this chapter analyzed the teacher's oral CF and the students' subsequent responses to the CF in the Chinese DLI learning context.

CF Studies in Language Immersion Classrooms

One of the pioneering researchers who investigated CF and learner responses in a language immersion learning context was Chaudron (1977). His study included the analysis of three teachers' CF in 8th and 9th grade French immersion classrooms for English-speaking students in Canada. The study intended to investigate the relationship between different types of CF and the rate of correctly modified student output. The study results showed that the type of CF which employed only a segment of the student's utterance and highlighted the student error, seemed to more successfully elicit correctly modified student output. Moreover, CF which utilized emphasis, such as using stress or question intonation to mark the error, also resulted in a high student correction rate. In contrast, CF which located or indicated the fact of the student error, in addition to repeating the error, yielded very little success in student error correction. Another pioneering CF study in the immersion context was conducted by Hamayan and Tucker (1980), who switched the focus from CF effectiveness in terms of correction rate, to the nature and frequency of CF. Hamayan and Tucker found that the French immersion teachers in Canada tended to provide explicit CF and the frequency was much higher in earlier grades. Since the pioneering work on CF, a systematic taxonomy of CF was not developed until almost two decades later by Lyster and Ranta (1997). The researchers developed the error treatment sequence model in which they identified six categories of teacher CF (explicit correction, recast, clarification request, metalinguistic feedback, elicitation and repetition). In terms of student responses, the researchers used the terminology, 'uptake', in their model, which refers to 'a student's utterance that immediately follows the teacher's feedback and that constitutes a reaction in some way to the teacher's intention to draw attention to some aspect of the student's initial utterance' (1997: 49). Two types of uptake are identified. One is needs repair, which includes uptake that shows the student's recognition of receiving the CF and or uptake that illustrates the student's failed attempts in correcting the error (e.g. made the same or different error, or did partial repair). The other type of uptake is repair, which involves the student correcting the error they made after receiving the teacher's CF. Using the error treatment sequence model, Lyster and Ranta investigated teachers' CF and learner responses in four elementary French immersion classrooms in Canada and reported that the most frequently used CF type was recasts; however, they also stated that recasts resulted in a low percentage of uptake. On the other hand, elicitation was reported to lead to 100% uptake. In addition, elicitation, along with metalinguistic feedback, were found to be the two most effective forms of CF in eliciting student-generated repair (self and peer repair). A different CF study in the immersion context, but with a distinct target language, was conducted by Mori (2002). The researcher analyzed the interactions in three fourth and fifth grade Japanese immersion classrooms in the United States and reported results similar to Lyster and Ranta's study in the distributions of CF types, which was that recasts were most frequently used by the teachers. However, Mori found conflicting results in the students' uptakes compared to the findings in Lyster and Ranta's study. While recasts elicited a low percentage (31%) of student uptake in Lyster and Rant's study, they produced the highest percentage of student uptake (61%) in Mori's study. The contradictory results prompted Lyster and Mori (2006) to theorize the factors which contributed to the learner response differences in the different immersion learning contexts. They stated that one factor could be the different distances between French and English, and between Japanese and English. Considering that the Japanese language has a greater difference to English in terms of its structure and typology than the French language, it is more likely that the Japanese immersion classrooms were more form-oriented, while the French immersion classrooms were more meaning-oriented. Another factor was related to the social contexts where the immersion programs resided. The French programs in Canada are in a second language setting, where the students could be exposed to the target language outside of the classroom, whereas the Japanese programs in the US are in a foreign language setting, where Japanese is identified as a less commonly used language. Such social context difference also might have contributed to the different communication orientations in the classrooms. In the form-focused Japanese immersion classrooms, the students responded promptly to recasts as they contained reformulated correct forms of the student's erroneous utterance that the students had been focusing on learning. On the other hand, in the meaning-focused French immersion classrooms, the students ignored more of the recasts as they were more focused on getting their meaning across, rather than correcting their errors. To summarize Lyster and Mori's (2006) study findings, the distance between the native and the target languages, and the social context where the learning takes place, are two main factors influencing the focus of classroom interactions, which then affect how students respond to CF. These findings suggest that CF study results from one immersion learning context may not be applied in another immersion context with a different target language in a different social setting. This implication prompted the investigation of CF and learner responses in this chapter, as the Chinese immersion context in the United States has not been examined.

The Instructional Setting

The student participants in this study were from class A in cohort one (for more details, see the focal teacher and student participants in chapter one). The teacher participant was the second author of this book. Audio-recordings and observations were employed in the daily Mathematics and Chinese Language Arts classes, which accounted for the majority of the instruction time in the first grade Chinese DLI. During the time of the study in the mathematics class, the students were learning how to collect data and make graphs, how to identify and build with shapes and figures and how to make equal parts. In the Chinese Language Arts class, the covered topics included features of animals, food and drinks, objectives in the classroom, shopping, and sports. According to the observation notes, the majority of time in both the math and Chinese classes was communicative-based, except for the times when students were focusing on solving math problems individually on the work sheets or when they were practicing writing Chinese characters. These tasks without interactions were excluded from the recordings for data collection. Learning activities regularly observed in the classroom included games, interviews, small-group work, and role-playing.

Data Collection and Analysis

The interactions between the teacher and her learners in the classroom were audio-recorded over a four-week time period in the spring semester. The digital recorder was placed in the teacher's pocket and was carried by the teacher in her pocket when she moved around in the class to give instruction. In addition, a research assistant (RA) observed the interactions as a non-participant in the back of the classroom. His observation notes were used as supportive data to strengthen the reliability of the findings. A total of 1293 minutes of teacher-student interactions were recorded. The recordings were transcribed by a Chinese native speaker and verified by us. Episodes of the teacher–student interactions were coded using the error treatment sequence model developed by Lyster and Ranta (1997). Each episode began with the identification of a student's erroneous utterance. This study took the definitions of language students' error types from Yoshida (2008) in categorizing the kinds of student errors generated in the teacher–student interactions in the Chinese DLI classroom. Four major types of errors were found: (1) morphosyntactic errors refer to errors made in grammar, such as particles and word order; (2) phonological errors refer to pronunciation errors (including errors in tone); (3) lexical errors refer to the use of L1 or inappropriate use of vocabulary; and (4) semantic errors refer to students' utterances without errors, but which were not understood by the teacher. The data of the error types was provided as the contextual information for this study and was not the main focus of the study. Following a student's erroneous utterance, we observed whether the teacher provided CF. In the cases where the teacher provided feedback, the CF was classified into the six categories identified by Lyster and Ranta. The classifications and definitions follow.

(1) Explicit correction: The teacher explicitly points out the error and offers the correct form.
(2) Recast: The teacher paraphrases the student's erroneous utterance in the correct form.
(3) Clarification request: The teacher informs the student in some way that his or her utterance contains an error and that repeating or reformulating it is needed.
(4) Metalinguistic feedback: Without providing the correct form, the teacher responds to the student's erroneous utterance by providing comments which give an indication that there is an error and hints (e.g. definition of the erroneous word or grammatical metalanguage referring to the error) which help the student form the utterance correctly.
(5) Elicitation: One of these three techniques may be involved. The teacher may pause her own utterance and prompt the student to complete the utterance, ask questions to prompt for the correct form or ask the student to reformulate their utterance.
(6) Repetition: The teacher repeats the student's error without any change and often with a stressed intonation.

The current study added a seventh CF, multiple feedback, after observing instances of the teacher using a combination of two CF in response to a single error.

Next, the teacher's feedback was followed by the student's uptake or no uptake. In the cases when a student produced an uptake, it was categorized into needs repair or repair. Needs repair includes: responses that acknowledge the CF; illustrate hesitation; are off target; or contains a different error, same error, or partial repair. A student uptake is counted as repair when it matches the description of one of the following four categories:

(1) Repetition: A student's repetition of the teacher's CF.
(2) Incorporation: Student incorporates the correct form into an expanded utterance.
(3) Self-repair: A student's self-correction after receiving the teacher's feedback without the correct form provided.
(4) Peer-repair: A correction offered by a peer.

After the CF episodes were transcribed, the data were analyzed separately by us. Reliability was achieved by the percentage of the coding agreements between the two of us. Before our discussion on the instances without coding agreements, the inter-rater reliability for the learners' error types was 98%, for the CF types, it was 96%, and for the learner uptake and repair, it was 95%.

For data analysis, frequency and percentage of different types of errors were calculated to give readers more background information on what the teacher's CF attempted to prompt the learners to repair. Next, a Chi Square Goodness of Fit test was run to determine whether a significant difference was found in the frequency of different CF types. In addition, Test of Independence Chi Square analyses were run to detect if CF types and learner uptake/learner repair were related. All tests assumed the null hypotheses at an alpha level of $p < .05$. Moreover, in order to more accurately make a decision about a cell's contribution to significance, adjusted standardized residuals $(+/- 2.0)$ instead of the standardized residuals were used (Haberman, 1973).

For the data analysis for the heritage speaker, since there was only one heritage speaker in the classroom and the amount of data related to her interactions with her teacher was not sufficient to run statistical tests, we simply tallied her data and used examples to interpret the results.

Students' Errors

Table 8.1 shows the percentages of the numbers and the types of errors made in the Chinese DLI classrooms during the four-week study period.

Table 8.1 illustrates that the students made a total of 942 errors. Among those, 547 (58%) were lexical errors, followed by morphosyntactic (27%), phonological (12%) and semantic (3%). Compared to other CF studies in elementary levels, which also reported the students' error types, the students in the current study generated many more lexical errors. For example, in Lyster's (1998) study in the French immersion context in Canada, and in Choi and Li's (2012) study in the ESL setting in New Zealand, the most frequently made student errors were grammatical.

This difference between studies could be explained by the distinct study contexts. First, in the current study, although the target language, Chinese, was taught with extensive time daily as a second language, it was taught in a community environment where Chinese is a rarely used language. It was not easy for the students to find opportunities outside the classroom to acquire additional vocabulary or to reinforce the use and memorization of learned vocabulary. In contrast, the target languages in the aforementioned studies, French and English, were commonly used languages in their respective social environments. Those students had

Table 8.1 Students' errors

Error Types	Frequency
1. Morphosyntactic error	255 (27%)
2. Phonological error	114 (12%)
3. Lexical error	547 (58%)
4. Semantic error	26 (3%)
Total	942 (100%)

more opportunities to have authentic conversation practice outside the classrooms in order to increase the target language fluency.

Under the different circumstances in the learning environments, it is reasonable to assume that the students in the previous studies knew more vocabulary words (hence making fewer errors in lexical items), but still needed to work on the accuracy of the target languages, which was evident as they made a lot of morphosyntactic errors. On the other hand, the high number of lexical errors made by the Chinese DLI students, who had exposure to Chinese only in the classroom, illustrated that they had yet to develop their lexical knowledge. Lacking the vocabulary knowledge to communicate was evident in the data. Many examples, such as that shown in Excerpt 1, illustrate that the students did not know how to say certain words in the target language to continue the conversation. In Excerpt 1, the students were asked to tell their friends where they went by using the word, 到 [to arrive]. In the excerpt, the teacher noticed a student who could not finish the utterance and offered CF to help.

Excerpt 1

David: 我到... [I went to...]
Teacher: 你到...? [You went to...?]
David: ...
Teacher: 你到哪裡? [Where did you go?]
David: ...
Teacher: 沒關係, 你想一想。 [It's OK. You can think about it.]

Teacher's CF Types

This study recorded a total of 632 CF to the students' errors. This means that sometimes the teacher did not provide any CF to some of the errors. The teacher did not provide CF in the following situations: First, the teacher was helping other students and did not hear when a student produced an erroneous utterance. Second, when the teacher felt that the teaching needed to continue so that the teaching schedule was not delayed, she ignored some of the students' errors. Third, when the students' language productions were not focused on the lesson topics, and/or the utterances had the purpose of catching people's attention instead of learning, their errors were ignored.

The test result on the frequency of the teacher's CF types, $\chi^2(6, N = 175) = 1234.5$, $p = .000$, revealed a statistically significant difference in the types of feedback provided by the teacher. Table 8.2 illustrates that the preferences of the teacher's CF, in decreasing frequency, are as follows: recasts (62%), clarification (13%), explicit correction (12%), multiple feedback (5%), repetition (4%), elicitation (2%) and metalinguistic feedback (1%).

Table 8.2 Frequency of the teacher's CF types

	Observed N	Percent	Expected N	Residual
Explicit Correction	75	12%	90.3	-15.3
Recast	392	62%	90.3	301.7
Clarification request	84	13%	90.3	-6.3
Metalinguistic feedback	4	1%	90.3	-86.3
Elicitation	15	2%	90.3	-78.3
Repetition	28	4%	90.3	-62.3
Multiple Feedback	34	5%	90.3	-56.3

It is obvious that the teacher preferred to use recasts as the primary CF. The teacher reflected on the teaching and explained that the first graders had very limited vocabulary knowledge. When the lack of vocabulary impeded the communication, she felt that telling her students the correct words to use (recast) was the most efficient way to prompt her students to imitate her utterances (student repetition) and learn the words. The high frequency of recasts was evident in both the math class and the Chinese language arts class. Excerpt 2 is an example of a successful use of recast. In the excerpt, Anthony was supposed to name the animal pictured on the board and incorporate it in his utterance.

Excerpt 2

Anthony: 老師, 我是kangaroo. [Teacher, I am a kangaroo.]
Teacher: 袋鼠。 [Kangaroo.] (recast)
Anthony: 袋鼠。 [kangaroo.]
Anna: 你是誰? [Who are you?]
Anthony: 我是袋鼠。 [I am a kangaroo.]

Anthony did not remember how to say 'kangaroo' in Chinese; however, after the teacher's recast, he repaired it by repeating the correct form and later incorporating it in the original erroneous utterance.

On the other hand, the other types of CF were much less frequently used: clarification request (13%), explicit correction (12%), multiple feedback (5%), repetition (4%), elicitation (2%) and metalinguistic feedback (1%). Different reasons explain why the teacher decided not to use each of these CF types as often as recasts. First, the teacher felt that the use of recasts was more time-efficient, which aided the flow of the classroom. It was also effective in eliciting student uptake; therefore, unless the teacher was unsure about the meaning the student attempted to convey, she would not use clarification request to correct errors. Second, the teacher did not believe that the use of explicit correction was as effective as recast, as her students liked to imitate saying the answers she said. Excerpt 3 shows how the teacher tried to use explicit correction to fix the student's erroneous utterance, but the student repeated everything she said resulting in an utterance that still needed repair. In Excerpt 3, Francis was writing Chinese characters and wanted to tell the teacher that he had not finished writing yet.

Excerpt 3

Francis:	我不好了。	[I am not good.]
Teacher:	不是'我不好了', '我還沒有好'。	[It is not 'I am not good.', 'I am not finished yet.'] (explicit correction)
Francis:	不是'我不好了', '我還沒有好'。	[It is not 'I am not good.', 'I am not finished yet.']

Instead of repeating only the correct form, 'I am not finished yet', the student repeated everything the teacher said including the sentence used for the explicit correction, 'It is not "I am not good"'. The ineffectiveness of explicit correction prompted the teacher to use more recasts to provide the correct form.

Third, the results of the data analysis showed that in the 34 multiple feedback instances (all were combinations of two different CF types), half of them had recasts in the combinations. A closer look at the combinations revealed that recast was used immediately when the first CF type used was ineffective. Excerpt 4 shows such example.

Excerpt 4

Fanny:	我喜歡喝…	[I like to drink…]
Teacher:	喝_____?	[Drink___?] (pausing for a few seconds)
	喝汽水。	[Drink soda.] (Elicitation & Recast)
Fanny:	喝汽水。	[Drink soda.]

This excerpt shows the teacher attempting to use a CF type other than recast, and switching to recast when the first CF did not generate student uptake or repair.

Fourth, the use of repetition as CF was rare as the teacher felt that it was so subtle that the students did not notice that she tried to correct their errors. In Excerpt 5, Sonia was chatting with the teacher and produced an utterance with grammatical errors, in which she tried to express that she loved her father, but did not see him often.

Excerpt 5

Sonia:	我愛爸爸我沒有看爸爸多。	[I love dad I did not see a lot of dad.] (Incorrect grammar)
Teacher:	我愛爸爸我沒有看爸爸多。	(Repetition)
Sonia:	… (no uptake)	

Fifth, elicitation was rarely used as the teacher thought that it was only effective when used with students who had high motivation and cognitive ability. In Excerpt 6, the teacher successfully elicited the correct form of a full sentence from Katie.

Excerpt 6

Raye:　　你想不想喝可樂? [Do you want to drink coke?]
Katie:　　想… [Yes…]
Teacher:　我想_____ [I want to___.] (elicitation)
Katie:　　我想喝可樂。[I want to drink coke.]

Finally, metalinguistic feedback was the least used CF (only four instances). The reason was that, as the class instruction was purely in Chinese, the teacher felt that offering definitions of words or grammatical metalanguage in the target language would involve too much jargon that the young students would not know.

The Relationship Between CF Types and Learner Uptake

Table 8.3 shows that on average, the rate of learner uptake was 69%. The result of the Chi Square test, $\chi^2(6, N = 632) = 39.710$, $p = .000$, indicated a significant difference in the types of teacher's CF in relation to eliciting student uptake; that is, certain types of CF were more effective than others in eliciting uptake. As shown by the adjusted residuals in Table 8.3, elicitation CF, with a positive residual of 2.0, was significantly

Table 8.3 Relationship between CF type and learner uptake

		Uptake	No Uptake	Total
Explicit Correction		56 (75%)	19 (25%)	75 (100%)
	Adjusted residual	1.1	-1.1	
Recast		274 (70%)	118 (30%)	392 (100%)
	Adjusted residual	.4	-.4	
Clarification request		65 (77%)	19 (23%)	84 (100%)
	Adjusted residual	1.7	-1.7	
Metalinguistic feedback		3 (75%)	1 (25%)	4 (100%)
	Adjusted residual	.2	-.2	
Elicitation		14 (93%)	1 (7%)	15 (100%)
	Adjusted residual	2.0	-2.0	
Repetition		6 (21%)	22 (79%)	28 (100%)
	Adjusted residual	-5.6	5.6	
Multiple Feedback		20 (59%)	14 (41%)	34 (100%)
	Adjusted residual	-1.4	1.4	
Total		438 (69%)	194 (31%)	632 (100%)

more effective than others in eliciting learner uptake while the CF type, repetition, with a negative residual of 5.6, was significantly less effective than other types in eliciting learner uptake.

As the teacher mentioned earlier, elicitation was not often used, as she thought it was effective only with students who learned the material well and could better recall knowledge learned. However, the fact that elicitation was most successful in eliciting learner uptake illustrates that the teacher's strategic use of the CF with specific students was effective. On the contrary, repetition CF was rarely used; and most of the time that it was used, students did not notice the correction. As mentioned earlier, one reason for the low rate of uptake from repetition was that this type of CF could be too subtle for the students to notice. In addition, this result could be easily understood by providing more details about the teaching context. Both the observation notes from the research assistant, and the data recordings, showed that in some of the repetition instances, the teacher's repetition was accompanied by praise to the student, which could make the student think that his or her utterance was correct. In Excerpt 7, the teacher walked by the student, who was supposed to find different friends to practice oral skills. The student stopped the teacher to interact with her.

Excerpt 7

Harrison: 因為我的椅子很多人坐下。 [Because my chair had many people sitting down.]

Teacher: 很好! 因為我的椅子很多人坐下。 [Very good! Because my chair had many people sitting down.] (Repetition)

Harrison: … (No uptake)

The student's utterance was both false (no one was in his chair) and erroneous in grammar. However, the teacher not only did not correct his error, but also praised him. The teacher explained that the students were required to speak only the target language in school, which created a lot of stress for them. They sometimes cried when they were corrected or when they did not know what to say in Chinese in front of the class. In order to boost their confidence, the teacher decided that if the errors were not the key points she was teaching and did not impede communication or class flow, she would praise the students' erroneous productions instead of correcting them.

Despite the significant results found in elicitation and repetition in relation to student uptake, the other types of CF led to student uptake more or less with the same frequency.

The Relationship Between CF Types and Learner Repair

The test result of the relationship between the teacher's CF type and learner repair, $\chi^2(6, N = 462) = 54.571$, $p = .000$, revealed that certain

CF more or less effectively elicited learner repair. The adjusted residuals shown in Table 8.4 illustrate that recast, with a positive residual of 5.2, and elicitation, with a positive residual of 2.0, were significantly more effective than other types in eliciting learner repair. In contrast, clarification request with a negative residual of 6.2, and multiple feedback with a negative residual of 2.6, were significantly less effective than other types in eliciting learner repair.

A closer look at interactions involving recasts shows that the majority of the repairs after receiving recasts were repetitions (181 incidences) rather than incorporation (56 incidences). As the teacher mentioned earlier, the students liked to imitate (repeat) the teacher's utterances. This phenomenon was especially frequent when the students noticed that there was a distance between their and the teacher's utterances when the teacher gave recast CF.

The other CF type that elicited significantly more repairs than others was elicitation. In fact, all 14 elicitations which led to student uptakes in this study also all led to student repairs. This result shows that elicitation not only successfully elicited student uptake, but all erroneous utterances were self-corrected by the learners. However, as the teacher said, elicitation was only used with highly motivated and highly capable students; hence, the repair result was only from a small group of the participants and should be interpreted with caution.

In contrast, clarification requests significantly elicited fewer repairs. This was evident in the recording data, which showed that when

Table 8.4 Relationship between feedback type and learner repair

		Repair	Needs Repair	Total
Explicit Correction		44 (79%)	12 (21%)	56 (100%)
	Adjusted residual	.0	.0	
Recast		237 (86%)	37 (14%)	274 (100%)
	Adjusted residual	5.2	-5.2	
Clarification request		32 (49%)	33 (51%)	65 (100%)
	Adjusted residual	-6.2	6.2	
Metalinguistic feedback		2 (75%)	1 (25%)	3 (100%)
	Adjusted residual	-.5	.5	
Elicitation		14 (100%)	0 (0%)	14 (100%)
	Adjusted residual	2.0	-2.0	
Repetition		4 (67%)	2 (33%)	6 (100%)
	Adjusted residual	-.7	.7	
Multiple Feedback		11 (55%)	9 (45%)	20 (100%)
	Adjusted residual	-2.6	2.6	
Total		343 (74%)	119 (26%)	462 (100%)

clarification requests were used, instead of correcting the errors, the students often repeated the same erroneous utterances or gave brief answers such as yes or no. Excerpts 8 and 9 illustrate such incidences. In Excerpt 8, the teacher was pointing to a picture on the board and expected the student to tell her what the object in the picture was.

Excerpt 8

Teacher:	這個是什麼? [What is this?]
Page:	抽(with 4th tone)屜。 [Drawer.] (The student used the wrong tone with the first character.)
Teacher:	什麼? [What is it?] (Clarification)
Page:	抽(with 4th tone)屜。 [Drawer.] (The student repeated the same incorrect tone.)
Teacher:	抽屜。 [Drawer.] (Recast)
Page:	抽屜。 [Drawer.] (The student used the correct tone.)

After the teacher tried to clarify what the student said, the student still used the incorrect tone. This error was not corrected until the teacher used recast to provide the correct tone information. In Excerpt 9, the teacher was teaching how to write the character, 飯 [rice; meal], and reminded the students that the first stroke of the right portion of the character was not a horizontal stroke.

Excerpt 9

Cindy:	蔡老師我沒有這個。 [Teacher, I don't have this.]
Teacher:	沒有什麼?沒有橫? [Don't have what? Don't have a horizontal stroke?] (Clarification)
Cindy:	對。 [Yes.]

The student wanted to confirm with the teacher that she did not write a horizontal stroke, but did not recall how to say it. After the teacher's clarification, the student simply answered, 'yes' to the teacher without correcting herself.

Multiple feedback also elicited significantly fewer repairs than other CF types. The teacher speculated that it could be that more than one type of CF provided at the same time resulted in too much information and language input for the young learners. The students appeared not to understand the feedback, or were not sure which part of the utterances they needed to correct. Prior to the conversation in Excerpt 10, Brian asked Charlie, 'Are you a girl?', Charlie said, 'No, I am not a girl.' In Excerpt 10, Brian needed to answer the same question.

Excerpt 10

Charlie:	你是女生嗎? [Are you a girl?]
Brian:	我也不是...男...生。 [I am also not a boy.]

Teacher:	我也不是男生. 我也不是_____ [I am also not a boy. I am also not a ____.] (Repetition + Elicitation)
Brian:	不是... [not a ...]
Teacher:	女生。 [girl] (Recast)
Brian:	女生。 [girl]

When Brian made the erroneous utterance, the teacher repeated the same utterance followed by elicitation. Brian's response to the teacher's multiple feedback was the repetition of the last two characters said by the teacher. It seems that he wanted to repeat the teacher's words, but was unsure where the starting point was. In the end, the teacher used recast to help him complete the sentence and was successful in eliciting student repair. This example shows that using more than one CF at the same time to correct an error could be confusing to learners and that recasts with short correct forms seemed to work effectively in eliciting student repair.

The Heritage Speaker in the Class

The heritage speaker, Alice (pseudonym), made 43 (48%) morphosyntactic, 41 (46%) lexical, three (3%) phonological and two (2%) semantic errors. Compared to the other students in the class, who did not know Chinese before entering the program, Alice's errors were much more equally distributed between grammar and vocabulary, with only a few in pronunciation and semantic areas. A closer look at her interactions with the teacher revealed that the kinds of lexical errors she made were distinct from the ones made by her peers. As mentioned earlier in the results section, when the students made lexical errors, it was mostly when they did not know, or could not recall, how to say a certain word. However, Alice's lexical errors contained mostly inappropriate use of lexical items. For example, in Excerpt 11, Alice was writing using writing sheets that had square boxes for Chinese writing. The students were told that each box could only fit a single character or a punctuation mark.

Excerpt 11

Teacher:	等一下妳的逗點,這個逗點。 [Wait, your comma, this comma.]
Alice:	逗點要在一個箱子裡面 。 [The comma should be in the box.]
Teacher:	對!在一個框框裡面,知道嗎? [Yes! In a frame, got it?]
Alice:	知道 。 [Yes.]

In Excerpt 11, the teacher tried to point out to Alice that a comma she made was in the wrong place. Alice realized it and responded that it should be in a box. However, she transferred the term 'box' directly from English to Chinese. In Chinese, box has a narrower definition and refers only to a container with a flat base and sides. The box Alice referred to (a space enclosed within straight lines) takes a different term, 框框

[frame]. The direct transfer from English to her heritage language also occurred often in her morphosyntactic language errors. In Excerpt 12, Alice wanted to ask for permission to say something in English in the hallway.

Excerpt 12

Alice: 老師我要跟你說件事在英文。[Teacher, I want to tell you something in English.]

Teacher: 好。[OK.] (The teacher went with her to the hallway.)

Alice used the character, 在 [in], to indicate that the language she wanted to use was English; however, in Chinese, 在 [in] is a verb specifically used to indicate locations (e.g. 我在中國。[I am in China.]. Alice's erroneous use of 在 [in] in Chinese complied with the grammatical rule in English and seemed to be a result of the language transfer from English to Chinese. In sum, rather than having a very low target language repertoire that still needs to be developed like her peers, Alice had sufficient language knowledge in both English and Chinese to make language transfer.

In terms of the CF types Alice received, there were 38 (54%) recasts, 19 (26%) clarification requests, five (7%) repetition, four (6%) explicit corrections, four (6%) multiple feedback and one (1%) elicitation. Similar to her peers, recast was the primary CF Alice received; however, Alice received more clarification requests than her peers. An analysis of the data shows that this result could be due to her frequent English to Chinese transfer in her language production, resulting in the teacher's need to clarify her meaning. Excerpt 13 is an example.

Excerpt 13

Teacher: 為什麼你們很快樂? [Why are you so happy?]

Alice: 因為我們跑步很多。 [Because we run a lot.]

Teacher: 你們常常跑步是不是? [Do you mean you often run?]

Alice: 嗯。 [Yes.]

In Excerpt 13, Alice transferred the sentence structure of English to Chinese and produced a grammatically incorrect sentence, which could be interpreted by a Chinese native speaker as 'Because we run for a long distance' or 'Because we run often'. The ambiguity of the erroneous sentence prompted the teacher to clarify what Alice meant.

With respect to Alice's uptake and repair, the results of the tallies show that out of the 71 instances of the teacher's CF, Alice's uptake rate was 73%. In addition, 62% of the uptakes contained repair (see Table 8.5).

Compared to her peers, Alice's overall repair rate (62%) was a bit lower than her peers' (74%). A comparison between Alice's and her peers' repair rate for each type of the CF confirms that in each type,

Table 8.5 Number and percentage of Alice's uptake and repair

	Repair	Needs Repair	No Uptake
Explicit correction (n = 4)	1 (25%)	1 (25%)	2 (50%)
Recast (n = 38)	20 (53%)	8 (21%)	10 (26%)
Clarification request (n = 19)	7 (37%)	9 (47%)	3 (16%)
Metalinguistic feedback (n = 0)	0 (0%)	0 (0%)	0 (0%)
Elicitation (n = 1)	1 (100%)	0 (0%)	0 (0%)
Repetition (n = 5)	1 (20%)	1 (20%)	3 (60%)
Multiple feedback (n = 4)	2 (50%)	1 (25%)	1 (25%)
Total	32 (62%)	20 (38%)	19 (27%)

Alice had a slightly lower rate for providing repair. This finding could be explained by the different focus of the teacher–student interactions. In other students' interactions with the teacher, the focus appeared to be more centered on using the correct form. This is evident as the study results showed a high rate of student repetition after the teacher's recasts. In contrast, Alice's interactions with the teacher seemed to be more meaning-focused. In Excerpt 14, Alice was describing a dog her mother had.

Excerpt 14

Alice: 我的媽媽有一隻小狗,他的名字是小白,因為他是白色,然後明天他就死掉了。 [My mom had a dog. His name was Little White because he was white. And then tomorrow he passed away.]

Teacher: 他之後就死掉了。 [After some time, he passed away.] (recast)

Alice: 對。它很可愛。 [Yes. He was very cute.]

Alice made an error regarding the description of time, but after the teacher provided the correct form, she answered 'yes' to confirm that it was what she meant and continued with her description.

Discussion

The finding of the study in this chapter illustrates that recasts was the most frequently used CF type in the Chinese DLI classroom. This finding is aligned with the findings in other studies with an immersion context (Lyster & Ranta, 1997; Mori, 2002; Sakurai, 2014). Lyster and

Ranta pointed out that recast is a modeling technique that teachers commonly use and that it is especially heavily used when the students have a lower degree of proficiency. This phenomenon was apparent in the current study. The students (except the heritage student) in this study only learned Chinese for less than a year and often lacked vocabulary for smooth interactions. It seems that the teacher's frequent modeling through recasts helped the students try to reach their ZPD. Unlike the finding in Lyster and Ranta's study, in which the students did not notice the modifications in the recasts and did not repair the errors most of the time, the extremely high repair rate (86%) of recasts in this study shows that the purpose of recasts was clear to the students and that recast seemed to be a fairly successful and appropriate CF method in aiding the students to maximize their ZPD. These result differences once again confirmed Lyster and Mori's (2006) hypothesis that the distance between the students' native and target languages, and the social environment where the language is taught are the factors influencing the patterns of the student repairs. These factors explained the reasons why the findings of the current Chinese DLI study were much more similar to the ones in Mori's (2002) Japanese DLI study than Lyster and Ranta's French DLI study. The Chinese DLI teacher–student interactions observed were more form-focused due to the distinct language features of Chinese compared to the students' native language, English. The scarcity of the Chinese language in the social environment where it was taught and the newness of the language to the student also directed the students to pay more attention to form than meaning. In Excerpt 3, in which the student mistakenly repeated everything the teacher said, including her words for explicit correction showed that the student was eager to learn the correct form from the teacher's modeling, but overlooked the meaning of her utterance.

On the contrary, the analysis of the interactions between the teacher and the only heritage speaker, Alice, showed that they tended to be more meaning-focused compared to the rest of the class. Alice's repair rate was lower than her peers' and her responses often started with an uptake followed by the continuation of the conversation. In other words, she recognized the teacher's corrections, but she did not intend to fix the error, as she was more interested in conveying more information to her teacher. An analysis of her errors revealed that many errors were the result of negative transfers from English to Chinese (see Excerpts 11–13 for examples). Her excerpts illustrate that she was able to find words (appropriate or not) in her Chinese repertoire for her to transfer English sentences into Chinese, which was something her peers were not capable of mastering at the same level yet. According to Vygotsky (1962), language transfer is a sign of cognitive activity, which helps learners build on the knowledge for both languages and increase their awareness of the functions and interplay of the different language structures. To accommodate Alice's advanced language level, the teacher included more clarification requests in her CF. However, due to Alice being the only heritage learner in the class, who was at a more advanced level compared to the others, the feedback she could receive was solely from the teacher. Although this study did not have a focus on peer feedback, it was found that in the conversation recordings, peer feedback occurred occasionally, especially when the teacher was busy talking with a student and could not provide another student CF when the student made an error. In total during the four-week study period, 34 instances of peer feedback occurred; however, Alice received none. In such a DLI setting where one type of student is the minority and the other type is the majority, the learning opportunities between the two groups become unequal. The minority students' opportunities are more limited as their learning needs and ZPD are different from the majority and sometimes full accommodations by the teacher could be difficult to achieve. In the case of Alice, no peer was comparable or more capable than her to guide her Chinese development; hence, she needed to fully rely on her teacher for feedback. If there were a more equal number of heritage and non-heritage speakers, or even just a couple more heritage students in the class, Alice would have had more learning opportunities and resources from other heritage speakers.

Teaching Implications

In the current study context, where classroom communication was mainly focused on form, it seemed appropriate that the teacher chose to use recasts to scaffold the students, as it was especially efficient in developing the students' lexical knowledge in the long run. However, Lyster and Mori (2006) proposed the counterbalance hypothesis, which stated that in order to achieve high effectiveness in learning, teachers should use interactional activities and feedback that is the opposite of the classroom's overall communicative orientation. In other words, if the class is form-focused, the teacher should offer more activities and feedback that direct students' attention to meaning, whereas if the class is meaning-focused, the teacher should provide more activities and feedback that lead students to notice the form. In the case of the Chinese DLI classroom, as the students developed more basic lexical knowledge, the teacher could slowly transfer the students to more meaning-focused activities, such as task or mission-based activities. On the other hand, for the heritage student, whose communication was focused on meaning, the teacher could direct her to do form-focused activities, such as sentence puzzles or categorizing words by their functions. In combining the counterbalance hypothesis with the concept of ZPD, a learner needs to be fully guided by a more capable person in both the areas of form and meaning in language learning. A lack of guidance in either area will not result in an optimal learning condition, but rather, it might hinder the learner in reaching their highest ZPD. In sum, a more ideal learning situation would be to include equal numbers of heritage learners whose communications focus more on meaning, and non-heritage learners who focus more on form, in the same classroom, where form and meaning could be more balanced in learning.

References

Annett, J. (1969) *Feedback and Human Behavior*. Middlesex: Penguin Books.

Chaudron, C. (1977) A descriptive model of discourse in the corrective treatment of learners' errors. *Language Learning* 27 (1), 29–46.

Choi, S.Y. and Li, S. (2012) Corrective feedback and learner uptake in a child ESOL classroom. *RELC Journal* 43 (3), 331–351.

Gass, S. (1997) *Input, Interaction, and the Second Language Learner*. Mahwah, NJ: Erlbaum.

Haberman, S.J. (1973) The analysis of residuals in cross-classified tables. *Biometrics* 29, 205–220.

Hamayan, E.V. and Tucker, G.R. (1980) Language input in the bilingual classroom and its relationship to second language achievement. *TESOL Quarterly* 14 (4), 453–468.

Krashen, S.D. (1981) *Second Language Acquisition and Second Language Learning*. Oxford: Pergamon.

Li, S. (2010) The effectiveness of corrective feedback in SLA: A meta-analysis. *Language Learning* 60 (2), 309–365.

Long, M.H. (1996) The role of the linguistic environment in second language acquisition. *Handbook of Second Language Acquisition* 2 (2), 413–468.

Lyster, R. (1998) Negotiation of form, recasts, and explicit correction in relation to error types and learner repair in immersion classrooms. *Language Learning* 48 (2), 183–218.

Lyster, R. and Mori, H. (2006) Interactional feedback and instructional counterbalance. *Studies in Second Language Acquisition* 28 (2), 269–300.

Lyster, R. and Ranta, L. (1997) Corrective feedback and learner uptake. *Studies in Second Language Acquisition* 19 (1), 37–66.

Mori, H. (2002) Error treatment sequences in Japanese immersion classroom interactions at different grade levels. Unpublished doctoral dissertation, University of California, Los Angeles, CA.

Nassaji, H. (2016) Anniversary article: Interactional feedback in second language teaching and learning: A synthesis and analysis of current research. *Language Teaching Research* 20 (4), 535–562.

Sakurai, S. (2014) Corrective feedback and student uptakes in English immersion classrooms in Japan: Is the counter-balance hypothesis valid? *TESL-EJ* 18 (1), 1–27.

Schwartz, B.D. (1993) On explicit and negative data effecting and affecting competence and linguistic behavior. *Studies in Second Language Acquisition* 15 (02), 147–163.

Swain, M. (1995) Three functions of output in second language learning. In G. Cook and B. Seidlhofer (eds) *Principle and Practice in Applied Linguistics: Studies in Honour of H.G. Widdowson* (pp. 125–144). Oxford: Oxford University Press.

Vygotsky, L.S. (1962) *Language and Thought*. Ontario: MIT Press.

Vygotsky, L.S. (1978) *Mind in Society: The Development of Higher Mental Process*. Cambridge, MA: Harvard University Press.

Yoshida, R. (2008) Teachers' choice and learners' preference of corrective feedback types. *Language Awareness* 17 (1), 78–93.

9 Translanguaging: A Documentation of How Emergent Bilinguals Use Translanguaging in Their Daily Communication

The Traditional View of Bilingualism

The traditional view of bilingualism has always treated languages as separate systems with different linguistic features. In accordance with this view, a 'true' or 'balanced' bilingual is defined as an individual who knows how to use two languages separately and never mixes the two (Valdés, 2003). García (2009a) referred to this traditional view as monoglossic ideologies of language use, which believes that languages are bounded and autonomous rather than flexible, dynamic and fluid. In the United States, monoglossic ideologies dominate the implementation of the majority of bilingual education programs. It is common to see such programs complying with language separation policies in daily teaching (Palmer et al., 2014). As Palmer et al. explained, due to the traditional view of bilingualism and the dominance of English in the United States, bilingual programs have been attempting to nurture minority languages by designating a specific space, time and teacher for communication only in the target language. Taking the DLI programs in Utah as an example, English and the target languages are kept separate by using only English or the target language for half a day. Language separation strategies are criticized as non-natural and not supportive of bilingual development (Lee et al., 2008; Reyes, 2001).

Hornberger and Link (2012) noted that although language separation ideologies had been practiced for a long time in bilingual programs, classroom research has shown that bilingual learners often resisted the ideologies in order to use languages more fluidly and robustly to accomplish their learning tasks. Indeed, it is the norm that bilinguals or multilinguals 'pragmatically draw on their entire linguistic repertoires to maximize understanding and performance across a variety of contexts, to shape experiences, and to make sense of the world' (Gort & Sembiante, 2015: 8). As researchers and educators realized the discrepancies between the traditional view and the authentic language practice of bilinguals, the concept of translanguaging emerged, which challenges the traditional conceptualization of bilingualism, and advocates the integration of one's available language resources in language learning.

Translanguaging

Translanguaging is a term originally used in Welsh by Cen Williams (1994) to refer to a teaching practice where his bilingual students were instructed to use one language to read and the other language to write to maximize their learning. The developing idea of translanguaging as a bilingual and multilingual phenomenon and teaching approach was popularized when Baker (2011) and García (2009a), along with other researchers, attempted to conceptualize and research the term in practice in different contexts. According to García and Kleyn (2016), translanguaging refers to 'the deployment of a speaker's full linguistic repertoire, which does not in any way correspond to the socially and politically defined boundaries of named languages' (2016: 14). Translanguaging should be seen as a natural bilingual languaging behavior that integrates 'diverse languaging and literacy practices in different social and semiotic contexts to maximize communicative potential' (Gort & Sembiante, 2015: 9). Wei (2011) stated that a translanguaging space where bilinguals utilize their different personal history and experience, practice their attitude, belief and ideology, and apply their cognitive and physical capacity, helps them generate new ideas, values, identities and practices. In applying the concept of translanguaging in the bilingual education context, teachers and students engage in dynamic and discursive communication when they draw on multiple languages or language varieties. Baker identified four potential advantages of translanguaging in education settings: (1) learners gain a better understanding of the subject matter; (2) learners are able to develop the weaker language; (3) it helps facilitate connections between school and home; and (4) it helps integrate learners at different language levels.

Despite the recent discussions and positive results found in translanguaging research, some argued that the use of translanguaging by emergent bilinguals, who are in the initial learning stages of becoming bilingual, may not be effective, as their language repertoire is not well developed (Lewis et al., 2012). However, García (2009b) explained that as emergent bilinguals develop their new language, translanguaging is utilized as a supportive context and communicative web to integrate the new language into their dynamic bilingual repertoire. In other words, 'new language practices can only emerge in interrelationships with old ones, without competing or threatening an already established sense of being that languaging constitutes' (García & Wei, 2014: 79). Hence, translanguaging is a natural and dynamic process which any bilingual individual on different points along the bilingual continuum takes to become a more capable bilingual user.

Drawing upon García's (2009a, 2009b) conceptualization of translanguaging of emergent bilinguals, this chapter documented whether and how, under the strict language separation policies of Utah DLI programs, the first-grade Chinese-English emergent bilinguals used translanguaging in their daily oral communication throughout the whole academic year.

Learners' Use of Translanguaging in DLI Programs

The current literature regarding learners' use of translanguaging in DLI programs has two foci. Some studies emphasized translanguaging as a pedagogical strategy, and researched the effectiveness of the strategies used by teachers (Alamillo *et al.*, 2017; Creese & Blackledge, 2010; Gort & Pontier, 2013; Gort & Sembiante, 2015; Palmer *et al.*, 2014). Others documented translanguaging as a natural phenomenon of the learners, with some of them observing translanguaging even when language separation policies were imposed in the programs. This chapter has a focus on the latter; therefore, a brief review of the current studies regarding the natural occasions of translanguaging by emergent bilinguals in DLI programs is discussed.

García *et al.* (2011) investigated the use of translanguaging of five- and six-year-old emergent bilinguals, who entered a two-way Spanish bilingual program speaking predominantly in only English or Spanish. They found that even with the implementation of language separation policies (e.g. separate rooms for separate languages and language teachers), the learners used translanguaging for six different meta-functions to help develop their bilingualism. They include (1) to mediate understanding among peers; (2) to co-construct meaning; (3) to self-construct meaning; (4) to include others; (5) to exclude others; and (6) to demonstrate knowledge. García *et al.* gave a good example of how learners' use of translanguaging to co-construct meaning led to language learning. In the classroom, a boy looked out the window and said to his peers in Spanish that it was raining. Later he realized that some of his peers were English-speaking, therefore tried to convey his meaning by saying that it was washing. A girl understood him and told him the correct word, 'raining', which the boy then repeated to himself. This example shows that translanguaging enabled the peers to communicate and learn the target language without the involvement of the teacher.

Esquinca *et al.* (2014) conducted a three-year ethnographic study in a fourth-grade Spanish two-way DLI program in Texas. Similar to the findings reported by García *et al.* (2011), the researchers documented frequent use of translanguaging in the classrooms, despite language separation policies imposed at the district level. The students were often observed using their full range of language repertoire to learn science content regardless of which language (Spanish or English) the teacher used to deliver instruction. The specific translanguaging practices used in the classrooms were translating, multimodality, paraphrasing and code switching, which were enacted in every class meeting. The researchers therefore pointed out that translanguaging was the tool to mediate understanding of the science content and to develop academic discourse.

The phenomenon of translanguaging is observed not only with school age emergent bilinguals as described in the aforementioned studies, but was also reported in an infant Spanish DLI classroom in California by Garrity *et al.* (2015). Infants as young as six to 11 months old, who were not bound by language rules and not yet socialized to practice monoglossic ideologies, were reported to use multiple languages (Spanish, English and baby sign language) to construct meaning of their environment, to connect with others and to learn about the multilingual world.

Based on the results of the current studies, translanguaging is not only a natural practice of emergent bilinguals as young as infants in DLI programs, it is also an essential tool used to help learners socialize and learn. Hence, the implication of the studies rejects the idea of dual or parallel monolingualism (Fitts, 2006; Heller, 1999), which produces learners who 'function similarly to monolingual speakers of two distinct languages' (Palmer *et al.*, 2014: 758). However, translanguaging research is still in its infancy, considering that the concept was popularized only approximately ten years ago and that translanguaging research is still limited. For example, most of the current translanguaging research in DLI has a focus on two-way Spanish programs. Chinese one-way programs in the Utah context, where the majority of the learners are English-only speakers, were left uninvestigated. Therefore, this chapter (Chapter 9) contributes to the current literature by researching a language and program type rarely studied.

The Study Context

Similar to the majority of DLI programs in the United States, Utah DLI programs set rules to separate the use of English and the target language. In addition to separating the use of two languages by keeping the learning of the languages in different classrooms, during a specific period of instructional time, and a specific instructor, in the *DLI Program Fidelity Assurances Grades 1–6* (Utah Dual Language Immersion, 2018) document given to DLI teachers, the target language teachers were instructed to 'communicate in the target language in the classroom at all times and in front of his/her students in all school environments' (2018: 1). This means that the target language DLI teachers need to avoid speaking English to the students or to an English-speaking individual (e.g. non-Chinese DLI students, English partner teachers or non-Chinese speaking parents) in front of the students in order to avoid revealing their English-speaking ability to their students. In other words, the target language teachers were expected to act as monolinguals. The same rule was listed again, accompanied with a Chinese translation of the rule in a different handout given to teachers titled, *Utah DLI Classroom-Level Non-Negotiables*.

As for students, the DLI programs suggested that first-graders use the first semester to adjust to the target language environment. After January 15th in their first academic year in the programs, the students needed to strictly follow the language separation policies stated in the *DLI Program Fidelity Assurances Grades 1–6* document, which said, 'There are clear, enforced, and reinforced expectations that students communicate in the target language in the classroom' (2018: 2). The Chinese DLI teachers would receive an email reminder regarding the time they needed to start practicing the language separation rules when the spring semester started.

The student participants in this study were from both classes in cohort two. The teacher participant was the second author of this book (for more details, see the focal teacher and student participants in Chapter 1).

Data Collection and Analysis

Since the language policies were loosely practiced in the first semester and then were strictly reinforced in the second semester in the first-grade classrooms, it was deemed important to try to capture the translanguaging phenomenon at different points in time: (1) two weeks in October when the policies were loose; (2) two weeks in January when the students were transitioning to Chinese-only in the classrooms; and (3) two weeks in March when the students were used to the Chinese-only policy.

The teacher carried an audio-recorder in her pocket daily to capture her interactions with her students and student–student interactions she observed. Specifically, she left the recorder on during early morning study sessions, regular instructional hours, lunch break and recess time. In this way, translanguaging in both formal and informal settings was captured. Pseudonyms are used to protect the identities of the students in the excerpts in this chapter. In addition, the teacher wrote down daily reflection notes to document the context in which translanguaging occurred. The reflection entries included the following information: time, date, the physical environment, participants involved in the interaction and the topic of interaction. Both the audio-recordings and the reflection notes were analyzed for translanguaging themes that emerged during the three study periods. In order to build a dependable analysis, we listened to the recordings and individually open-coded the episodes of translanguaging initiated by the students. After that, we compared the coded data for consistencies and contradictions, which resulted in collaboratively coming up with new categories or modifying the current coding themes to better reflect the function and meaning of the translanguaging episodes. Through synthesizing the data from different data sources and analyzing it both separately and jointly, a trustworthy study is more likely to be assured. Finally, the incidences of the different translanguaging themes found were tallied and reported as results.

Translanguaging in the First Period

An analysis of the two-week data in the first period illustrates that the students' translanguaging practice can be categorized into 14 different themes, with seven of them (items 8–14 in Table 9.1) observed only once, a few (items 5–7) a handful of times, while four of them (items 1–4) were practiced much more frequently.

To offer information or opinion

As the students had been learning Chinese in the program for about two months, they gained some basic vocabulary for daily communication. With the use of Chinese-English translanguaging, they were able to offer information or opinions to their teacher and peers. The following example shows two students complimenting the teacher's hair using translanguaging.

Table 9.1 Translanguaging in the first period

Translanguaging Themes	# of Incidences
1. To offer information or opinion	84
2. To learn the target language	81
3. To be a translator	55
For other students in class (46 incidences)	
To show their Chinese knowledge (8 incidences)	
For non-DLI students (1 incidence)	
4. To confirm with the teacher what she said in Chinese	33
5. To offer or ask for help	11
6. To answer questions	6
7. To ask for the teacher's permission	5
8. To self-correct	1
9. To ask a question	1
10. To explain a math problem	1
11. To express lack of understanding	1
12. To give invitation	1
13. To give warning	1
14. To express needs	1
Total	282

Excerpt 1

Brielle: I love your 頭髮。
                        [hair.]
Cindy: 你的頭髮 is nice。
                [Your hair]
Teacher: 谢谢。
                [Thank you.]

Although the sentence structure and vocabulary used in the compliments were short and simple, the students successfully conveyed their meaning to their teacher.

To learn the target language

It was often observed that after the teacher told the students how to say a certain phrase in Chinese, the students would voluntarily switch their language from English to Chinese by repeating what the teacher taught them to say. Excerpt 2 is an example of such incidences.

Excerpt 2

Matt: Can I go to the bathroom?
Teacher: 我可以上廁所嗎?
                [Can I go to the bathroom?]
Matt: 我可以上廁所嗎?
                [Can I go to the bathroom?]

The switch from English to the target language by repeating the target sentence that the teacher wanted the student to know is considered an effective cognitive learning strategy. Speaking practice, such as imitating a native speaker, is essential in language learning (Oxford, 1990).

To be a translator for other students in class

Since the first day the first-graders entered the DLI program, the Chinese teacher could speak only Chinese to them. The analysis of the recording and reflection data shows a trend of peer-assistance using translanguaging when some of the students were not sure what the teacher tried to communicate with them. Excerpt 3 took place when some of the students did not pay attention to the teacher's instruction.

Excerpt 3

Teacher: 很多人玩他們的頭髮、玩他們的鞋子。
                [Many people are playing with their hair or shoes.]
                不可以玩你的頭髮, 不可以玩你的鞋子。
                [Don't play with your hair, don't play with your shoes.]

Luke: Don't play with your 頭髮。Don't play with your 鞋子。
                       [hair]   [shoes]

The student translator, Luke, translated parts of the utterance from Chinese into English and left two words, hair and shoes, in Chinese. The translanguaging decision was probably due to his judgement that all students were familiar with the vocabulary, hair and shoes, as those were the target vocabulary recently learned in class, but were less familiar with the sentence structure, 'Don't play with _____'. In this two-week period, being a translator for peers to facilitate the understanding of class instructions was the most frequent use of the translator category (46 out of 55 incidences). The rest of the translation purposes were either to show that they understood their Chinese teacher by translating what she said into English (8 incidences), or to translate their conversation in Chinese with their teacher to English to a non-DLI friend (1 incidence).

To confirm with the teacher what she said in Chinese

As Chinese was a brand-new language for the students, it was observed that in the study period, the students often felt the need to confirm with the teacher what she said in Chinese. The conversation in Excerpt 4 occurred after the teacher taught the students to write the character, 下 [down].

Excerpt 4

Teacher: 圈起來'一'。
           [Circle 'Yi' (a radical in the character)]
Amy: Wait, is it 圈起來全部?
                       [Circle the whole thing?]

In addition to the frequently observed translanguaging practice described above, translanguaging was used sparsely, but with diverse functions such as to offer or ask for help, ask or answer questions, ask for the teacher's permission, self-correct, explain a math problem, express lack of understanding, give an invitation, give a warning and express needs.

Translanguaging in the Second Period

The two-week data in the second period of study shows the translanguaging practice in mid-January, during the time when the Chinese-only policy was recently made stricter. Table 9.2 illustrates that the translanguaging incidences decreased compared to the first period (282 in the first period vs. 219 in the second period); nevertheless, the frequency rankings of the translanguaging themes mostly remained the same, with offering information or opinion being the most frequently occurring theme, followed by learning the target language and being a translator.

Table 9.2 Translanguaging in the second period

Translanguaging Themes	# of Incidences
1. To offer information or opinion	68
2. To learn the target language	44
3. To be a translator	33
For other students in class (31 incidences)	
To show their Chinese knowledge (2 incidences)	
4. To answer a question	22
5. To confirm with the teacher what she said in Chinese	19
6. To ask a question	13
7. To offer or ask for help	11
8. To express lack of understanding	4
9. To explain a math problem	1
10. To address a problem	1
11. To correct a peer	1
12. To provide the correct answer	1
Total	219

The main difference observed between the first and second periods is that the students asked and answered many more questions using translanguaging in the second period. The questions were asked by the students to the teacher, which usually were related to the content of or the behavioral policies in the class. Excerpt 5 is an example of a student using translanguaging to ask a question regarding the content the teacher just taught to them.

To ask a question

In Excerpt 5, the teacher was teaching numbers in Chinese and used numbers to indicate age.

Excerpt 5

Teacher: 蔡老師一百歲。
            [Miss Tsai is a hundred years old.]
Lucy: Are you really 一百?
                        [a hundred]

In Excerpt 5, Lucy was surprised that the teacher said that she was a hundred years old; hence, she used translanguaging to ask if the statement was true. The use of English grammar structure with a new Chinese vocabulary word effectively conveyed her meaning to the teacher.

To answer a question

In the second period, the students also answered many questions, the majority of which were questions other students had about the class. Excerpt 6 shows Ryan answering Travis' question that the teacher was not able to answer due to the Chinese-only policy.

Excerpt 6

Travis:	Is this 功課? (looking at the teacher)
	[homework]
Teacher:	哼? (Acting as if she didn't understand the question because the student was not supposed to use English in class)
	[Huh?]
Ryan:	It is 功課 (Ryan whispered to Travis)
	[homework]

As it was time to strictly enforce the Chinese-only policy during the second period, the teacher sometimes acted as if she did not understand the students when they spoke in English or used translanguaging. The lack of response from the teacher triggered their peers to help answer questions.

Translanguaging in the Third Period

In the third period, the translanguaging incidences had decreased significantly compared to the first or the second period, with only 87 incidents found in a two-week period (see Table 9.3).

Although the overall number of incidences was diminished, the top two translanguaging themes, to learn the target language and to offer information or opinion, were identical to the last two periods. A close analysis of the incidences under the two themes illustrates that the students used translanguaging the same way to learn the target language; however, translanguaging used to offer information or opinion was different.

To offer information or opinion

In the first and second periods, the students mostly used English sentence structures with some Chinese vocabulary to convey their meanings, but in the third period, they used more Chinese structures filled with one or two English vocabulary. Excerpt 7 shows such an incidence.

Excerpt 7

Teacher:	給蔡老師功課。現在趕快給我。
	[Turn in homework to Teacher Tsai. Turn it in to me now, hurry.]
Eric:	我沒有 do 我的功課。
	[I did not] [my homework]

Table 9.3 Translanguaging in the third period

Translanguaging Themes	# of Incidences
1. To learn the target language	25
2. To offer information or opinion	18
3. To accommodate interlocutors and space	8
4. To ask a question	8
5. To answer a question	7
6. To be a translator	6
For other students in class (2 incidences)	
For other students when they were outside the classroom (3 incidences)	
For a non-Chinese speaking peer at school (1 incidence)	
7. To address a problem	4
8. To offer explanation	3
9. To express one's understanding	1
10. To give warning	1
11. To describe a situation	1
12. To describe a plan	1
13. To argue with a peer	1
14. To make a complaint	1
15. To introduce a family member	1
16. To report an incident	1
Total	87

> **Teacher:**   喔，不可以說英文。　'我沒有寫我的功課'
> [Oh, don't speak English. 'I did not write my homework.']

Even though Eric's communication was effective to the teacher, due to the Chinese-only language policy, there was zero tolerance of using translanguaging in the third period, as the teacher's response was focused on making the student aware of his violation and not related to the content of the original conversation about homework. Indeed, in the third period, the teacher made it very clear that English was not allowed in the Chinese classroom. In a few incidences in which the students tried to use translanguaging in the classrooms, the teacher immediately requested the students to use Chinese only. Excerpt 8 shows an example.

Excerpt 8

> **Brady:**   Can I read 毛毛蟲書?
> 　　　　　　　[the book about worms]
> **Teacher:**   什麼? 你可不可以說中文？
> 　　　　　　　[Excuse me? Can you speak in Chinese?]

Brady: 我可以看毛毛蟲書跟你嗎?
[Can I read the book about worms with you?]

Initially, Brady used translanguaging to ask the teacher if she could read a certain book, which was not acceptable in the classroom; therefore, the teacher requested the student to ask in Chinese.

To accommodate interlocutors and space

During the third period, most of the students were familiar with the teacher's expectation and knew to switch languages between spaces and among different interlocutors. In Excerpt 9, April initially was chatting with a non-Chinese speaking friend in the hallway in English, but as soon as she stepped into the Chinese classroom, she started speaking Chinese.

Excerpt 9

(After lunch, April wanted to show marbles to her friend in the hallway.)

April: They're very special. Let me show you.
(April stepped into the classroom and ran into her teacher.)

April: 可以有這個(行為表)在我的家?
[Can I take this (behavioral chart) home?]
Teacher: 可以。
[Yes.]

Other than the aforementioned translanguaging themes, just as in the second period, the students occasionally practiced translanguaging to ask or answer questions, and to be a translator in the third period. However, these incidences mostly occurred outside the Chinese classroom and the frequencies were much lower. In addition, it seems that even though the students used translanguaging more sparsely in compliance with the language policy, it was observed that they used it more broadly for different purposes outside the classroom. The data analysis illustrated that the students used translanguaging to address a problem, to offer explanation, to express one's understanding, to give warning, to describe a situation or a plan, to argue with a peer, to make a complaint, to introduce a family member and to report an incident.

The Heritage Learner's Translanguaging Practice

The only heritage learner of cohort two, Laura, had a much higher Chinese language level compared to others and was observed to use translanguaging in different ways; hence, her data was analyzed separately from others. During the first period, the students were new to

Table 9.4 Laura's translanguaging practice

First Period	#	Second Period	#	Third Period	#
1. To communicate with peers in class	8	1. To translate for peers requested by the teacher	4	2. Requested by the teacher to switch to English	2
2. To communicate with her Chinese teacher	5			3. To translate for peers	2
3. To translate for peers	3				

speaking Chinese, hence, Laura often used translanguaging to communicate between her peers and her teacher (see Table 9.4 above). To be specific, she might start a conversation with the teacher in Chinese and switch to English when a peer started another conversation with her or vice versa. Excerpt 10 shows such example.

To communicate with peers and her Chinese teacher

Excerpt 10

(During lunch time...)

Teacher:　你喜歡中國食物還是美國食物?
　　　　　[Do you like Chinese or American food?]
Laura:　　美國食物。我從小就是在美國出生,小時候有回去中國一下,從小到大就是在美國。
　　　　　[American food. I was born in the United States. I went to visit China for a short while, but I have lived in the United States since I was born.]
Sydnee:　This is yummy.
Laura:　　This is pretty cold.
Teacher:　什麼?
　　　　　[Excuse me?]
Laura:　　這麵包有一點冷。
　　　　　[The bread is kind of cold.]

Excerpt 10 demonstrates how easily Laura was able to switch between Chinese and English to accommodate her interlocutors.

To translate for peers requested by the teacher

In addition to using translanguaging when she talked to both her teacher and her peers, Laura also used translanguaging to translate for her peers, which was usually requested by her teacher. Excerpt 11 illustrates the translation requested.

Excerpt 11

Teacher:	來, Laura。 我跟他說話，你幫我跟他說英文。
	[Come, Laura. I am going to talk to him and you need to help me speak with him in English.]
Teacher:	Bob, 你下課沒有聽我吹哨子。你還在外面玩。
	[You didn't listen to my whistle. You were still playing outside.]
Laura:	You did not listen to the teacher's whistle and you still stay outside.
Teacher:	蔡老師很遺憾你的臉受傷了。
	[I am sorry that your face got hurt.]
Laura:	The teacher is sorry that you got hurt.
Teacher:	以後妳沒有聽蔡老師吹、沒有排隊,那你就要去辦公室坐下。
	[In the future if you ignore my whistle and do not get in line, you will need to sit in the office.]
Laura:	If you won't listen to Ms. Tsai blowing the whistle, then you have to sit in the office.
Bob:	(nodding his head)

This example shows that the teacher had difficulty giving detailed behavioral directions to the student as the teacher was not permitted to show her English ability, even when she needed to deal with class management or behavioral issues and needed Laura to be the mediator. The example also demonstrates Laura's advanced Chinese proficiency level. Laura's translanguaging theme of translating for peers requested by the teacher helped the teacher comply with the language separation rules and at the same time made effective communication between the teacher and the non-heritage students possible. The translating requests from her teacher to Laura continued in the second and the third periods.

Requested by the teacher to switch to English

In the third period, the teacher was observed on two occasions outside the classroom (e.g. lunch or recess time) asking Laura to switch to English when she could not express herself in Chinese. This was due to the teacher feeling that Laura obeying the Chinese-only policy had made her a passive learner when it came to expanding her vocabulary in Chinese. The recording data shows that when Laura did not know how to say a word in Chinese, she would either be silent, say something else in Chinese, which did not convey the original meaning she wanted to express, or tell the teacher that she did not know how to say it in Chinese. Excerpt 12 is an illustration of such incidents.

Excerpt 12

(Laura is chatting with her friend.)

Laura: There is a ghost!
Teacher: 你剛剛說什麼?
          [What did you just say?]
Laura: 那裏關起來了。
          [It is closed there.]
Teacher: 你剛剛說那裏有什麼?
          [You said there was what?]
Laura: 我不知道中文怎麼說。
          [I am not sure how to say it in Chinese.]

Laura did not know how to say 'ghost' in Chinese, and in order to comply with the language policy, Laura was discouraged from using translanguaging to ask the teacher how to say the word in Chinese. Rather, she substituted the original sentence with something completely different to respond to her teacher. In fact, the strict language policy discouraged not only the heritage learner from mixing languages for effective communication, but also transmitted the negative message to all of the students that the use of any English, including translanguaging in the Chinese classroom to facilitate communication, was not a good thing to do. In Excerpt 13, a student was caught using English and was reported by his peer and questioned by the teacher.

Excerpt 13

Carson: 蔡老師, Matt說英文。
          [Ms. Tsai, Matt spoke in English.]
Teacher: Matt, 為什麼說英文?
          [Why did you speak in English?]
Matt: 對不起...沒有很多很多很多。
          [Sorry...I didn't say much.]
(Matt stepped into the hallway to explain in English why he spoke in English.)

Matt: I accidentally spoke an English word.
Teacher: 以後不可以, 好嗎?
          [Do not do it again, OK?]

Discussion

This chapter investigated the translanguaging practices of first-grade Chinese DLI learners at three different times during the academic year. In the first period, the study results revealed how the emergent bilinguals used the little amount of new Chinese language knowledge just gained to practice translanguaging for different purposes. For example, they frequently used English structures with Chinese words to express themselves, switched from English to Chinese to repeat what the teacher tried to teach them to say, and mixed English with Chinese to translate the teacher's instructions for other students and confirm whether they understood the teacher's instructions correctly. These findings are very similar to the findings in García *et al.* (2011), in which students used translanguaging to co-construct meaning and demonstrate knowledge. The findings are also similar to the ones in Esquinca *et al.*'s (2014) study in terms of the specific translanguaging practices used such as translating, paraphrasing and code-switching.

With regard to the heritage learner, Laura's translanguaging, it was observed that she could readily switch between languages since the first period to accommodate different interlocutors. Due to her advanced language level, she was always picked as the translating helper by the teacher to translate detailed teacher directions for other students.

The number of translanguaging practices significantly diminished in the second and especially in the third period with only 87 incidences in a two-week period. The diminishing number showed how the translanguaging space was suppressed because of the strict implementation of the Utah DLI programs' language policies. For instance, a close look at the conversations that occurred in the second and third periods revealed that the teacher pretended not to understand translanguaging, or translanguaging was corrected with reinforcement of the Chinese-only policy, regardless of whether communication through translanguaging was effective. As a result of such emphasis on language separation, negative effects were found. The students felt the need to inform their teacher of policy infractions by their peers (see Excerpt 13), and the students who practiced translanguaging felt the need to be apologetic to their teacher. Moreover, the heritage learner, Laura, strategically avoided translanguaging to comply with the language policy; however, she lost opportunities to ask and gain new language knowledge from the teacher. By not using translanguaging, and only saying what she already knew in Chinese, she became a less active learner, who could only use part of her language repertoire to explore and learn.

As García and Kleyn (2016) stated, 'Once educators start looking at language from the point of view of the bilingual learner and not simply at the named language with its prescribed features, everything changes' (2016: 17). While monoglossic ideologies still dominate in bilingual programs in the United States, the study results of this chapter illustrate how the practice of these ideologies limits students' learning. Hence, this chapter urges program leaders to re-evaluate the level of effectiveness of monoglossic-based bilingual programs, and consider creating a translanguaging space, where students can bring their own experiences, values, beliefs, learning styles and full linguistic repertoire into the classrooms, and freely utilize them to co-create knowledge.

References

Alamillo, L., Yun, C. and Bennett, L.H. (2017) Translanguaging in a Reggio-inspired Spanish dual-language immersion programme. *Early Child Development and Care* 187 (3–4), 469–486.

Baker, C. (2011) *Foundations of Bilingual Education and Bilingualism* (5th edn). Bristol: Multilingual Matters.

Creese, A. and Blackledge, A. (2010) Translanguaging in the bilingual classroom: A pedagogy for learning and teaching? *The Modern Language Journal* 94 (1), 103–115.

Esquinca, A., Araujo, B. and de la Piedra, M.T. (2014) Meaning making and translanguaging in a two-way dual-language program on the US-Mexico border. *Bilingual Research Journal* 37 (2), 164–181.

Fitts, S. (2006) Reconstructing the status quo: Linguistic interaction in a dual-language school. *Bilingual Research Journal* 30 (2), 337–365.

García, O. (2009a) *Bilingual Education in the 21st Century: Global Perspectives*. Malden, MA: Blackwell.

García, O. (2009b) Reimagining bilingualism in education for the 21st century. Paper presented at the NALDIC Conference 17, University of Reading, 14 November.

García, O. and Kleyn, T. (2016) Translanguaging theory in education. In O. García and T. Kleyn (eds) *Translanguaging with Multilingual Students: Learning from Classroom Moments* (pp. 9–33). New York, NY: Routledge.

García, O., Makar, C., Starcevic, M. and Terry, A. (2011) Translanguaging of Latino kindergarteners. In K. Potowski and J. Rothman (eds) *Bilingual Youth: Spanish in English Speaking Societies* (pp. 33–55). Philadelphia, PA: John Benjamins.

García, O. and Wei, L. (2014) Translanguaging and education. In O. García and L. Wei (eds) *Translanguaging: Language, Bilingualism and Education* (pp. 63–77). New York, NY: Palgrave Macmillan

Garrity, S., Aquino-Sterling, C.R. and Day, A. (2015) Translanguaging in an infant classroom: Using multiple languages to make meaning. *International Multilingual Research Journal* 9 (3), 177–196.

Gort, M. and Pontier, R.W. (2013) Exploring bilingual pedagogies in dual language preschool classrooms. *Language and Education* 27 (3), 223–245.

Gort, M. and Sembiante, S.F. (2015) Navigating hybridized language learning spaces through translanguaging pedagogy: Dual language preschool teachers' languaging practices in support of emergent bilingual children's performance of academic discourse. *International Multilingual Research Journal* 9 (1), 7–25.

Heller, M. (1999) *Linguistic Minorities and Modernity: A Sociolinguistic Ethnography*. New York, NY: Longman.

Hornberger, N.H. and Link, H. (2012) Translanguaging and transnational literacies in multilingual classrooms: A biliteracy lens. *International Journal of Bilingual Education and Bilingualism* 15 (3), 261–278.

Lee, J.S., Hill-Bonnet, L. and Gillespie, J. (2008) Learning in two languages: Interactional spaces for becoming bilingual speakers. *International Journal of Bilingual Education and Bilingualism* 1 (1), 75–94.

Lewis, G., Jones, B. and Baker, C. (2012) Translanguaging: Developing its conceptualisation and contextualisation. *Educational Research and Evaluation* 18 (7), 655–670.

Oxford, R. L. (1990) *Language Learning Strategies*. New York, NY: Newbury House.

Palmer, D.K., Martínez, R.A., Mateus, S.G. and Henderson, K. (2014) Reframing the debate on language separation: Toward a vision for translanguaging pedagogies in the dual language classroom. *The Modern Language Journal* 98 (3), 757–772.

Reyes, M.D.L.L. (2001) Unleashing possibilities: Biliteracy in the primary grades. In J.J. Halcón and M.D.L.L. Reyes (eds) *The Best for Our Children: Critical Perspectives on Literacy for Latino Students* (pp. 96–121). New York, NY: Teachers College Press.

Utah Dual Language Immersion (2018) DLI Program Fidelity Assurances Grades 1–6. See http://eastlake.jordandistrict.org/files/2013/10/Utah-DLI-Assurances-Grades-1-6.pdf (accessed 27 April 2018).

Valdés, G. (2003) *Expanding Definitions of Giftedness: The Case of Young Interpreters from Immigrant Communities*. Mahwah, NJ: Laurence Erlbaum Associates Publishers.

Wei, L. (2011) Moment analysis and translanguaging space: Discursive construction of identities by multilingual Chinese youth in Britain. *Journal of Pragmatics* 43 (5), 1222–1235.

Williams, C. (1994) *Arfarniad o ddulliau dysgu ac addysgu yng nghyd-destun addysg uwchradd ddwyieithog* [An evaluation of teaching and learning methods in the context of bilingual secondary education] (Doctoral dissertation, University of Wales, Bangor, UK).

10 Conclusion

The research studies in the Utah Chinese DLI context in this volume make a timely contribution to research and practice in bilingual education in the United States. It offers greater understanding of all (e.g. students, parents, teachers and administrators) involved in the Utah Chinese DLI education process and helps fill the lack of research in DLI studies other than Spanish. The purpose of this final chapter is to synthesize the findings in the previous chapters to view them holistically through the utilization of two overarching theoretical frameworks: an ecology metaphor and the sociocultural perspective.

An Ecology Metaphor for Educational Policy Analysis

The rapid boom of the Utah DLI programs would not have been possible without Utah Senate Bill 41; hence, it is appropriate to view the results found in the Utah DLI phenomenon through an educational policy analysis. This chapter used an ecology metaphor to conceptualize the foundation and growth of the DLI programs. An ecology metaphor is 'an appeal to researchers to theorize and account for the many interconnections that create, sustain, hold off, or destroy policy formation and implementation' (Weaver-Hightower, 2008: 154). Drawing upon the concept of an ecology metaphor, the Chinese DLI programs can be analyzed through four main ecology elements: *environments and structures*, *actors*, *relationships* and *processes*.

Environments and structures

The *extant conditions* (e.g. economy, society, culture and foreign relations) in the environment and the social and institutional structures are the base of an ecology. Within the Chinese DLI context, globalization and the rising economic power of China both contribute to the framing of the Chinese DLI ecology. According to the article, *Dual Language Immersion: Origin Story* on The Senate Site (2018), the creation of the Utah DLI programs was inspired by Senator Stephenson's trip to China in 2000. While in China, Senator Stephenson was impressed with the Chinese students' superior English skills and inquisitive nature on meaningful topics. In order to prepare globally competitive citizens like the ones seen in China, Utah Senate Bill 41, which funds dual language programs in languages identified as critical for the economic future and security of the US, was passed in 2008. While Utah is eager to ensure that DLI education equips their students with sufficient skills and knowledge for the global market, China also has its own agendas, which are to expand its international influence and create its positive image through language and culture teaching (Cheng, 2015). Three Confucius Institutes have been set up in Utah, providing Chinese DLI teachers with regular training and Chinese DLI students with numerous Chinese language and culture learning opportunities throughout the year. In addition, the Confucius Institute Headquarters, Hanban, sends many Chinese-speaking teachers each year to serve in the Utah Chinese DLI programs. In sum, the Chinese DLI ecology emerged and operated under the conditions of the increasing interdependence of world economies and the growing global influence of China.

Actors

Actors are individual or group agents with varying power and positions within an ecology. Determining the agents who are powerful actors is often an essential task, as they are the ones who assist the process to work (Weaver-Hightower, 2008). The most influential *actors* in the Chinese DLI context are the state lawmakers, who made funding possible for the programs, and the educational administrators and researchers at the state level who created rules and policies for the programs. The 'origin story' told by The Senate Site (2018) – the Utah DLI one-way design to benefit the majority in the ecology, the English-native speakers, and the state's decision to collaborate with Hanban – all reflect the powerful *actors*' ideologies and decision-making, influenced by the extant conditions of global competitiveness. In fact, even large numbers of the other *actors* (13 of the 25 teachers and 11 of the 20 parents interviewed in Chapters 2 and 3) within the Chinese DLI context identify future work opportunities as the top benefit of Chinese DLI programs. This finding could be attributed not only to the *extant conditions*, but also how the powerful *actors* set up and promote the programs. The fact that the state created mostly one-way programs for English speakers learning a second language and also made promotional materials whose main discourse targets only the benefits of English-speaking students learning a second language divert attention away from the needs of Utah's minority language communities (Valdez *et al.*, 2016), the less powerful *actors* in the DLI ecology. This is evident when we found that the few parents with Chinese heritage background who participated in our studies were the only ones who voiced the need to preserve the minority language and culture.

Relationships

The *actors* in an ecology do not merely share space, but form complex relationships. All of the Chinese DLI students, parents, teachers, administrators and Hanban are in a relationship of *cooperation* as all of them work toward the common goal of the students becoming superior bilingual and bicultural individuals when they exit the programs. Nevertheless, the *actors* identified many hurdles that need to be overcome. These challenges came down to the needs for others in the ecology to be more supportive and to have better communication. For example, the teachers asked the administrators to provide more resources, lessen the frequency of curriculum changes, and reconsider the large class size in DLI programs and the effectiveness of the Chinese-only policy set by the state. The teachers also expressed the need for the parents to be more supportive of their children's learning at home and for better communication between Chinese and English teachers. From the position of both the school and the state administrators, better communication and supportiveness were also the two key terms in their relationship of *cooperation*. All administrators recognized the cultural barriers between Chinese teachers and English teachers and administrators, and asked all to have more understanding and tolerance toward each other. Finally, DLI parents also asked for more support from the teachers and the administrators. They needed more supplementary reading materials, after-school programs, and to know ways to support their children's study at home and learn about their children's learning progress. The study in Chapter 5 regarding how to create an effective and supportive DLI class can serve as a guide for successful teacher–teacher and parent–teacher relationships of *cooperation* in the Chinese DLI ecology. For instance, Chapter 5 identified that communication through multiple channels, using support tools, learning each other's cultures and fairly sharing responsibility were all principles of a good relationship of *cooperation* in DLI.

In addition to the relationship of *cooperation* within the Chinese DLI ecology, the Chinese DLI parents and students had a relationship of *competition* with the non-DLI parents and students within the school ecology. Some of the non-DLI students had hostile feelings toward the Chinese DLI students when they learned that certain programs or activities were designed only for the DLI students. Moreover, some of the Chinese DLI parents showed an attitude of superiority, which made the non-DLI parents uncomfortable.

This relationship of *competition* leads to one of the school administrator interviewees' discussion regarding how the current lottery system used to help decide the DLI enrollment created bitter feelings from the parents who desired to have their children in the DLI programs, but could not. The administrator mentioned a key point that public schools should not exclude children. Indeed, to view Utah DLI programs on a larger scale, based on the statistics provided in Chapter 1, most of the Chinese DLI programs (eight out of 12 school districts) were located in above average income areas, serving mostly white middle-class English-speaking students. In many areas where minority and ELL student population were dense, DLI was not an option. Viewing it from the policy ecology lens, this is described as a relationship of *predation*, in which certain *actors* eliminate the others for the benefit of a particular group. In the case of the Utah DLI programs, the legislators provide funding for a DLI program type suitable for English-speakers learning a second language, and the state implements most of the programs in wealthy areas, where only a few minorities and ELLs benefit from the programs.

Processes

An ecology goes through different *processes* depending on the influences and pressures received. The Chinese DLI ecology was in the process of *emergence* when some of the *actors* went through the process of *anticipation* of future needs. In this case, the state legislators foresaw the global competitiveness and responded with the funding of DLI programs. Although the Chinese DLI ecology has issues to overcome, it has been a functional ecology, where all actors tried to work closely together to achieve the common goal. However, the findings in this volume also illustrated how the particular group of *actors*, namely, the heritage speakers and ELLs, were ignored by the powerful *actors* in the processes of the ecology. With all of the findings in this book and the other studies in mind, we call out to the powerful *actors* of the state in the DLI ecology to re-evaluate the set-up of the programs, and consider initiating a process of *conversion* to change the basic structures and dynamics in the ecology. It is recommended that the state should make efforts to set up DLI programs where language majority and minority students learn from each other and should actively advertise that the Utah DLI programs not only have the benefits of becoming fluent in a second language and competitive in the future global market, but also help preserve minority languages and cultures.

The Sociocultural Perspective

This section views the findings in this volume through the sociocultural perspective grounded in Vygotsky's (1978) theory, which treats language learning as a sociocultural process. Two important notions in the theory, mediation and zone of proximal development, are discussed below.

Mediation

Mediation stems from the concept that one's consciousness is associated with the use of cultural, social, historical and linguistic tools or signs that have been passed on from generation to generation (Yoon & Kim, 2012), and that mediation is only possible through interaction with experts who are knowledgeable about the tools and signs. When novice members participate in joint activities with more knowledgeable members, they actively appropriate tools and signs and construct their meaning. This sociocultural process to form one's consciousness including identity is evident in Chapter 4 regarding the DLI Chinese teachers' identities. All four teacher participants in the study identified several events and incidences since childhood which helped form their current teacher identities. For example, as a young child, Tony looked up to his grandmother and Linda admired her elementary teachers and they saw them as teacher role models. The same study also found that the teachers' culture played an important role in mediating their teacher identities. This is evident when the teachers of Chinese origin used quotes from Confucius to help elaborate their teaching beliefs. While some of the teacher participants were already experts in teaching prior to working in the DLI context, they found themselves becoming novice members again when the teaching setting changed. For example, the teachers of Chinese origin noticed a difference between US and Chinese students' learning styles, and tried to modify their ways of teaching. In addition, they were seen by the parents as English language novices, and were the less preferred persons to whom the parents reached out to address student issues. These examples demonstrate that as teachers moved to a new sociocultural context, it is likely that they need to go through a new process of sociocultural formation to fit into the new setting, regardless of their expertise in a different setting. This means that in the case of the DLI context, educational administrators need to bear this issue in mind and provide any necessary assistance to help newly arrived teachers to be acculturated into the DLI programs.

Mediation occurs through tools and signs. The classroom studies in Chapters 6 to 9 have many good examples on how the teacher used tools and signs to mediate and support the learners' language learning. In Chapter 6, the teaching strategies used and the learning strategies directed for student use by the teacher not only helped the learners build on their language level, but also advanced their use of learning strategies. In Chapter 7, the chunking method experimented in the study was identified as a good tool for learning Chinese characters. In Chapter 8, the teacher's use of different types of corrective feedback helped cultivate the learners' oral language ability. In Chapter 9, we observed the naturally occurring language phenomenon of translanguaging and how it mediated the learning of the emergent bilinguals in the DLI setting.

All of the tools and signs were used by the teacher and the students through the concept of scaffolding. The next section details the concept and how it applies to the current studies.

Zone of proximal development (ZPD)

ZPD involves the concept of scaffolding, which refers to a learning scenario where a teacher or a more knowledgeable peer provides necessary support and guides while a student learns. In Vygotsky's (1978) original quote, ZPD 'is the distance between the actual developmental level as determined by independent problem solving and the level of potential development as determined through problem solving under adult guidance or in collaboration with more capable peers' (1978: 86). This definition implies that learning is more effective when it occurs with an expert's adequate guidance, rather than by the learner alone. In order to provide adequate guidance to learners, a few conditions need to be met. First, teachers need to learn the students' current independent level in order to provide the appropriate tools to guide them toward the level of potential development. For example, Chapters 6 and 8 of this volume found that certain strategies and oral corrective feedback types were more effective than others due to the learners' novice Chinese level. Another example is that in Chapter 7, we found that although the tool of chunking was effective, it might not have exerted its full strength with novice learners, and future research is needed with more advanced learners. In Chapter 9, due to the imposed Chinese-only policy, the translanguaging study found that the learners who tried to avoid utilizing Chinese-English translanguaging could not maximize their learning potential. Hence, knowing students' current levels and providing suitable tools and signs accordingly are essential.

The second condition toward successful reach of ZPD is knowing that individual students might be at different levels; therefore, teaching needs to be differentiated and tailored amongst students. The results of a couple of the chapters of this volume have demonstrated this need. For instance, Chapter 6 illustrated that the heritage learner, Alice, who was more advanced than her peers, used mainly compensation, metacognitive and social strategies, while her peers used more cognitive and memory strategies. In addition to strategy use, Chapter 8 also found that Alice made different types of oral language errors compared to her peers. These differences show that the heritage learner was at a different place on the learning continuum and needed specific guidance to meet her level. A good example of the teacher's differentiated instruction could be found in Chapter 8, in which the teacher was observed to use more meaning-focused, rather than form-focused, oral corrective feedback to aid the accuracy of Alice's oral production.

Finally, ZPD can be easier to reach when the current background knowledge of the student is recognized. In other words, the cultural, social and linguistic knowledge students bring into a classroom should be seen as crucial resources that can be used to mediate learning (Yoon & Kim, 2012). In Chapter 4, many Chinese DLI teacher participants recognized heritage learners' expertise in Chinese as bringing extra learning opportunities and positive influences to their DLI peers. However, one teacher participant was particularly concerned about the heritage learners' own learning progress. She pointed out that the absence or very low number of heritage speakers in her classes each year might have caused the heritage learners' Chinese learning to regress, which was evident in their oral communication with their teacher and on the Chinese tests. In other words, while the few heritage learners in the Chinese DLI programs served as more capable peers in collaboration with others, their own learning was marginalized and not supported by the programs. One suggestion to remedy this issue is to bring more heritage learners into the programs. More balanced numbers between heritage and non-heritage groups offers a more balanced mode of learning. Both groups can bring in their own expertise and learn from each other. The peers within the same group can also support and maintain their expertise. Another suggestion is a reminder to DLI teachers and programs that even though currently only a very few heritage learners are enrolled in the one-way Utah DLI programs, the attention and response to their learning needs should not be neglected.

Conclusion

Bilingual education, having been going through a long period of controversial debates in the United States, has recently become a favored subject due to the impact of economic globalization. The rapid growth of one-way DLI programs for English-speaking students in Utah and the state programs serving as models for other states are unprecedented. However, despite the many benefits DLI programs could offer, such as fluent bilingualism, cognitive development and open attitudes toward other cultures, we question whether economic globalization, the main cause for which the state of Utah designated funds for DLI programs, is a sufficient reason to rapidly create programs and whether actual economic benefit will be gained from it. According to Bell and Stevenson (2006), studies have found that it is difficult to find a cause-effect relationship between economic gains and additional or a specific type of educational investment. There are other factors at play, such as investment in research and development or infrastructure. More importantly, while the state is busy implementing one-way DLI programs to increase the level of global competitiveness, it loses sight of the needs of minority communities. Cribb and Gewirtz (2003) stated that an educational policy (e.g. Utah Senate Bill 41) should execute distributive and cultural justices. Distributive justice refers to the allocation of resources across various social groups and cultural justice is concerned with valuing all cultures and languages within a society. Indeed, maintaining one's language is one of the basic linguistic human rights and becoming bilingual is essential for minorities to execute other basic rights and needs (Skutnabb-Kangas & May, 2007). As Wiley (2007: 89) explained,

> It is necessary to distinguish between the right to access an education that allows for social, economic, and political participation, and the right to an education mediated in one's mother tongue(s). For language minority students, both rights are essential if they are to participate in the broader society and maintain continuity with their home/community language.

Through our study findings, we ask the state leaders to recognize the benefits of including more heritage learners in DLI programs and urge the leaders to face and challenge inequalities in the current system. After all, education equality rooted in social justice is a much more valuable reason than economic benefit to create or expand educational programs.

References

Bell, L. and Stevenson, H. (2006) *Education Policy: Process, Themes and Impact*. New York, NY: Routledge.

Cheng, A. (2015) Teaching Chinese in the global context: Challenges and strategies. *European Review* 23 (2), 297–308.

Cribb, A. and Gewirtz, S. (2003) Towards a sociology of just practices: An analysis of plural conceptions of justice. In C. Vincent (ed.) *Social Justice, Education and Identity* (pp. 15–29). London: RoutledgeFalmer.

The Senate Site (2018) Dual language immersion: Origin story. See http://senatesite.com/utahsenate/dual-language-immersion/ (accessed 27 May 2018).

Skutnabb-Kangas, T. and May, S. (2007) Linguistic human rights in education. In T. McCarty and S. May (eds) *Language Policy and Political Issues in Education* (pp. 125–141). Cham, Switzerland: Springer.

Valdez, V.E., Delavan, G. and Freire, J.A. (2016a) The marketing of dual language education policy in Utah print media. *Educational Policy* 30 (6), 849–883.

Vygotsky, L.S. (1978) *Mind in Society: The Development of Higher Mental Process*. Cambridge, MA: Harvard University Press.

Weaver-Hightower, M.B. (2008) An ecology metaphor for educational policy analysis: A call to complexity. *Educational Researcher* 37 (3), 153–167.

Wiley, T.G. (2007) Accessing language rights in education: A brief history of the US context. In O. García and C. Baker (eds) *Bilingual Education: An Introductory Reader* (pp. 89–107). Clevedon: Multilingual Matters.

Yoon, B. and Kim, H.K. (2012) *Teachers' Roles in Second Language Learning: Classroom Applications of Sociocultural Theory*. Charlotte, NC: Information Age Publishing.

Index

Printed in the USA
CPSIA information can be obtained
at www.ICGtesting.com
JSHW011921061224
74951JS00003B/25